THE LAST COMMANDER

THE LAST COMMANDER

The Once and Future Battle for Afghanistan

SAMI SADAT

Published by Bombardier Books
An Imprint of Post Hill Press
ISBN: 979-8-88845-875-4
ISBN (eBook): 979-8-88845-876-1

The Last Commander:
The Once and Future Battle for Afghanistan

Cover Design by Jim Villaflores

All people, locations, events, and situations are portrayed to the best of the author's memory. While all of the events described are true, many names and identifying details have been changed to protect the privacy of the people involved.

Post Hill Press
New York • Nashville
posthillpress.com

Published in the United States of America
1 2 3 4 5 6 7 8 9 10

Dedicated to my friend Lt Gen Giles Hill. Thank you for saving my life and that of my family. When you reached out it was the darkest moment of my life. You saved many Afghan lives, for that we are grateful, and we will never forget.

Your friendship, advice, and support after the fall of Afghanistan gave me the strength to restart my mission to free our country again.

As I look into the future, men like you will always be needed in this world to guide, support, and bring people together so they can live in freedom.

I am grateful for the assistance of
David Loyn in writing this book.

TABLE OF CONTENTS

All Afghanistan

TAJIKISTAN
KUNDUZ
Kunduz
TAKHAR
BADAKHSHAN
BAGHLAN
PANJSHIR
NURISTAN
Bagram Airfield
Kabul
Sarobi
Jalalabad
NANGARHAR
LOGAR
PAKTIA
KHOST
'P2K'
PAKTIKA
NORTH WAZIRISTAN
SOUTH WAZIRISTAN
PAKISTAN
N
W
E
S
AFGHANISTAN
0
50
100
150
Miles

Chapter One

TWO BETRAYALS (2021)

"Commander. Last night, a group of Taliban again came looking for me."

The voice was quiet, urgent, as if afraid of being overheard.

"I managed to escape from that house, but I can't go back."

The man on the phone, let's call him Ahmed, not his real name, was one of my senior staff when I commanded in Helmand, southwest Afghanistan, until the Taliban takeover in August 2021. Since then he has been on the run, moving seven times, always just one step ahead of the Taliban as they go house to house.

Every day I get messages and calls from honorable and brave warriors who fought alongside American troops, like "Ahmed," who have become fugitives, fearful of contacting relatives in case the Taliban come to find them, not knowing who might betray them. If they are identified they will be shot at once.

I am powerless to help. Over a few short days in August 2021, I turned from being the most powerful general in Afghanistan into a refugee. The pressure has never let up and, if anything, the noose has tightened around people connected with the pre-Taliban administration. In early 2023 the Taliban ramped up their searches, looking especially for former special forces soldiers connected to me. I found a way to get some of my soldiers out to Iran, but Ahmed had a wife and child, and neither had a passport. Translators who worked with us and Afghan soldiers who trained with our special forces are the most vulnerable, but anyone connected with the former government is a target.

Even in neighboring countries former soldiers are not safe. The last brother of one of my officers, Bashir Achakzai, was killed by Taliban assassins in the Pakistani town of Quetta. Two men on a motorbike drew up alongside a car they thought Bashir was driving, but it was his brother they killed, injuring his mother in the back seat. He had already lost five other brothers killed fighting the Taliban in Helmand.

Ahmed is just one of the thousands of trained warriors now in hiding in fear of their lives. No one is safe. The Taliban may have seventh-century minds, but they use twenty-first-century technology to monitor social media, jailing people for anything they consider opposed to their crazed worldview. Women activists are routinely jailed and beaten. In Kandahar, that precious jewel of the Pashtun heart in the south of the country, bodies were left lying outside, with families too scared to give people a decent burial as Taliban gangs roamed the streets. The Taliban have even desecrated our dead, tearing apart the grave of my good friend General Raziq, a famous warrior in Kandahar. In Uruzgan, they dug up the body of a police chief, Shah Muhammad, and played with his skull. And in Panjshir they destroyed the shrine of the legendary mujahidin commander Ahmad Shah Massoud and danced on the burial site.

Obsessed with total control of the hearts and minds of men, banishing women from public view, they rule by fear, allied with al-Qaeda. They are the same unimaginative bigots who destroyed the country when last in power in the late 1990s. And we know how that ended, with the attacks on the American homeland on 9/11, planned out of a cave in the Tora Bora mountains of Afghanistan. If the Taliban remain in power, another 9/11 could happen at any time.

A week before the fall of Afghanistan in 2021 I was still holding Helmand, the province the Taliban most wanted to take, while the rest of the country collapsed. I was ordered back to Kabul, first to command all Afghan special forces, and the next day to stage a last-ditch defense of the capital itself. But it was too late. By the time I arrived nothing functioned. When President Ashraf Ghani fled from the presidential compound in a helicopter, telling no one, it was all over. The government imploded. I was the last commander still standing, trying to coordinate the defense of the capital after government ministers ran away. Even the air force had gone as pilots saved their aircraft and flew across the northern border to safety into neighboring Central Asian states.

So who was to blame for the collapse? Direct responsibility lies with the US, and specifically with former president Barack Obama and his Democratic successor, Joe Biden. Obama, who from the outset was clearly intent on withdrawing the US from the global War on Terror launched by President Bush, spent the whole of his first year in office delaying any decision about Afghanistan. Finally he agreed to send more troops, but only on the condition that they left on a strict timetable. This emboldened the Taliban, who knew they had only to wait it out and America would leave. The Taliban had a saying: "Americans may have a watch, but we have the time."

Back in 2009 Afghan forces were not yet ready to take on the fight for ourselves, and while we were still building our military strength, America's generals constantly argued for enough troops to fight alongside us—ready to stay until the job was done, not on a short-term artificial timetable. A new generation of generals, David Petraeus and Stanley McChrystal foremost among them, had studied counterinsurgency and wanted to put it into practice in Afghanistan.

They knew it would need sustained support in terms of numbers of troops and time. But the strict timetable doomed their best efforts. Just as they reached the peak of the increase, troops began to leave on a downward slide due to finish in 2014. Revealing the date when Americans would leave the battlefield gave the Taliban a huge advantage.

But the long years of training made a difference. In 2019, Afghan forces went on the offensive, taking and holding ground for the first time on our own. I was one of a group of younger Western-trained Afghan generals put into senior positions by a new and ambitious defense minister, who decisively changed the course of the war in our favor, winning across the country. I am convinced that if we had retained consistent US air support we would have seen a dramatic increase in ground securely held by our forces, while the Taliban would have been reduced to a small insurgency, no longer a strategic threat by 2021. We had better troops, better equipment, and had developed the ability to mount many complex operations on our own.

But we still needed American planes to engage the most difficult targets, and a whole lot else besides. And in 2020 once again that support became conditional, time-limited, when President Trump agreed to a bad deal with the Taliban in Doha. It was a withdrawal deal, not a real negotiation to end the war. As a result, we were forced to release thousands of high-value Taliban prisoners from jail with only a vague promise from the Taliban to sever their links with al-Qaeda. We learnt a new English verb, "retrograde"—meaning taking out all the American military hardware in the country. It was later used as the title of a documentary about my last months in command.

When he came into office, President Biden could have taken a breath after the Trump years and reviewed Afghan policy. The Taliban had broken both the public and secret terms of the Doha deal. They had not severed links with al-Qaeda, many of those released from jail were back on the battlefield, and there were attacks on US bases and provincial capitals across the country. These attacks were not publicized at the time, however.

Trump had drawn the number of American troops down to just twenty-five hundred at the end of his presidency, and Biden was under pressure from his generals to keep them there. Along with troops from a number of allies, notably Turkey, Germany, Italy, and the UK, there were around ten thousand international troops in all—enough to give Afghan forces the basic support we needed to take the fight to the Taliban, if we had been allowed to do it.

A month after Biden's inauguration, in February 2021, General Joe Dunford, the former chairman of the Joint Chiefs of Staff, who had commanded in Afghanistan, wrote an influential report arguing that keeping troops at this level for the medium term was a wise and affordable insurance policy. Otherwise, he wrote, international terrorists, including al-Qaeda and IS-K, would be able to "rebuild their capabilities in the Afghanistan-Pakistan region such that they might be able to attack the US homeland within eighteen to thirty-six months."

Biden was not listening—and was evidently not getting intelligence that would have told him how bad this withdrawal would be. In a reverse of how intelligence should work, under Biden the White House tells the CIA what the president wants to hear, regardless of its importance or level of threat to the US and the rest of the world. Policy became a show rather than a program to save lives and make the world a safer place.

Our American military partners were as frustrated as we were. On a visit to Navy SEAL headquarters in Camp Dwyer, in a remote corner of Helmand in the southwest in January 2021, General Scott

Miller and I sat in a secret operations room where the SEALS briefed us that they continued to track Taliban positions across the country. "If the peace talks fail," a SEAL commander said, "we could destroy the Taliban in nine days in Helmand."

But the talks between the Afghan government and the Taliban did fail, and Biden turned his back on Afghanistan nonetheless. Beyond a pause to extend the off-ramp so the final out date was September, not May, he had no appetite for longer involvement. He may have lost the argument for a drawdown in the Obama White House in 2009. Now that he was in charge, his withering contempt for my country came to the fore.

On April 14, 2021, after announcing the final out date in the Treaty Room in the White House, where President George W. Bush had launched the war in 2001, Biden walked in light rain along lines of graves in Section 60 of the Arlington cemetery, where the dead of America's recent wars are laid to rest. He said that the final withdrawal had not been a hard decision to make. To him it was "absolutely clear." With the defeat of al-Qaeda and the death of Osama bin Laden, there was no reason to stay in Afghanistan, a country that in his words had "never been united."

Biden handed another propaganda victory to our enemies by choosing September 11, 2021, as the date the last soldier had to leave. This is a day celebrated by terrorists around the world as they remembered the attacks on America in 2001. It was as if Osama bin Laden had come back to life and asked for this date, so they could celebrate another victory against America. He was forced to bring it forward to August but the damage was done.

The idea that we were beyond hope or help betrayed not only Afghanistan. Biden also betrayed the thousands of American troops and development workers who had been alongside us since 9/11, not always spending money wisely, not always fighting with effect, but in the end building a different life for a new generation of Afghan men and particularly Afghan women who wanted something different from those who came before.

Biden was wrong, too, in another criticism, when he said, "Afghan forces are not willing to fight for themselves." We were more than willing and increasingly capable, but he took away our ability to fight. For eighteen months before the collapse, we were starved of ammunition and told to stop offensive operations. And then when the troops left, they took out the last supports, the seventeen thousand contractors who supported our forces in the field by maintaining the modern equipment provided by America. Our forces were trained using the US military model based on highly technical special reconnaissance units, helicopters, and airstrikes. That capacity depended on sophisticated maintenance and software. When the troops went, the contractors went too. Black Hawks, C-130 transport planes, surveillance drones, and so much else, lay idle.

We did not lose capacity only in the air. Our forces used sophisticated software systems similar to that of our US partners. The contractors took that proprietary software and those weapons systems with them. They physically removed our helicopter missile-defense system, and the loss of software meant that our ability to track our vehicles, weapons, and personnel disappeared, along with real-time intelligence on targets.

This felt like an attack on our capability from the inside. The technical way of fighting that we had adopted under American supervision immediately became useless, and the Taliban, backed by Qatar, Pakistan, Iran, and China, achieved superiority. Since we could not resupply without helicopter support, our soldiers often lacked the necessary tools to fight, so the Taliban overran those bases. Entire units surrendered, not for lack of will but lack of weapons, ammunition, and other enabling capacity that was now taken out from under our feet. We had already been fighting with one hand tied behind our back when we were told to stop offensive operations and "give peace a chance" in the days after the Doha deal, and were now further disabled by the loss of military contractors, ripping out our capacity to fight a modern war overnight.

The swiftness of the collapse in the wake of the US withdrawal meant that we handed the country over to primitive fundamentalists. The Taliban are not only cruel but incompetent and have failed in the basics of statecraft again, as anybody could see they would. The economy has collapsed. Streets are full of people attempting to sell basic household items to buy bread. Money is physically in short supply. Some people are reduced to selling their kidneys or their daughters to survive.

It took the Taliban a while to impose their harshest rule. They are obsessed with clothing and behavior for both men and women, with women treated far worse, but initially did not introduce their strictest demands because they did not understand what Afghanistan had become. When they returned to power in Kabul it was an alien place to them—not the ravaged ruin they left behind when their government was defeated after 9/11, but a thriving Central Asian capital, with coffee bars and bowling allies. They did not know how to deal with this very young society equipped with smart phones. It was an Islamic culture, but in their distorted, perverted, and violent view of our faith they did not recognize a functioning modern Islamic city. As is accepted in modern Islamic countries, women were everywhere—at the top levels of government and running businesses, as well as in more traditional women's roles in teaching and medicine. Women covered their heads, but not with the full-face veil and all-encompassing *burqa* that the Taliban imposed.

The Taliban were as ignorant of the ways of government as of society. When they took over, fighters went room to room in ministries asking where the money was, as if government were run like a militia, where the commander had a box of cash under the bed. They threw away twenty years of reforms, obsessed not with getting the economy moving again, but imposing their dark vision on the lives of men and women. They piled on restrictions day after day, with more than thirty specific new laws preventing women from almost all work or any role outside the home. Even for a visit to the shops women need a male *mahram*, escort, who has to be a close relative. Widows without sons have it hardest.

Male Taliban fighters pull up the outer clothing of women in the streets and beat them if they are wearing Western trousers, and, not content with stopping girls going to high school or university, more unspeakable dignities were thought up. Women have been hired to go into elementary schools and conduct intimate examinations on girls as young as nine. If they show signs of puberty they are sent home. All contraception is banned from sale. Beauty salons have been closed, throwing fifty thousand women out of work, tailors have been banned from making clothes for women, women "adulterers" face public flogging, and just as in the 1990s, executions are staged in front of large crowds in the football stadium.

For many years the Taliban have had an unholy alliance with the criminal drug gangs, and that did not stop when they were in government. More than 80 percent of the global supply in illegal heroin comes from Afghan poppy fields, and the proceeds dwarf the legitimate economy. The Taliban did announce a ban on poppy *growing*, but that did not immediately stop exports as there were huge stockpiles, and there was no ban on trade. The ban had the effect of ruining many small farmers, while those who controlled the trade grew rich as prices rose with dwindling stocks.

And as General Joe Dunford foresaw, Afghanistan has once again become a safe haven for international terrorism. Any illusion that the

Taliban might be sticking to their Doha commitment to cut links with al-Qaeda disappeared in the smoke of the missile that killed al-Qaeda leader Ayman al-Zawahiri in downtown Kabul eleven months after the Taliban returned to power. He was staying in a guest house that had been seized by the Taliban deputy leader Sirajuddin Haqqani, who was next door at the time. Since then the Taliban have deepened their links with al-Qaeda and other groups who threaten stability in the region as well as the West.

Afghanistan is once again a crucible of terrorism again as it was in the 1990s. A handful of al-Qaeda commanders based there later went onto to significant roles in international jihadi organizations. Apart from Osama bin Laden and Ayman al-Zawahiri, Afghanistan was the crucible that turned out the current global leader of al-Qaeda, Saif al-Adel; the founder of ISIS, Abu Bakr-al-Baghdadi; the butcher of Iraq, Abu Musab al-Zarqawi; and the 9/11 mastermind, Khalid Sheikh Mohammed. Members of this group carried out 9/11, butchered Iraqis and international soldiers, captured Yemen with Houthis, and captured Afghanistan with the Taliban. As well as the Middle East, they are strong across a number of countries in Africa—Libya, Somalia, Syria, Iraq, Niger, Kenya, Burkina Faso, and Mali.

Under Joe Biden, al-Qaeda is winning the war on terror. In 2001, before 9/11, they had less than four thousand men spread across the Arab world in small groups of less than one hundred, most without lethal capabilities; now they have more than one hundred thousand fighters on three continents and sixty bases in nineteen countries. Then they were a small network of avengers focused on dictatorship in their own Arab homelands. Al-Qaeda is now the largest and the most powerful non-state military actor in the world. Allowing them to retake Afghanistan with the Taliban in 2021 gave them a new rallying call. This is now their most important hub.

There are eight hundred al-Qaeda commanders in Afghanistan, the majority seasoned battle leaders, more sophisticated than their seniors in the 1990s. Under them are some sixteen thousand fighters, coming from Africa, the Arab world, and Southeast and Central Asia. Half are al-Qaeda main, and half are an affiliate, "al-Qaeda in the Indian Subcontinent," AQIS, rapidly becoming the most powerful terrorist group in the world. Their manpower increased hugely after the fall of Kabul, enabling them to project violence into Pakistan and India from their new safe haven in Afghanistan.

The current emir of AQIS, Usama Mahmood, is a Pashtun Pakistani who first worked with the Pakistani Taliban for more than a decade before coming over to al-Qaeda. When I worked in Afghan intelligence we called him "Zawahiri's gatekeeper," as he used his Pakistan connections to keep al-Zawahiri safe after he took over from bin Laden.

Usama Mahmood lives in Kandahar, where he and Abdallah bin Laden, the son of Osama bin Laden, are frequent visitors to the Taliban leader, Sheikh Haibatullah Akhundzada. They are the key voices urging that the Taliban hold to policies that will keep Afghanistan isolated from the West. His involvement has strengthened ties across the frontier with Pakistan, forging deeper links between the Afghan and Pakistani Taliban. The State Department has designated him a global leader of terror, an impotent gesture after the catastrophe of withdrawal that opened the door to Mahmood and thousands of young fighters inspired by his call.

Al-Qaeda commanders from Yemen, Iraq, Syria, and North Africa routinely travel to Afghanistan via Iran and Pakistan to regroup with their fighters, friends, and family; some have moved their families to Afghanistan since the Taliban takeover. For the past two decades the al-Qaeda leadership was separated from communicating with their operational echelon thus limiting their abilities to operate as a cohesive organization with strategic direction. But today the al-Qaeda leader Saif al-Adel and his commanders meet openly in Iran, train openly in Afghanistan, and travel freely across the Middle East to north and east Africa.

So al-Qaeda not only survived but adapted to the changing policies of American administrations, waiting the West out of Iraq and Afghanistan and watching the US attack their Islamic State rivals in the Middle East. This was all clearly predicted by the American military establishment. When he pulled out in the way that he did in 2021, Biden ignored the advice of his generals who told him that Afghanistan would once again become a willing host to international jihadi groups if the Taliban came to power again. And against all other evidence he has deluded himself into believing that the Taliban are America's allies in sharing intelligence against Islamic State.

For four days after Kabul collapsed, I focused on bringing to safety key personnel from special forces and from my command in Helmand, as Taliban fighters roamed the streets of the capital. But then I had to look after myself. I had been privately nursing a shrapnel wound for a week, changing the bandages alone every night. I feared the loss of morale if anyone knew I was injured. The wound had become badly infected and was causing real pain. I had done all I could and accepted the offer of treatment at a British army medical center set up by the international force that had arrived to secure the airport—and a ride out.

While I stood on the tarmac that day, watching chaos engulf my beloved country, I knew it would be hard to recover. In the months after the collapse any thought of a quick return collided with the harsh reality of the scale of the defeat. A number of former Afghan Army troops tried to stand their ground across the country, but none succeeded. The vice president of the Afghan republic, Amrullah Saleh, who might have been able to rally forces if he had been given any notice of President Ghani's flight, turned up across the border in Tajikistan, defeated and in exile. The Taliban even wiped out most resistance in the Panjshir Valley, the natural fortress surrounded by protective peaks to the northeast of Kabul, which had held out against them when they last took most of the rest of the country in the late 1990s.

The country was demoralized. The Taliban had seized power by mobilizing opinion against the Ghani presidency, calling it corrupt and Westernized. As religious clerics railed against the mismanagement of the state, tribal leaders hedged their bets, supporting neither the president nor the Taliban. And when America pulled the rug from under us as we fought, and incompetence and cowardice in the Ghani team led to their collapse, the new Taliban state was accepted in 2021 by tribal and religious leaders for want of anything better.

"Sit down and hold onto the ropes as if your life depended on it." The British-accented order was shouted over the heads of men, women, and children who filed up the steep metal ramp through the back door of the grey Royal Air Force C-17. A plane designed to carry weapons and people to war was repurposed to take out civilians fleeing their country for an uncertain future.

Joining them on that August day in 2021 was the most difficult choice of my life. I was leaving my country, and felt like I was leaving my soul behind. I had to put a stone in my heart and kill all my emotions to sit in the cavernous hold of that plane. I was put into one of the few canvas seats bolted along the inside but gave it up for a woman with two small children and took her place, squatting on the floor, reaching down to hold onto cables designed to secure cargo. British troops picked their way carefully through the people sitting on the floor, handing out basic supplies for kids and bottles of water.

I felt humiliated. Why was this happening to me? Why was I sitting on the floor of an airplane, clutching a cable among women and children and elderly people? Only a few days before I had arrived at that airfield in my own helicopter and driven in an armed convoy with my own guys. Now I was just a refugee. I felt lonely, disconnected, and humiliated.

The plane took only twenty minutes to load. As soon as the ramp was pulled up to close the back door, the giant aircraft began to rumble along the tarmac. With no windows, I could not see the beautiful mountains that I knew so well to the north of the city. I remembered the pride I felt when my father, Habibullah Sadat, came through those mountains in command of his militia force when they defeated the Taliban after 9/11. I thought back over the years when I had worked in the secret world of spying and been promoted into the military, quickly becoming one of the country's youngest generals. To push through reforms I had faced down veterans from the past—figures from Afghanistan's former wars who blocked progress as they sat in senior jobs both in the spy agencies and the military. I had always led from the front and promoted the people and values of a new generation, my generation, who wanted to build a new Afghanistan after decades of war. For all the failings of democracy and the corruption that ate it from the inside like a cancer, with more time and support we could have made it work. As I left my beloved country I vowed to commit myself to do everything I could to end Taliban rule. We can and will take our country back—and end the cycles of war that have gone on for so long.

Chapter Two

AFGHANISTAN'S FOREVER WAR

I saw into the heart of the Taliban's perverted and violent worldview when I was arrested by them before 9/11. At the time they did not hold the whole country. I was captured while trying to cross their front line to go to the north to see a mentor and friend of my family, Professor Burhanuddin Rabbani, who wanted to send me abroad for education. I was just fifteen years old and the Taliban accused me of being a spy.

At the time the northeast was out of their hands. I was stopped at a Taliban roadblock where they asked me why I wanted to cross the front line.

They mocked me. "Why is a young man going to the other side?

"There are members of my family there. I'm going to check on them." I could hardly say I was going to see Rabbani, who was the overall leader of the northern forces opposing them. But the Taliban quickly found out that my father had been fighting against them and took me to their commander, Mullah Fazal. He was a senior Taliban member who would later be arrested and held in Guantanamo for thirteen years before being released as one of five leading Taliban figures exchanged for the missing American soldier, Bowe Bergdahl.

Fazl looked at me intently. "Where's your father?"

"I don't know," I said.

"I'm about to launch an attack on the other side. That's why the road is closed. So I don't have time to find out what you are really doing."

Then his eyes flashed underneath his black turban. "But if I was not planning an attack, even if you were the son of God I would make you talk."

They drove me from Takhar province to Kunduz, put me on an old Russian plane, and flew me to Kabul, where I was handed over to their Military Commission, who were responsible for security. A man called Mullah Ismael asked me what I was doing in the north. I will never forget the look in his eyes when he said, "We know you've been spying."

It was in vain that I replied, "I don't know anything."

He called over two men who tied my hands and feet and lay me face down. While one sat on my head and the other on my feet, Mullah Ismael started beating me with a bunch of large sticks cut from a tree. When one broke, he just picked up another and carried on hitting me on my back and thighs.

At one point, bleeding profusely, I fell unconscious, and when I came round I could not feel anything, just watch my blood flow. I drifted in and out of consciousness. And every time I opened my eyes, I cursed Mullah Ismael.

After he had broken all the sticks, there was a weird mad argument about Islamic theology. His deputy looked at my bleeding body, and said without emotion, "This kid is going to die, and under the religious code we should not kill minors." But Mullah Ismael found a loophole by citing the principle of *baligh*, where a child could be considered an adult because they were wise and could take responsibility for their actions. "He knew what he was doing when he went to the north, so religiously, we can kill him because of his father." For that they needed approval, so although it was evening they took me to the ministry of justice. I could not walk and they did not have a stretcher. The two fighters who had been holding me down rolled me onto a shawl and carried me like a dead body.

The minister, Nuruddin Turabi, took one look at me and said, "What did you guys do to this kid? He's bleeding a lot." And they said it was because of my father, and the talk went this way and that as I drifted in and out of consciousness. Then after a visit to the attorney general I was put in a jail in the center of town. It was full of children, from seven years old upwards. I was thrown into a cell with about six boys, wise beyond their years, forced to grow up fast in this terrible place. They attended to me and helped me clean my wounds, take a shower, and change my clothes. I never saw a doctor, and it was a week before I could walk again.

While I was recovering I had a fight with a boy from another cell, and when guards came to break it up, we were both sentenced to sixty slashes on the hand with a stick. They planned to do ten on each alternately, and the other boy went first. I sat listening to the terrible cracks on his hand. He immediately began to cry. My body was still in such pain from the first beating that I could not even take ten. As they cut into the palm of my hand, one, two, three…, my eyes blurred and I lost control and grabbed the guard, pushing him up against a wall. The other guards held me and took me to the head of the prison who ordered my punishment to be carried out in front of the whole jail.

They gathered all the other boys into a courtyard. Four of my roommates stepped forward and said, "Sami can't take any more. We'll take his hits for him." That was friendship. They took ten each, and I had to endure only twenty.

Every moment living in that place was torture. They left the lights on at night, and I quickly learnt from the others that if you tied a wet handkerchief round your eyes and locked it from behind, that was an effective eye mask, so we could sleep. They woke us early and after lining up in the cold to wash we had to attend morning prayer led by an Egyptian member of al-Qaeda. After prayers he would give us religious instruction until 7:00 when they brought us tea with sugar and bread. That was our breakfast: half a piece of bread, one cup of tea, and one spoon of sugar. After breakfast we would immediately start another class. Some of the teachers spoke Pashto, others only Arabic with a translator. They spoke about Islam, the Holy Prophet, and the nature of jihad; how to cleanse sins, how to become a good Muslim and fight for Islam. They were trying to cut us off from the world we knew, the material world and our families. They said that we came from corrupted fathers and mothers and the only way to cleanse ourselves was to disconnect from all we knew and work for Islam and be prepared for *Shahada*, holy death.

Their twisted logic led down just one path: martyrdom, self-sacrifice, which they said was the only way of righteousness, all that was open to us to be good Muslims and reach heaven. We had to die fighting as jihadi warriors. They spoke of nothing but sacrifice and martyrdom. That is how the Taliban became a death cult, so that by 2021, when they took power again, they were so perverted that they celebrated suicide bombers as the most honorable of their fighters. Their supreme leader, Haibatullah Akhundzada himself, was proud that his own son died as a suicide bomber.

It was the most ineffective brainwashing. It did not work with any of us. As soon as the teachers left we would curse them and start joking and being naughty. We were just young kids. Nobody liked the Taliban. Nobody liked the teachers. We were stuck in this constant routine of indoctrination, prayer, follow-up prayer, evening meal, then we had the last prayer of the evening. And the food was terrible. We never had meat, but maybe okra for lunch, and potato or beans for supper. And then back to sleep with our handkerchief eye masks, and it all began again.

After several weeks of this I came to know that a man called Shamsul Haq, who had served with my father, lived in the same street as the prison. He was now working with the Taliban. I managed to get a letter out to him and he came to meet me. And two weeks later I was called in to see the head of the prison to be told I would be released. That same Mullah Ismael, who had nearly killed me when I was arrested, was sitting with him. And he looked at me and said, "So, are you a human being now." I looked him in the eye and said, "I was always a human being." He got mad and started shouting, and said that if he ever saw me again he would throw me back in jail. I guess he already knew that one day my family would come after him.

Going out on the streets again was so strange. Even in that short time out of sunlight my brain had reprogrammed itself. My eyes could not compute real life; I felt like the cars were driving upside down. I took a taxi home and that was when I took a vow to myself that whatever else I did in life, all I wanted to be was a warrior who would kill Taliban every day. I saw through their hypocrisy, the way they were treating children.

Islam is the way of peace. But what they did was not the way of peace, it was a cruel distortion of our faith. I saw only cruelty—small kids beaten if they did not know how to recite the Holy Quran or remember the Hadith. We did not know Arabic and were beaten for it. How they behaved was so different to the language of Islam. They used the words that Islam is a religion of love. We have to love Muslims. We have to unite. We have to get together. We have to sacrifice for each other. Yet they were not sacrificing anything. They were beating us every day, giving us bad food, and treating us like animals.

I had seen into the dark heart of the Taliban and knew from that moment that Afghanistan would never be safe until they were destroyed.

CROSSING THE FRONT LINE

I had already made one trip across the front line to see Professor Rabbani the year before when I was only fourteen years old. He was one of the most important figures in modern Afghanistan. Educated in Egypt, he had founded an Islamic opposition party in the 1970s that developed into one of the most effective groups fighting against the Russian invasion after 1979. He became president after the Russian-backed government fell in 1992, but when the anti-communist coalition fell apart into civil war, he returned to his home in the northeastern province of Badakhshan—next door to where my father had grown up. If anyone could help to get my father out of a Taliban jail it was Professor Rabbani, who had contacts across the country, including in Taliban territory.

He sent me back with letters to people he thought could help and $303 for my travel expenses. I guess that was how much he had in his pocket. I unpicked the threads holding the label of my jacket and sewed the letters and the six bills, three hundreds and three single dollars, in behind it. I was robbed on the way back south and the hiding place survived a search. When the robbers could not find anything, they stood me in the snow, told me to close my eyes, and one stood back and pulled back the charging handle on his AK-47.

The moment I closed my eyes, I remembered a very fluffy pillow at our house. I was tired; we had been walking for hours. I just needed to rest, even if it meant dying. When the shooting started, I remembered that pillow and my mother smiling. A man standing next to me let out a cry and I thought he had been shot. But they had shot down into the snow in front of us and we were spattered with stones and mud. The robber came close again and asked, "Are you afraid now?" When I answered no, he asked, "Why not?" And I said, "I am the son of a warrior." At that they let us go.

Further on I found myself with a group of traveling Uzbek nomads, who put my bag onto a donkey. A woman was carrying a baby and I took it for her, wrapped it in a big shawl on my back, and walked in the middle of them. It was good disguise as the nomads were not molested by robbers. We passed by another group of travelers being beaten and robbed at the side of the road. That was Afghanistan under the Taliban in the late 1990s: a broken country with no honor or safety. I took Rabbani's letter appealing for my father's release to a tribal leader to Helmand who was close to him and also had good contacts with the Taliban. But the traditional ways of doing business no longer worked; the tribal elders had no sway in the Taliban regime.

Failing to negotiate, we had to sell our house to raise a ransom for my father's release. And a month later I came south to Kandahar where I met a Taliban fighter in a café. I was carrying ten million Pakistani Rupees, worth about $25,000, which I gave him in a bag. After quickly checking the bag he nodded and said, "Go home, it's not safe for you here."

I had carried other letters as well, to commanders in the south who were loyal to Rabbani although currently allied with the Taliban. America never understood the complex, fluid, shifting loyalties that people had during the decades of conflict. When Russia invaded Afghanistan a generation before in 1979, the countryside rose up, inspired by Islamic preachers to become mujahidin fighters, under the leadership of men like Professor Rabbani. This was not the distorted cruel Islam that the Taliban would later adopt. It was employing the centuries-old virtues of our faith to come to the defense of the country at a time of acute crisis.

But there was not a neat mujahidin/communist binary separation of the nation; it defied easy analysis, and loyalties were fluid. If you lived in a village you had to be in the Islamic mujahidin or leave as a refugee. On the other hand, if you were in a city, as we were at the time, you were expected to join the communist party and back the Russians, or flee to Pakistan.

It was my father, Habibullah Sadat, who taught me to be a patriot, opposed to extremism, loyal only to the country, and not to any passing cause. He was a special forces brigadier general and famous for being outspoken. When I became an officer myself, he never second-guessed my judgement. He did call me just once during the Battle of Helmand in the last days of the republic to tell me to be careful not to cause civilian casualties.

While he was a commander with the Russian-backed forces, he was never doctrinally a communist. He was doing the best for his family. My mom used to joke when he was saying something she did not like, "You learned that from those infidel Russians." There were divided families like ours across the country. My father had initially fought for the communist-backed government in the 1980s against the insurgency led by Rabbani, but he later joined him to fight against the Taliban. I had an uncle who was close to Rabbani and helped him found the Islamic political group that later became the Jamiat-i Islami party. The uncle was pushed out of a helicopter by the communists and his body never found.

HELMAND CHILDHOOD

My father was stationed in the early 1990s in Helmand in the southwest, where I remember an idyllic upbringing in what now feels like a lost country. There was not much fighting where we were; the war seemed far away. We never played war games at school. We lived in a large brick house originally built for an American engineer in the Helmand Valley scheme, a huge American-backed project from the 1950s and '60s to provide hydro-electricity to the south and irrigation canals for agriculture. We had about three acres of land down to the canal where there were ducks, and every day we had fresh milk from our own cows. There were no fences between us and our neighbors. I used to climb up and look at the explosives, machine guns, and hand grenades in a tall guard tower built in the corner of our land, stored in case the compound was attacked. But we never needed to use it.

I returned to the house when I was commanding in the south thirty years later, and it was surrounded by blast walls and barbed wire. The garden was reduced to dust, and the irrigation canals now provided water for fields of opium poppies.

The Russian-backed Afghan forces in the south, including my father, held out for two years after Kabul and the north fell to the mujahidin in 1992. But the day came when the ammunition ran out, and Helmand fell to the mujahidin. Hundreds of pickups, crammed with fighters, coursed into town. Unlike the neat uniformed soldiers of the national army, they were wearing Afghan *shalwar kameez*, flowing white pajamas, with long hair and beards. They were not the freedom fighters of legend who had risen up after the 1979 Russian invasion to defeat the infidels. By now they had deteriorated into little more than bandit gangs.

They came to our house and looted it, taking TVs, carpets, and all the dishes and silverware from the kitchen. When my father came home, they took him outside into the yard and wanted to shoot him in front of us. They were Hezb-i Islami, a group with a ruthless reputation. His life was saved when fighters from the other main mujahidin party, Jamiat-i Islami, arrived. I was only seven years old and the Jamiat men said, "You can't kill this guy in front of his kid and his wife." In the end Jamiat prevailed, and after they all left we made our way to Kabul. When the Taliban emerged shortly afterwards, my father, a soldier by trade, joined Professor Rabbani's forces to fight against the Taliban.

The rivalries between mujahidin groups diminished their effectiveness. By the time we arrived in Kabul much of the city had been destroyed in random rocket attacks as they fought among themselves. They did not unite even after the Taliban swept across the south and by 1996 were threatening the capital. As the mujahidin could not mount a united defense, the city fell to the Taliban for the first time, and I learnt an early lesson in how disunity was so self-defeating.

But this complexity was never grasped by the American forces who marched into Afghanistan in 2001 with a simplistic take—the Taliban were bad, and other militia leaders, sometimes called warlords, were good. They remembered that the non-Taliban "warlords" had been America's allies in the war against Russia in the 1980s. This ignored the complex history of the lives of Afghan families like ours, who had picked sides to survive. Worse, the US took no account of how many members of the once-heroic mujahidin had morphed into little more than gangs fighting for turf.

When 9/11 happened my father called from the north, where he had been fighting against the Taliban, to tell me to prepare food and supplies. I did not know anything about America. I asked many questions about America and what my father thought would happen. "Son, if I can sum it up for you," he said, "there is a monster, and it has been awakened by the Taliban. And this monster will swallow all of the Taliban at once. This is how we will take our country back."

He wanted to make sure the family would get through the hard times ahead. "Buy food items and medical supplies for a couple of months," he told me, giving me a list. So I went to the market and stocked up with provisions in case everything closed.

A few days later, the first B-52s flew in daylight high and slow over Kabul, untouchable, leaving four distinct vapor trails. We were in awe at their accuracy as they hit only the Taliban. Once we knew the bombs were not random I ran round the city with my school-friends watching where they fell. We were scared after one bomb fell into a residential area until we heard it was targeted at the Qatari-owned TV station Al-Jazeera, so there was no wider danger. We lived in Khair Khana, the gateway to the north from Kabul, and had a ringside seat as wave after wave of F-14 Tomcats lined up to bomb Taliban front lines in the plains to the north of the city. The mighty Taliban and their holy warrior allies collapsed in a matter of days, running for their lives like rats.

ARRIVAL OF AMERICA

All of a sudden, a month after the first American bombs fell, there was continuous gunfire throughout the night, and in the morning we were told that the Taliban had left, heading south for their stronghold in Kandahar in fleets of pickups. I went down with some friends to Shahr-e Naw park in the center of the city. We were told not to go too close as there was a firefight, and we saw men shooting up at the trees, where some Taliban fighters had climbed for refuge. Later we saw the bodies of Pakistani fighters who did not know that the Taliban leadership had gone. Elsewhere stranded Taliban were killed by civilians. We watched a crowd gathering around one group and beating them to death with sticks and stones. I had one errand I urgently needed to do: to save the life of Shamsul Haq, who had secured my release from jail and would be vulnerable as a Taliban sympathizer. I went to his house and brought his family to come and live with us.

At the time it was the holy month of Ramadan, when we were fasting from dawn to dusk. In the evening my father arrived, dusty from the last battle for Kabul. He came with about thirty of his men and told us to cook food for them. We did not have space in the house, so we took blankets outside, and they sat in the street in long lines while we served them food. And that was the routine for many weeks. Sometimes we were feeding more than fifty soldiers every night.

The sense of freedom was exhilarating. The Taliban had banned TV, and making up for lost time, we bought two satellite dishes—one for Asia and one for Europe. We would sit at night and if somebody wanted to watch Asia, they would go upstairs with the family. If they wanted to watch the BBC and other European channels they went downstairs where Shamsul Haq and his family were now living.

It felt as if a great weight had been lifted from the city. There were lines of men outside barbers' shops. The Taliban had not allowed men to shave, but now everybody wanted to clean up for this new world. The streets were thronged with trucks and cars, with luggage and furniture piled high, as people returned from exile. Foreigners arrived, wanting to rent houses, paying translators $1,000 a day, the annual income of an Afghan middle-class family at the time. I went with my schoolfriends into the new Western restaurants that opened, and we ogled the menus. What was "steak," or "mushroom kebab"? Of course we would eat pizza, we soon understood that. And then we branched out and started eating Chinese food. It was so strange after the monochrome tedium of the Taliban years.

Our new president, Hamid Karzai, was a gifted politician who could communicate well to different levels of Afghan society. He drew support for the new republic from traditional authority figures in the countryside as well as more modern sources of power. His pleasant, easy manner and ability to engage people at all levels of society appealed to religious and tribal leaders, and he also appealed to young people—an important new element in the politics of a country with a big youth bulge. Democracy was a great leveler and brought together people from many sides of our recent conflicts, so that former mujahidin, communists, and even some ex-Taliban could coexist in peace.

As international aid rolled in to help reform the country, the Taliban lost their ability to influence events and began to realize they would not quickly return to power. So they changed the dynamics to carve out space for themselves with an assassination campaign targeting those religious and tribal leaders who were working with the state for progress and development, particularly in their heartland in the south.

When my father was appointed as deputy head of the army division in charge of protecting the presidential palace, I met my first American soldiers: huge, bearded men wearing baseball caps, bulked out even more with body armor, carrying weapons I had not seen before, with sidearms strapped to their legs. All I knew of America were pictures of high-rise buildings from an English course I followed. The soldiers chatted to me, and at first I did not understand, but I learnt more as I talked to them. I would run to the presidential palace every day after school. It was not just language but behavior and cultural values that I was learning. They were different to us, and I wanted to crack the code. I could see that this was going to be an essential skill going forward.

WORLD OF WORK

By the time I left school, aged eighteen, I had good enough English to work for a Provincial Reconstruction Team that had set up in the northeast. These were joint international civil/military bases that helped rebuild our country. The one I joined was German, but the main language used was English. The head of the civilian side, Torulf Pilz, became a mentor to me. I quickly learnt the difference between Afghan and German ideas of punctuality. One morning I turned up for an 8:00 a.m. meeting at one minute past, and Torulf would not let me in. "One minute past eight is not eight," he said impassively.

But the most important lesson I learnt there was how winning a war was not just about fighting. The country could not recover from the Taliban without help. It opened my eyes into how there needed to be a follow-on after the shooting was over.

I liked the way the Germans did things. They had a long history in our country. In the long decades of peace in the twentieth century before the Russian invasion, Germany was our most constant support, from links forged after Afghan kings turned to them in the 1920s and '30s, deliberately shunning the former imperial power Britain.

The Germans I worked with had expertise from other developing countries in Africa and Asia, applying those lessons to rural Afghanistan, and as translator I was witness to every decision. They held meetings with our various civilian departments in order to get schools, economy, labor, and agriculture back up and running after the years of Taliban brutality. There was a big difference between them and the one American in the camp, who was from USAID. He talked in terms of spending millions of dollars, while the Germans worried about thousands. Their approach was much more appropriate to a poor rural economy, which could not absorb the kind of cash the Americans were spraying round without a lot of it going astray. The Germans would go and ask people what they wanted; the American would do his own survey and then tell them the answer. It was a big difference. And worse than that, the American was always looking for the one powerbroker, the strong man he could work with, while the Germans wanted to support society as a whole.

After a year working with them, the Germans put me on a fast-track military training program they had set up for Afghans who wanted to become officers in the army. It was in a remote former Nazi military base close to the Austrian border. As a Muslim I struggled with the diet. There was pork in everything, even the breakfast croissants. On weekends I would drive to the nearest town with an American base and eat burgers.

We were learning NATO standard theory and tactics, how to work with allies, information warfare, and so on. I enjoyed the studies, but I did not enjoy the field training where this American drill sergeant would curse us all the time.

"You motherfucker, why are you running like a chicken?" he yelled.

"What did you fucking say?" I replied.

"Fifty push-ups."

When I refused, the military police were called and I complained that the sergeant was cursing me. I did not like to be humiliated. It is not the Afghan way. They said, "He's not singling you out. It's like, this is how we talk in the military. It's how we train recruits." So I learnt this different mindset, and he went on cursing.

I came back to Afghanistan having learnt basic tactics and how to swear like a American drill sergeant. I moved to the ministry of interior, which was responsible for a large force of armed police. With my slight exposure to the West, after a year with the German reconstruction team and military training I found I could grasp some concepts better than many in the department who were far older. The first program I worked on was aimed at building coordinated district centers, with a police house and a compound for the district governor. It was very locally focused and involved training of district governors and police chiefs and providing vehicles and equipment. I thought it was a really good plan, but like a lot of development schemes during the twenty years of America's intervention, it was not followed through. The American military did not like it, they had their own ideas, and we completed the infrastructure for only a quarter of the district centers in the country before the program was canned.

I then went to work in the minister's office and helped draft a program to increase the size of the Afghan National Police. I had no formal training in writing policy papers or proposals, but again what little knowledge I had went a long way. After another short NATO command course, this time in Poland, I came back to work in the ministry of interior and was soon promoted to be policy adviser to the minister, Hanif Atmar. I would have a lot to do with him in my career, and at one point he would try to have me killed. But that was down the line.

Atmar was a former communist who had lost a leg fighting in the battle of Jalalabad in 1989. Because he spoke beautiful English he was always given a free pass by foreigners. But in the department we knew better. He was smart, and could formulate strategy, but had no idea how to build an effective team to deliver it. He let his ego get in the way. He was an authoritarian leftist by nature, wanting central control of everything, including information. While most Afghans could move on from the past, because we knew what compromises had to be made to survive, Atmar could never get on with the former mujahidin. No amount of foreign advice changed that. He made policy in his office then threw it into other departments to do delivery, and often there was no follow-through. These were called "Atmar plans," which we knew would never be implemented.

It was while working in his office that I had my best break. I was nominated for one of two Afghan places on a prestigious course for military officers destined for high command at Shrivenham in the south of England. After passing the language test, I met the British official running the scheme, Steve Brooking. All the other candidates from the ministry of interior failed. Steve was open-mouthed and did not hide his surprise when he saw me.

"Are you Sami Sadat?"

"Yes. What did you expect?"

"Oh my God, you're far too young for this program."

"So what does age matter," I replied. "Is this a program for an older man?"

"No, no, no. You're probably the best candidate."

But he did not like it—and kept on talking as if to himself to justify it. "No one else has your experience, but you're so young. No one else has your English or your experience despite your age. This is for the military and you already have military background. But this is for leadership of the ministry of interior. So are you too young?"

In the end he argued himself round and I went to England with two guys from the army who had also passed. The course was in a futuristic modern building in the heart of the countryside, set in rolling green farmland. I was the youngest student in the history of the course, while most of my fellow students were British officers in their forties. Some of their children were not much younger than me, and I would play soccer with them at weekends.

ADVANCE COMMAND COURSE

When I first arrived I saw the disbelief on people's faces. The first thing they said to me was, "How old are you?" When I said twenty-four they would laugh. And it became more hostile in the evening in the bar when they were drunk and could not hide it. They would say things like, "You got your rank and came on this course because probably you're connected to some high family, or maybe you paid your way in." I hated that and I said, "No, I fucking worked hard for my rank." I was a major, and during the course I was promoted to lieutenant colonel.

I had a good command of English by now and was able to hold my own. I did not say much in class, but sometimes I was provoked. One day a student was trying to explain his experience in Africa, where he met a soldier engaged in corruption. He said, "He was a young kid, but a colonel, just like Sami here." I could not let that go. "What the fuck," I said. "Are you comparing me with this African gangster?" I was popular and if a lecturer spoke well of Pakistan and against Afghanistan I would raise my hand. The other students would chant, "Sa-mi, Sa-mi, Sa-mi," because they knew that I had learned how to debate like the British. I could be brutal and loud, while making a rational case against what the lecturer had said.

There were other foreign soldiers on the course, and we had British sponsors to keep an eye on us. When I first met my sponsor, Major James Sunderland, who later became a member of parliament, I could see he was worried because I was so young. I allayed his fears after the first exam when I got a merit and he had a pass. I was passionately keen to learn and was studying hard, while also going to London often to make what contacts I could.

It was on that course that I went to the US for the first time. We arrived at the military camp at Norfolk, Virginia, at night, and when

I woke the next morning I was in what felt like a substantial town, with regular roads and traffic lights and so on, and I wondered where I was. It took a while to realize I was not in a city but an enormous military base. Everyone I could see, as if to the horizon, was working for the military. The scale was on another level from anything in my experience. I had seen British aircraft carriers which were big, but nothing like the Nimitz-class ship we boarded on my first day at Norfolk. A thousand feet long and weighing one hundred thousand tons, I was told there were five thousand people working on it, with their own hospital and the ability to travel for as long as six months, all to carry one hundred aircraft to any place on the globe.

We did classes with the air force, marines, and the navy. And I was awestruck by the depth and breadth of their military capacity. They even had a Space Command. Its commander gave us a presentation about the future threats in the space, and America's response, although just beginning, was to spend tens of billions of dollars a year to keep up in this new arms race.

Our hosts also wanted to show the sacrifice their fellow Americans had made in the cause of freedom. In addition to the Lincoln Memorial, they took us to see the lines of graves in in Section 60 in Arlington Cemetery, where the fallen of Iraq and Afghanistan had their final resting place. I walked along the graves looking at the names of those who had died for the freedom of my country. It balanced the rest of the tour. There was a price to be paid for keeping America's place as the biggest and best in the world.

That trip changed my perception of the world. Back home in Afghanistan, there were all kinds of conspiracy theories about the war: the Americans had come to take our precious stones, and extract coal, gas, and oil; or they were planning to stay forever and have permanent bases across Afghanistan. Now I knew those stories were not true. I genuinely believed that America had come to help.

The British command course was the best thing I could have done to give me a new way to see the world. Through these practical demonstrations, but even more in the classroom, I learnt what war meant. It was as if everything that happens or will happen in the future is in some way connected to a former war or to prevent a future war. Global shipping routes, internet connectivity, the airline industry, mines, infrastructure—it all had a security component. The military were a key determining factor in so much of our lives.

And on that course my technical military understanding, too, moved onto a new plane. I learnt how to command thousands of troops, coordinate joint forces on the ground and in the air, and work with other countries on combined operations, while exercising leadership with civilians. I learnt the value of strategic communications and what it means to connect with a global audience and other governments, as well as running information operations against the enemy. I came away with analytic skills that I had not imagined existed. I loved it, but it was very, very challenging. It took the best of me.

When I graduated in 2011 I gave my prayer rug as a gift to my sponsor, James, with some presents for his children, and walked away from that Staff College a completely different man ready to take on the world.

BACK IN KABUL

Afghanistan, too, had changed in the year I had been away. When I left, one of the best American commanders to serve in our country, General Stan McChrystal, had been forced out after careless gossip by his staff that appeared in Rolling Stone magazine. McChrystal had been the main architect of the "surge" of troops that a reluctant President Obama had agreed to in 2009. The president had cut the legs off the surge by announcing withdrawal at the same time. He signed off the increase to nearly one hundred thousand Americans, along with fifty thousand allies, only with the agreement of a clear timetable for it to end. An American political adviser in Kabul said it was "like raising in poker, while saying you're going to fold next round."

It was during the long arguments over the surge that Joe Biden's opposition to any Afghan involvement was revealed. He was vice president, and if he had had his way, instead of increasing troops, he would have cut the American troop presence in Afghanistan down to just one thousand, capable of doing limited special forces raids and protecting themselves but nothing else.

Biden's desire to pull out almost all troops and Obama's signaling of the timetable showed how little they knew about warfare or the complexity of regional matters in Central Asia.

The generals fighting the war became increasingly concerned that they were being asked to do a job but not given sufficient resources. On a visit to London to shore up allied support for the war, McChrystal called Biden's plan to cut troops a recipe for "Chaos-istan."

Meanwhile on the ground Afghans were dying every day, and we could see that imposing this deadline on the war was a disastrous mistake. Obama's way of waging war—set by the calendar, not conditions on the ground—sent out a signal that America was not committed in the long term and was damaging to the nation's standing in the region and the world.

When he was fired, McChrystal was replaced by the guru of counterinsurgency, General Dave Petraeus, who had literally written the manual for how to win in a complex battle space like Afghanistan. He came at the peak of the surge, but just as the Taliban were emboldened by the timetable for withdrawal. He was dealt a difficult hand, and it did not help that his relations with President

Karzai were terrible. He had a transactional approach and showed no respect—a quality that mattered in the Afghan context where courtesy was important. I knew that the president loathed him, and the feeling was mutual.

Increasing civilian casualties had embittered Karzai, who lashed out at a press conference. "History," he said, "is a witness to how Afghanistan deals with occupiers." The occupiers he was talking about were the international coalition in Afghanistan. Standing shaded by tall plane trees and larches in the large garden area of the Arg for a press conference on a fine May day in 2011, the president added to a growing catalog of complaints. He demanded an end to night raids; an end to all US military operations if not partnered by Afghan troops; an end to foreign-owned private security companies; and the closure of Provincial Reconstruction Teams, the joint military and development bases across the country, which he called a parallel state.

It was in that same garden that I had lunch with the president and his chief of staff soon after returning home. He wanted to talk about a letter I had written from England about how we needed to take back control of our country for ourselves. With the Obama administration heading for the exit, we needed a plan. I wrote that transition to Afghan authority would have three pillars. The first pillar was ensuring that the Afghan economy could stand up for itself without support. The second was transition of military affairs to our military, getting the best of American skills training, but taking responsibility for our own security. And the third pillar of transition was how to keep the US and the wider international community engaged in Afghanistan. Of course, we needed to focus on economic and military sovereignty, but we needed the longer-term engagement to keep on the right track.

Looking back, the consequences of failure in that third pillar are the most serious for my country. Even without the Ukraine war the world has turned its back on Afghanistan. I had seen the Israeli lobby in the US and wanted to use that as a model. Our lobbying in Washington had never been successful. Back in the days of the Cold War when the then–defense minister (and later president), Daud Khan, could not persuade America to provide economic and military support. At the time the CIA's main partner in the region was Pakistan, and Daud's failure had the disastrous result that Soviet involvement increased, leading to the catastrophe of the 1979 Soviet invasion.

"You know, I took your letter to the National Security Council," the president said. "I told them to implement all three of your pillars of transition."

His chief of staff, Abdul Karim Khurram, nodded in agreement. "It was good work," he said. "Sami, you've been in England, and briefly in America, and have seen American forces operating here. What are the differences between them?"

"Sir, I think the main difference is in their mindset," I said. "The British learnt from imperial experiences in India, Africa, and Malaysia, as well as their successful operation against an insurgency in Oman in the 1970s. The Northern Ireland conflict is still fresh in their minds. And what they take away from those experiences is that they may not need to totally defeat their enemy—but set the conditions where they can engage with them. It is an approach that can seem complex and frustrating."

Khurram said, "But it may be the best outcome. In the long term we need to engage with the Taliban, may even need to bring some into government."

I knew that the president had recently got into trouble for calling the Taliban his "brothers." I did not want them to get the idea that we should give them an easy ride.

"The approach is not soft," I said. "We need to be on the offensive every day. But the US could learn from the UK, who put a lot of conceptual mental power into studying the enemy, and working with society and the communities that support the enemy, with the aim of potential negotiations, while the American way is to use more force with the aim of total defeat."

No American commander was keener on defeating the Taliban than Petraeus. He was not interested in negotiations. His so-called "Anaconda" strategy was built to squeeze the life out of the Taliban, both on the battlefield and through economic and other means. But he lacked consistent support from President Obama. The language of President Obama's first speech on the war in 2009 signaled narrower aims than had been adopted by his predecessor, President Bush. At the start of the war Bush sent troops to Afghanistan "to destroy the Taliban and al-Qaeda," before moving to nation building. But under Obama the word "destroy" had gone. He wanted, "to disrupt, dismantle, and defeat al-Qaeda in Pakistan and Afghanistan and to prevent their return to either country in the future."

But just as Bush had never put in the right resources to "destroy" al-Qaeda, so Obama was not fully committed for the long-term engagement we needed to ensure stability. The paradox of the policy of short-term fixes was that it committed America to be in Afghanistan for the long term. During the arguments in 2009 over troop increases requested by McChrystal, the president was clear. "I'm not doing ten years. I'm not doing a long-term nation-building effort. I'm not spending a trillion dollars." The consequence of this short-term thinking was that America would indeed be in Afghanistan for another ten years, spending more than another trillion dollars, still without a plan for anything other than the short term.

"Perhaps because the UK has a monarchy they can take a longer view," I said over that lunch in the garden in 2011. "America's time horizon never goes beyond the next election. Every president does their own analysis, draws their own conclusions. And then they start eliminating or establishing new programs every four years."

Decisions would be made in Washington with little reference to reality on the ground, and ahead of American elections, both for president and the mid-terms, there would be uncertainty in Afghanistan. Our currency would fall, the economy would stagnate; long-term projects by the Europeans and NATO countries would go on hold until the election was resolved. The American political cycle killed momentum both towards fighting the Taliban and constructing a new country.

"The reason the whole US project is failing is not because what was applied was wrong," I said, "but any strategic vision was damaged by these constant swings and policy changes. Conceptually, the UK viewpoint is better and more effective, because it takes a long-term view involving society, and involving negotiation with the enemy. And that can neutralize opposition."

Karzai nodded, although reluctant to praise the British. He was educated in India and had a healthy skepticism about the colonial past. "When I first became president, the foreigners told me things to try to deceive me. Now I know better than to be taken in. People like you who have studied their approaches can help me understand better some of the military affairs."

I smiled and said, "Yes, I can help you if you want to invade Pakistan."

"So, what are we going to do with you?" He laughed. "You've been well trained now. You understand the ways of our international allies. You're competent with conceptual knowledge. I think you're best suited for the intelligence because you're smart."

He called Bismillah Khan Muhammadi, who had replaced Atmar as minister of interior while I was away, and told him to give me a good job. I wanted to be director of Interpol to connect Afghanistan to the global community in law enforcement.

"You're far too young for that," the minister said when I went to see him about the job, "and have no experience." He could not turn down the president entirely, so he offered me deputy at Interpol. But while these discussions were going on, I had to resign after a fight with a corrupt detective who was close to the minister. The detective had tried to demand a bribe from a friend of mine, Ajmal Abidy. I had a reputation for opposing corruption, and when Ajmal called for help, I immediately went with him to Kabul police headquarters to help sort it out.

Ajmal was trying to call in a loan of $50,000, but the man who had borrowed the money refused to pay it back. When he went to get help from the police department that dealt with fraud, a detective had asked for a bribe. We went straight to the office of the police chief, General Muhammad Ayub Solangi, who I knew well, who signed a letter approving the investigation. We took the letter down to the man who was supposed to deal with these things, whose office was a small filthy room in the basement of the building. He was not wearing a police uniform but stained Afghan clothes, sitting at a desk with just one other broken chair in the room. When we arrived he did not stand up or greet us in any way.

I waited a couple of minutes, standing in front of his desk, and then said, "Sir, we have a complaint letter."

He did not reply, so I went on, "Your boss instructed us to come to you. This is the letter, and this is your instruction."

"Who are you to tell my boss who should be investigated?"

"That doesn't matter," I said. "I could just be a taxi driver or any other guy off the street. It's a case of fraud, and it's your job to investigate."

He widened his bloodshot eyes. "I told your friend what I need."

"What did you tell him?"

That made him mad. "You rich pricks come in here and order people around. You take money from people, and when you lose a bit, you expect us to do your dirty work and get it back."

"Well, that's your job."

"It's not my job. We don't have anything. I am not working for you for nothing."

I picked up the piece of paper. "Look, your boss is clear about what you need to do."

"Well, why don't you go back to him," he said. "And tell him I am not going to do it. Unless I get my cut, there'll be no money for you." And he crumpled the piece of paper in a ball and threw it away.

At that I took a couple of paces forward, and, stretching over the desk, I punched him hard on the nose. Then I grabbed his head and smashed it down on the desk, causing his nose to bleed.

"You fucking need to do your job," I said, as we strode out and went back up to General Solangi's office. The detective appeared a few minutes later. He had torn his clothes along the way to make the attack look more dramatic. He changed his tone when Solangi's assistant told him that I was a friend of the police chief. He walked out and escalated the incident to the minister Bismillah Khan Muhammadi, who was his cousin.

I was summoned to the minister's office and now there was no chance of me getting a more senior role. The incident revealed a real problem at the heart of the republic. If the minister of interior was unwilling to stop this low-level fraud, it showed the deep roots of failure in our system.

Chapter Three

SECRET WORLD (2011–2013)

The bomb that killed my mentor and family friend Professor Burhanuddin Rabbani in 2011 was so small that it could hardly be heard even at the end of the street where he then lived in central Kabul. He had been appointed by President Karzai to head a government High Peace Council and scope a potential peace deal. A man claiming to be a Taliban intermediary made an appointment, and courteous as ever, Rabbani had greeted him in the Afghan style, embracing him. The intermediary leaned his head forward to touch Rabbani, and detonated a bomb hidden in his turban. Rabbani died for peace in the embrace of a suicide bomber.

I happened to be close by and had a call in my car that there had been a bomb. I quickly called the police control center.

"Sir, it appears the explosion was in Professor Rabbani's house."

"Do we know of any casualties?"

"There are no reports yet."

I went straight to the house and arrived at a scene of chaos. Rabbani's guards were crying, and two men were lying down in the road covered in blood. One had been beaten and shot. His injuries did not come from the bomb but from Rabbani's guards. One was now raising his rifle to shoot again. I quickly recognized the wounded man on the ground as the head of secretariate of the High Peace Council, Masoom Stanekzai.

"Don't shoot," I shouted.

The guard shouted back, "This is the guy who brought the suicide bomber to the house."

I ran over and pushed down his rifle barrel. "Don't be an idiot. This is the one person who can tell us anything about what happened and who was really behind this."

I went into the house, which was badly damaged. The windows were blown out, and I could see the feet of the suicide bomber. The carpets were covered in blood. I could not bring myself to see Rabbani's body. It was more important to keep those outside alive.

Stanekzai was a Pashtun and was now in mortal danger from Rabbani's loyal Tajik guards, who had fought alongside their leader in the mountains, followed him to Kabul when he was briefly president in the years after the Russians left, and were in blind rage after his death. I pulled Stanekzai into one of Rabbani's vehicles, his assistant and a wounded security guard into another, and drove them the short distance to the "Four Hundred Bed" military hospital, which was close by. The hospital had been built and named by the Russian occupiers in the 1980s.

Stanekzai was still not safe there. Rabbani had supporters everywhere. And there were Taliban sympathizers who might want to kill him to cover their tracks. I went with Stanekzai to a room on the top floor, while the other two were treated downstairs, and called the chief of staff of the army, General Karimi.

"Sir, we need your help. We need to transfer these guys immediately to Bagram Airbase. Stanekzai has already been shot and beaten. If they kill him and Rabbani's assistant, we'll never know the truth."

Karimi acted quickly, sending two helicopters to the hospital, which ferried the three men to the American military hospital at

Bagram. There they would be protected from those who wanted to kill them and be treated for their wounds. But even the short flight was tough to take. By the time we arrived Stanekzai had lost a lot of blood. He was immediately taken into one operating theater, while I was asked to go into another with the security guard to translate as a doctor punched a hole in his side and pumped out what seemed like an ocean of blood.

"What's happening?" I said, as the never-ending tide splashed on the floor.

"Don't worry," said the doctor. "It's OK. It's internal bleeding. We need to empty all the blood out of his stomach." It was a nervy night. The security guard, who I now knew to be a colonel by the name of Sattar, had shrapnel in his liver. And Stanekzai's leg was wounded so badly he would never walk normally again.

I was on the clinic floor when an American officer walked up to me to ask what had happened. I tried to explain what I knew, and he said, "Are you close to Professor Rabbani?"

I said, "Yeah, we were like family."

"I'm sorry for your loss," he said, clasping my shoulder. It was then that I saw the four stars on his collar, and I looked at the name on his chest, which read "Allen." He was a marine general and commander of all international forces.

"Oh, I apologize, sir. I didn't realize you were General Allen."

He smiled and said, "It's OK. What's your name?"

"My name is Sami."

And he said, "Sami, you have my condolences. We'll do everything we can to make sure the wounded men are saved." He walked away, and that was my one and only meeting with General John Allen.

Later I asked the wounded security guard, Colonel Sattar, how the bomber had gotten through. He told me he was carrying an audio recording from the Taliban leader, Mullah Akhtar Muhammad Mansour, which identified him as an envoy for peace.

"He came in a white Land Cruiser with Stanekzai. I know Stanekzai and I let him into the house, but I insisted on searching the Talib."

I was mad. "So how did you search him and he still had the bomb?"

Sattar started crying.

"I searched him all over. I would not let anyone harm the president." They still called Rabbani president. "I even searched his balls. I found nothing." The suicide bomber had counted on the fact that it was a sign of disrespect to interfere with a turban.

CHAOS AT THE FUNERAL

I returned from Bagram to Kabul the day after the bombing and went straight to the short street where the attack happened. I wanted to see Rabbani's son, Salahuddin, to pay my respects and tell him what had happened, as I had been the first witness after the bomb. But it was difficult to talk to him. There was an angry mood among the many Rabbani supporters who had gathered, jostling inside the house. Some were armed. There was a division between those from Badakhshan, Rabbani's home province in the northeast, and those from Panjshir, further south. Those from Badakhshan were not out for revenge. But the Panjshiris wanted to use the death to stir up trouble against President Karzai.

The leader of those wanting blood was Amrullah Saleh, a complex figure who had been trained by CIA during the mujahidin war and now wanted to take revenge from President Karzai.

"There is only one person to blame for this, and that is President Karzai," he said. "He may not have ordered the bomb itself, but he was jealous of Rabbani's growing power. Rabbani was a symbol of unity; Karzai wants to rule only for the Pashtuns. We Tajiks are being pushed out of the way."

There were calls in assent to this, not least from Ahmad Zia Massoud, the brother of the legendary Jamiat commander, Ahmad Shah Massoud, who had fought under Rabbani's leadership, and was killed by a suicide bomber two days before 9/11.

I spoke up against Saleh's provocations. "Sir, please remember that Professor Rabbani was killed by terrorists. If we divide now we'll only be doing their work."

That did not speak to the mood of the meeting. Rumbling dissent began to grow. I carried on regardless.

"We could make it worse if we fight after this. We'll betray the professor's memory." I cast around for the right image. "It'll be something like committing treason for his blood."

When I pointed out that politicians here held a grievance against Karzai I was not allowed to finish. Ahmad Zia Massoud cut me off. "This is our family matter. Who are you to get involved?" And he threw me out.

Rabbani's son Salahuddin came outside with me, and from that walk in the street the day after his father's death we developed a firm friendship. Away from the crowds in the house, he asked me what happened. After telling him what I knew, I warned him of how the death was going to be manipulated by Karzai's enemies for their own reasons, and he should not be used by them.

I gestured back to the house. "Everyone who has come here has a grievance against President Karzai, and if we follow their lead there could be more bloodshed. We would be saying that a Pashtun president has killed a Tajik former president, and this will divide the nation." He nodded in agreement.

Shortly afterwards, Karzai appointed Salahuddin to head the High Peace Council, replacing his father, and he asked me to work with him. He needed a friend inside the Afghan system. He was not from the mujahidin generation who had fought the Russians but had spent a lot of time in the West and wore Western suits. I said I would give him a year out of respect and love for his father.

But first we had to go through the funeral. It was delayed for three days to allow Karzai to return from New York, where he had been at the United Nations. And every day the cries for revenge grew louder. On the day of the funeral, the whole of central Kabul was sealed off to traffic as thousands of people made their way by foot to the site of the hero's tomb on the Bibi Maru hill, to the north of the center of the city, that had been given for the last resting place of this revered figure from the days of the struggle against the Russian invaders.

The funeral ceremonies began calmly enough behind the high walls of the presidential palace a mile away from the burial ground with a blessing by Abdul Rasul Sayyaf, another of the mujahidin leaders from the 1980s generation. But all the time the crowd on the hill was increasingly restless. Speaker after speaker took the stage and exhorted people to stand up and fight in revenge for the blood of Professor Rabbani.

Amrullah Saleh had now set up his own political movement, and thousands of his supporters pushed at the security fence to gain access to the heart of the ceremony. They were being held back by the presidential guard, one of the most professional security services in the country, but there were too many of them, and when they began to exchange shots in the air, the decision was made that it was too dangerous for Karzai to come to the site.

After the barricades collapsed as the presidential guard withdrew it was chaos: people threw rocks and there were many injuries. The coffin was pushed up the hill over the heads of the crowd, hand to hand, while bloodcurdling speeches continued from the podium. When Saleh forced his way to the front to take the microphone, I found some people able to cut the wires so the loudspeakers were silenced. Unfortunately it meant that Abdullah Abdullah, the former presidential candidate who had been close to Rabbani, one of the most senior people from the 1980s generation, was also unable to speak to the crowd. He always dressed immaculately, and that day was all in black—black trousers, black sweater, and black blazer. He was still trying to speak after the coffin was laid in the ground, but no one could hear him, and the event descended into a general riot.

In the days that followed, Saleh held a series of rolling protests against the Karzai government in a dangerous ethnic escalation. But, taking my advice, Salahuddin refused Saleh's invitation to join him. I could see it was a political trap. Salahuddin was not a war fighter; he believed in debate and discussion. He spoke both of our languages well and, like his father, wanted to bring unity to all the tribes. Although I agreed to join the High Peace Council with him, I did not trust the idea of peace because I knew the Taliban would not make peace. I took the job to support Salahuddin, who had been like a brother to me. I loved his father and wanted to help him.

While not a fighter, he did not lack courage. I saw this on one trip to Helmand in the southwest when we went out to a meeting in Sangin, a town which had seen some of the fiercest fighting of the war. The British and American ambassadors had come from Kabul with us but were unwilling to risk coming out of the secure army camp into the town. During the meeting rockets began to land nearby. I grabbed Salahuddin to take him to safety. He pushed me off, saying quietly, "These rockets can't go on. The third one has landed. That'll be the last one." People had been trying to flee, but they turned back when they saw him sitting there, unmoving as a rock. Cheers rang out celebrating his bravery, they returned to their places, and we continued the meeting. I have seen soldiers who were less brave and was very impressed.

"NOT AN ADEQUATE STRATEGIC PARTNER"

It was a difficult time to try to build peace in the country. Fighting was at the most intense of any time in the war and did not abate in the winter of 2011 and 2012, at the height of Obama's surge of troops. There was little trust between the American and Afghan administrations, let alone with the Taliban. President Karzai's relations with America were now at an all-time low.

The two main international leaders in the country, General Allen on the military side and Ambassador Ryan Crocker on the civilian side, were more emollient than their predecessors. But however good their personal relations, Karzai no longer trusted America.

Crocker had known Karzai since the first winter of the war in 2001, when he had been the first American ambassador after the fall of the Taliban, and on his return in 2011 the two would reminisce about the days when they met in the presidential palace, the windows shot out, with torn furniture to sit on, and only a primitive stove to keep out the harsh cold of a Kabul winter. Good personal chemistry could not hide a broken relationship: the Obama administration had given up on Karzai.

The brutal assessment of Crocker's predecessor, Karl Eikenberry, that Karzai was not reliable, "not an adequate strategic partner"—in a memo that inevitably leaked—was the real position of much of the Obama administration. Karzai was described as a corrupt figure at the top of a system where there was "little to no political will or capacity to carry out basic tasks of governance."

Eikenberry had correctly assessed that Karzai and those around him thought America would be there for ever. "They assume we covet their territory," he wrote, "for a never-ending 'war on terror' and for military bases to use against surrounding powers."

To me Karzai was a great Afghan patriot. But he did not know how to deal with the West. On one hand he wanted American support, but on the other was very harsh on them, and oftentimes unfair. He never understood American intentions to leave even when they were spelt out to him in clear terms. He thought that Afghanistan's strategic location, the bridge between Central and South Asia, was so important that America would not want to lose their foothold in our country.

Karzai's relations with the Obama administration had gotten off to a bad start at a dinner for Joe Biden, then the newly elected vice president, back in December 2008. It went down in Kabul legend. Karzai had been respected as a fellow head of state by President Bush, who would describe him as "My man Karzai." They talked by videoconference every two weeks. Karzai told me that Bush had been dignified. "In conversations, he would understand my point of view."

Biden made clear that things would be very different under Obama. With the US economy in meltdown following the crash, Karzai was told that American voters would no longer sign a blank check. Voices were raised on both sides—Biden repeated a jibe that Karzai had little control, he was little more than the "Mayor of Kabul." The vice president complained about corruption, referring to the ornate homes of many of those at the dinner that were on display in central Kabul.

Karzai told me that he had tried to get more American focus on Pakistan, asking the new vice president how they would approach a country which was clearly the "center of gravity for violent extremism in the region."

Biden replied, "Why do you think we should choose Afghanistan over Pakistan?"

"Because we are allies," Karzai responded.

"Make no mistake, Pakistan is fifty times more important to the United States than Afghanistan," said Biden. It was a ruthless reset of relations.

The breaking point in the conversation came over civilian casualties. There was a growing American sense that while the vast majority of Afghan civilian deaths were at the hands of the Taliban, those killed by international troops were given undue prominence by the president's very public complaints. Karzai pleaded that Afghans should be "partners and not victims." When Karzai said, "We are just poor Afghans, nobody cares," the evening abruptly ended with Biden throwing down his napkin, and stalking out of the room, saying, "This is beneath you, Mister President."

Biden would go on to be the most consistent critic in the Obama administration over continuing engagement in Afghanistan. This history makes the naiveté of the Ghani government in 2021 even less forgivable. They clung to some hope that Biden would listen to his generals and keep troops in the country. They should have remembered his contempt for Afghanistan, which he has repeatedly said is not really a country at all.

The appointment of Richard Holbrooke in a new role with overall control of policy for Afghanistan and Pakistan made things worse. Holbrooke's meddling in the 2009 election was overt. American officials spent months standing up other potential candidates before fixing on Abdullah as the man most likely to beat the incumbent.

The freeze in US/Afghan relations with the incoming administration damaged faltering attempts at peace talks with the Taliban. American negotiators held a series of meetings in early 2011 with a Taliban team in Doha, Qatar. But Karzai was enraged that he was not part of the talks process, and the talks stopped when Afghan officials leaked the name of the Taliban negotiator to the German media. The death of Osama bin Laden, tracked down to a house close to a major Pakistani military base in Abbottabad, complicated things further. Despite Pakistan's clear complicity in international terrorism, America never took the action they should have done against them. By the time I joined the High Peace Council with Salahuddin at the end of 2011, the talks process was on ice amid deep distrust between Obama and Karzai.

At the High Peace Council our role was not making peace at the strategic level. We were trying to give a role to former Taliban fighters who had surrendered. It was called the FRIC, the Forced Reintegration Cell, with the aim of integrating Taliban fighters into Afghan society. It never worked. International troops would, for example, fund the clearance of a canal, offering shovels to former Taliban fighters. But I do not believe that many joined the workforce and gave up the gun for good.

There were political divisions inside the High Peace Council which reduced our effectiveness. When Stanekzai recovered from his injuries he ran things his way. He was supposed to act under the leadership of Salahuddin, but he ran his own programs, his own relationship with President Karzai, and with foreigners. And of course he used patronage to bring his own people into jobs, following the money and building a power base, as were so many in the government.

INTO THE SECRET WORLD

During the year I worked at the High Peace Council, President Karzai would call me in for lunch every few weeks and ask my advice on provincial matters, particularly regarding Helmand. He wanted me back in government, and after nearly a year I was ready to agree.

"Look, Sami, the future of this country belongs to young people like yourself, especially those who are educated," he said. "I want our intelligence agency to become competent and become capable in this region, because intelligence is the most important function."

We had been in a big group at lunch, but this meeting was just one-on-one in his office after the meal. He was idealistic about the capacity of intelligence. "The most patriotic people who are smart and courageous join the intelligence agency of any nation. So I want you to go there, take a job, and then start reforming the NDS."

He was planning to bring in a new director general to head the NDS. For now the acting head was Rahmatullah Nabil, who called me to say that he had been told to hire some guy called Sami Sadat.

I went in to see him and he looked me up and down with that look I knew. He did not even need to say the words "you're too young."

"Are you Sami Sadat?" he asked. He did not get up or move from his desk to welcome me but gave me a peremptory handshake while sitting. "So what have you been doing?"

I explained my military background and training, as well as work in the ministry of interior. "And now I work for the High Peace Council."

He said, "Well, we have to start you in a job in a managerial position." That was more junior and clerical-sounding than I was expecting. I said, "I'm already a director in the Afghan High Peace Council," a more senior role than he was offering. He said, "Well, those directorates are small and not comparable with our directorates, which are led by brigadier generals. So I can offer you a managerial position, which is a colonel position, and you're a lieutenant colonel." I turned him down and went back to the High Peace Council. "If you change your mind," said Nabil, "give me a call."

When the president asked in their next weekly meeting what he had done, he said that he had met me but we could not agree on a role. "Sami wants a higher position, like a director position. And I think he's not capable and competent enough for that." At that the

President yelled at him. He said "Are you out of your mind? I told you this guy's capable, and how did you find out, meeting him for just five minutes, that he was not? So get out, find him, and hire him for the NDS."

I was about to board a plane to Brussels for a "key leader" engagement. It was the kind of thing that a lot of money was thrown at during the American-led intervention in our country. The people running the programs sought out potential leaders for networking and training. I was with my friend Matin Bek and the president's cousin Hekmat Karzai.

I got a call from Nabil. "Hi, Mister Sadat. Where are you?"

"At the airport. I am about to get on a flight to Brussels."

"Come to my office so we can discuss the job."

And I said, "I can't come. I'll come when I'm back."

"You don't understand." His voice began to rise in a slight panic. "You can't travel without the consent of the NDS. I just got your decree from President Karzai." It was my first taste of the reach and power of the NDS, a dark and deep world with a strict organizational culture. A couple of NDS men arrived and took my bag out of the hold of the plane, and I went straight to see Nabil who appointed me as deputy director for intelligence analysis, a senior enough role. I would come to value the support of Nabil. Behind a quiet and thoughtful manner, he was a risk taker who really understood how to work with the grain in Afghanistan. This was in sharp contrast to, for example, Hanif Atmar, as well as some others in the administration, who thought that there would be no progress without significant foreign input.

But at the time my appointment as deputy to Yama Karzai felt like an ambush. I was driven without ceremony to another NDS compound, one with a highly fortified inner compound. It was known as Department 44. I went inside to a dark austere office with a low ceiling, stone floor, and brick walls painted black. There were stylish black leather seats. A man rose from the gloom of the room and said, "Are you Sami Sadat?" I nodded, and he said, "I'm Yama Karzai."

This Karzai was the president's cousin, but he had a good claim on the role despite that family link. He had come into southern Afghanistan with his cousin Hamid before the fall of the Taliban in 2001 and worked for some years in counter-narcotics before going up through the ranks in intelligence. So he had earned his senior role, although there is no doubt that being the president's cousin helped.

I had not even had time to find out who was running the department for intelligence analysis before I came. When I realized, I thought Nabil had thrown me under the bus. Yama Karzai came with a maverick reputation—and was powerful enough not to obey Nabil as the head of the NDS. Nabil's calculation must have been that since the department was out of his control, he may as well throw another problem its way.

I could not have been more wrong. Yama Karzai took me under his wing, talking two or three hours a day about intelligence, sitting in the black leather chairs, and drinking black coffee all the day long. An introvert who rarely left the office, he had trained at the National Defense University in Washington, DC, and had studied the subject in depth. He told me of the daily intelligence cycle, how to manage input and output, and the map of different organizations—not just our own, but CIA, MI6, and the Germans, Canadians, and so on—who all fed us information. And we needed to monitor open-source intelligence. But he had not cracked a core problem: that they were gathering enormous amounts of raw intelligence but lacked the organizational capacity to manage it into actionable data for policymakers. It was a classic intelligence challenge.

Department 44 had more than one thousand employees in all thirty-four provinces of Afghanistan, and this was the place where all the other branches of NDS, including the central branches, the overseas stations, and the thirty-four provinces, reported their findings. Department 44 would then analyze the data and decide what to send where, classifying information all the while. As well as the enormous daily processing of material, at the time we were also doing special analysis of ongoing operations.

Now I could put into practice something I had learnt at the British officers' academy—that it was better to share information where possible and not hide it. In my first days in the department I brought in builders to tear down the internal walls. Until then analysts had sat in individual cubby holes, with wooden partitions between them, protecting information even from their own colleagues. I encouraged the analysts to share information and seek confirmation from their colleagues. If they were on the wrong track, others would quickly tell them. Working collectively the analysis would improve, because the pieces could be fitted together.

In what would become a trademark in every office I led, I bought a good coffee machine. And I promoted younger Afghans. Like many parts of the Afghan security sector, the NDS was full of old men who had come back from exile after 9/11 and were now working out their time before retirement. If I was going to change outcomes in our favor, I needed new blood. I put the younger analysts on courses so they could learn how to examine information and, crucially, how to follow trends, instead of events and incidents, and provide analysis based on a trend. That would equip them to see the future. The training brought in fresh ideas, helping the department to rethink and understand clearly its mission and vision.

One day Yama Karzai said, "The guys are coming over from Ariana today." That was code for the CIA station, based in the old Ariana hotel nearby. During the meeting one of the Americans asked a question about our sources, and Yama looked at him and said, "Are you on staff or a contractor?" And when he said he was a contractor he was asked to leave. That was Yama Karzai.

The CIA was really interested in what I was doing to make a change. "You can have whatever you want from us," one said. "We've been wanting to do this for a very long time, but there was nobody to partner with us." They assigned an officer to work with me, to sift through the 1200 pieces of intelligence we received every day for the fish we wanted in the middle of this large ocean—how to decide what was gold and what garbage. Until then too much intelligence had remained just raw material, lacking any analysis or understanding of its importance.

I wanted to start a daily briefing for the president, to focus our analysis towards him. He liked it, and it became an important conduit for NDS material. To help craft the product, the CIA sent someone from Washington who prepared briefs for President Obama. He said that every president had his own style. Some wanted long written briefings, others material on one side of paper. We had learnt that Karzai wanted it read out to him. Ours is a very oral culture, and he would issue guidance based on what he had heard.

Yama Karzai had a really interesting view of this relationship. The CIA briefer said that the president was our "number one client." He needed to buy the product and be fully aware of what the intelligence agency saw as threats. But Yama Karzai said it was the other way round. The president was a source to be recruited in order to be influenced. Any briefing implied a course of action to be taken against a threat. We were competing for the president's ear with countries in the region and the wider world, as well as other actors in Afghanistan. It was the job of the intelligence agency to be able to recruit the president in an attempt to keep him on our side, so that when we sent information he would take it seriously. That way our information influenced the president and other key decision makers in order for them to be able to protect the country from harm.

President Karzai asked who was preparing his daily digest and, when told it was me, he was pleased as he knew I was an Afghan patriot. But he had begun to mistrust the wider NDS, thinking it was increasingly under the influence of the CIA. He became more and more paranoid, retreating into conspiracy theories.

Yama Karzai also believed in conspiracies. He thought that dark forces were at work, and whatever Afghanistan did to clean up its democracy, foreign agents would always decide the outcome of elections. Though a brilliant spymaster, he thought America was constantly engaged in acts designed to harm Afghanistan, including an absurd story that America delivered weapons to the Taliban in order to justify the continuation of the war. This was the result of a successful Russian disinformation campaign that never went away. Reports talked of white helicopters that would arrive at night in the north of the country, dropping weapons to the Taliban. Yama Karzai wanted me to put the information into the daily brief.

"I can't do that. There's nothing in it."

"It comes from our director in Zabul," he said.

"I don't care. I know, and you know, this is wrong." And the disagreements would go on late into the night. Whatever we said, President Karzai believed the story. The Russians had dropped this disinformation bomb into enough willing ears for the rumor to spread on its own.

Apart from civilian casualties, which was a daily preoccupation of the president, his main outstanding issue was over a longer-term security deal with the United States once troops left. Negotiations over the Bilateral Security Agreement, the BSA, went on for years and overshadowed all other relations between our two countries. It assumed that some international troops would remain, and the deal guaranteed income for Afghanistan for rental for bases for them and committed them to support Afghanistan.

I was frank with the president. "We need to sign the BSA. It's good for Afghanistan."

"I know it's good for Afghanistan," he said. "But I want to know what the Americans are doing in this region. If they're looting the region, we want our share. If they're building the region, we want our share. I'm very suspicious about Americans in the region."

He did not like the BSA because it was not the mutual defense pact that countries like Japan or South Korea had. It did not commit the US to send troops if we were attacked by Pakistan. America would never give us that because of their long ties with Pakistan. But Karzai overplayed his hand and misjudged their intention, believing they would never leave because of the advantage that Afghanistan gave them in terms of their strategic footprint in the region—a fatal miscalculation.

I was only in that job for seven months, until Yama Karzai was promoted to be deputy director of NDS. I moved to be senior director for the covert action program, the psychological operation wing of NDS—one of the most important departments. In the right hands this was a powerful tool to influence people and unite the Afghans, while reading the enemy's mind. I soon discovered that in Department 44 I had only dipped my toe in the water of intelligence. Now I was thrown into the deep end.

Chapter Four

SPY GAMES (2014–2016)

By 2014, when I moved to head the covert action program at the NDS, President Obama had ended combat operations on his artificial timetable, changing the mission so that US troops and their allies were now configured to "train, advise, and assist" our forces. US air strikes went down markedly, and Obama did not change course when the Taliban took ground, and not even when some fighters took up the black flag of the Islamic State, more ruthless than the Taliban, who were by then sweeping across Syria and Iraq. In Afghanistan they called themselves "Islamic State-Khorasan Province" (ISKP), using a medieval name for land that is now part of modern Afghanistan.

The black flag and use of the term "Khorasan" were powerful lures for young men drawn to extreme violence in the name of religion, because of an Islamic prophecy that when the Mahdi comes ahead of the Day of Judgement before the end of the world, he will come out of Khorasan ahead of an army bearing black flags. American special forces did what they could to combat ISKP in the east where they began. But working under Obama's rules they were not able to use enough force to strangle this new threat at birth.

We needed to move fast to reform our intelligence capacity to fill the gap. The NDS occupied a large number of fortified buildings across the center of Kabul, a city within a city, a secret network built by the Russian invaders in the 1980s when the organization was called KHAD. The name may have changed, but many of the people had not. When I held my first meeting as director of Department 76, the covert action program, I faced ranks of communist-era officers with jet-black dyed hair, wearing ill-fitting suits. There was an air of dust and decay. I was the youngest person in the room.

Their programs were as out of date as their suits. Modern Afghanistan had passed them by. Outside the walls of the secret compounds was a vibrant city, swiftly modernizing, where young men and women lived radically different lives beyond the imagination of the old colonels. We were a country at war, needing to build a united identity for the present. But their idea of influence operations was through a network of local radio stations, usually in army bases. Along with patriotic songs and stories from soldiers there was relentlessly upbeat coverage claiming military success and bumper harvests.

The first thing I did was to close down the network. Everyone knew this was government propaganda. Instead we needed to better engage the free independent media, whose growth in what was then nearly a decade and a half of American intervention was one undoubted success story of the republic. The biggest independent network, TOLO TV, was an international player, with a production arm exporting programs and a twenty-four-hour news channel that competed with the best in the world.

Department 76 may have been called the "covert action" department, but much of what it did was out in the open. I had studied American and British doctrines of information operations, and I knew that in Afghanistan, language in this area was loosely used by people who had no grasp of what was meant. Terms like "Strategic Communications," StratCom, and "Psychological Operations," Psyops, were specific and defined in Western military terminology, but abused in the Afghan space. Afghan officials tended to take one of these words and stick it onto a program, while not changing their mindset that the state should control all information.

I could see that I would not be able to make the change I wanted without a change in personnel. Those lines of communist colonels with bad haircuts had their minds so deeply programmed they could not be reformed. Before I arrived, Department 76 was little more than a failed attempt for people to hold on to their jobs, with no change from communist-era thinking, where the media said whatever the intelligence agency at the time wanted them to say. The director's office was full of big colorful sofas that looked as if they were left over from a 1970s cigar lounge. There was a huge desk at one end and low lighting. It turned out that it had been built as a radio studio and taken over by the previous director.

The next morning I arrived very early and by lunchtime private contractors had arrived to tear down partition walls to make an open plan office, raising the ceiling and letting light in. A couple of CIA agents came over from Ariana. One was a guy with a white beard and a ready smile we called the professor, the other was a tall woman, let's call her Karen, not her real name. There were a lot of women in the CIA in Afghanistan: *Homeland* was based on real life. They were nervous and paced up and down, clearly worried about whether I could do the job.

"This is a complex department," Karen said. "There's a lot you need to know."

"So do you have some material I can read?" I asked. "Manuals, what worked, what didn't work?"

The professor went to an office the CIA had in our department and returned with a large stack of paper and documents. Karen gave me more from her bag. I asked them what problems they faced. They were concerned that the CIA and NDS did not share common aims.

"We work together on some projects. But the mission sometimes is different than we understand it is for the Afghan government. There is a lot of room for making mistakes." Not a good situation in the middle of a war.

When we met again three days later I had a full notebook.

"Now let me ask some questions," I said. "Has there ever been a conceptual manual or doctrine for this section, because any intelligence organization needs to cover distinct functions. The first branch should be able to collect and counter information. The second needs the ability to conduct influence operations and clandestine activities that are deniable. And I didn't find any documents even from the communist time on this. Am I missing something? Do you guys have anything?"

Karen looked at the professor, looked back at me, and said, "Are you telling me you read all those documents?"

"Yes, I have. And I think by now I know that for this department the first thing we need is a vision, mission statement, projects, objectives, and also a reform across the organizational structure because what we have is a remnant of something put together thirty years ago by the communist government with no connection to the real world."

She beamed a big smile. "Sami," she said, "We've been telling your predecessors hundreds of times that we need to review this. But even if they agreed, they could not make the changes needed because they would not get approval."

I said, "Well, I will make sure those changes are approved if we agree on a way forward." From that meeting I put together a new plan, splitting the department. One side would be Department 76 Overt, which would work in the open, giving information to the free media, having dealings with political parties and women's groups.

Agents there would be able to introduce themselves openly: "Hi, I'm NDS. How can we work together?"

The best people we had would go to a new Department 76 Covert, working inside the enemy, running deception programs behind enemy lines, recruiting vulnerable Taliban leaders, and so on. To make this work I needed wholly new structures. None of the existing managers had any background in information operations. They were from a world where the government had the right to arrest journalists and make them do the government's bidding. Their only communication idea was to spend more money on developing our own websites. I was dismayed at their level of incompetence. They were completely out of touch with our post-Taliban constitution that celebrated freedom of the press, freedom of speech, and a free market in ideas along with everything else.

Within weeks I had a new vision, mission statement, and objectives. The three most important objectives dealt with first, how to counter violent extremism; second, how to become more effective in uniting the Afghan tribes and building a vision for the republic; and third, how to garner support for Afghan security forces. Other objectives included countering foreign agent influences on Afghan media and political parties and civil society. We were in a tough neighborhood. Afghanistan bordered some of the most difficult countries in the world. China, Pakistan, and Iran were intent on bending things their way, while Russia, beyond the Central Asian republics to the north, had not given up its ambition to influence Afghanistan despite being kicked out in the 1980s.

The Americans were skeptical of my ambition. They knew how entrenched things were in the department. I told them, "Well, I'm gonna make a bet that I can do this thing." I prepared the ground well. I told the director general, Rahmatullah Nabil, that I wanted to make a presentation only to him, because it required some decisions that might be jeopardized if too many people saw the proposals. I knew that because this was such an important department, the senior staff were chosen by strong men in the country with influence deep inside the NDS. I was shifting people who had powerful friends.

He agreed that only he and his deputy, Massoud Andarabi, would see the presentation. I opened my laptop and put up a PowerPoint on the screen in his office, laying out the radical changes I would need to move lots of old-guard senior managers.

They were stunned. "Wow, these are big changes." Nabil said. "I've been trying to find someone who understands psychological warfare operations, and it seems Sami does."

But I could see that neither of them thought I would be able to carry this through.

"Boss, let's distribute tasks," I said. "You sign on it. And I promise this will be implemented if you back me. I'll bring a new team and good results after I've had time to train them."

I had brought the paperwork with me. I would not leave that room without a signature. Once he had signed it, I said, "When I've delivered these changes, we'll have a new department that's capable of serving the Afghan government pretty well."

MAKING THE CHANGE

I knew my most difficult task was to get the old guard out. I had tea with cakes and sweets brought in from outside to our large meeting room. And I invited by name only the managers affected—both those I wanted to promote and those I wanted to shift out. The older senior managers sat at the front with the younger new generation behind them. As I started speaking I felt the whole weight of the building sitting on my shoulders; it was more difficult than I had initially thought.

"I am talking to you with respect for your service," I had not really planned how to do this but knew how important respect was in our society.

"There are people in this room who've suffered in war in ways that some of us can only imagine. The pain of invasion, exile, losing friends and family and home. The pain of loss. I am second to none in paying tribute to the sacrifices many of you have made. Yours was the generation that paid a high price for what happened to our country."

The lines of faces looked at me deadpan. They did not know what was coming.

"But now we are in new times. And new times need new ideas. To move forward we need to freshen our approach to information operations. To do that we need new blood, new thinking."

I paused and took a deep breath.

"I don't want to damage our relationship. Out of respect for your talents and your long service, I've made a deal with the director general that all those who are leaving this department will be appointed elsewhere. New men will be promoted from inside the department to take your positions."

They didn't get it. One said, "What does it mean, sir?"

This was the critical moment in the meeting. "It means that except for finance and HR, every manager in the department will be replaced and you will be reassigned elsewhere."

The immediate response was silence. Then a very tall man with a mustache, who was a bit younger than the others, said, "You can't do that."

And I said, "Well, I already have. The director general has approved your transfers."

He raised his voice, quivering with anger. "I've been supporting the presidential campaign in favor of Ashraf Ghani. Now he's the winner you can't remove me."

He thought it his best play, but I responded calmly, looking him in the eye.

"Well, I asked for your reassignment, but based on what you just told me, that you have linked up with a political campaign, I will fire you directly, because NDS officers are not allowed to contribute to anyone's campaign."

That set them off. The meeting had been calm up to then, but he stood up and some others with him, and they started to yell. For a minute I thought they were going to attack me. But then I looked behind them and saw the younger ones who were appointed in their place as managers. They were smiling as they stood up as well, and I thought, "OK, so I have my team."

The advantage of the power of the NDS over its people, which I had seen when I was first recruited and hauled off that flight to Brussels, was that the director general's signature was law.

I tried to keep my nerve as they shouted in my face. "Look, you're only making matters worse. You will be reassigned to other departments; you will have good jobs. If you yell at me like this, and if you disrespect me for one second, I will make sure you're all fired. This guy is already fired, so he's not going to be a member of NDS anymore." They left the meeting room without any violence, leaving the new younger managers behind. We had succeeded in a generational shift.

"Come up to the front," I told them. "From now on your seats are around the table. I have put my trust in you guys. I'm your colleague, and your friend, and your boss as well. So never forget that I am your boss, but whatever you guys need from now on, there is no appointment, no waiting in the waiting room for the director. There is nobody outside my office with a gun, like the previous director. You just come in and we'll talk."

I made sure the outgoing managers left the building that day with only their ID cards and their personal belongings. For a while my CIA minders never left the safety of Ariana, fearing a riot at the NDS. Meanwhile I was called round the clock by supporters of the old communists.

"What are you doing?" said one. "Don't you know where you are?"

Another shouted down the phone, "This agency has eaten people's heads and buried people like you."

Among the callers was General Husamuddin Marzi, one of the deputy directors of the NDS. He had been head of military intelligence in the communist government in the early 1990s, until discovered selling information to Ahmad Shah Massoud, the mujahidin leader who was then besieging the capital. He was a lucky man, saved from the gallows when Massoud broke into the city and he was released. Now he was at the center of the web of old communists at the heart of the NDS.

"These guys are going to parliament to complain against you," said Marzi, "and I am backing them all the way." His intervention was the toughest challenge I faced. He went through the men I had moved one by one, detailing his family and military links to each of them. "You can't fire them. I'm sending them back to you. You will give them back their jobs."

"I can't accept nepotism," I said. "And I can't accept what you're saying. If they're your classmates, why don't you assign them as directors in other departments? Or actually, if you really trust them, then assign them as director in my place. I would be happy to go to another department." He would not call my bluff.

Word went out that there was this new guy at the NDS who's anti-communist and anti-older people. I bumped into the director of the Kabul region NDS, General Akhtar Ibrahimi, who snarled at me. "Oh, Mister Sadat, I hear you're firing communists. I'll hire all of them. You should know that I am a proud communist and will help my comrades if you keep firing them."

"General, I'm not against anyone. But if the communists are not adapting to our new constitution they should have no place in the NDS." I wanted to avoid confrontation but also give him a clear answer. We needed to make a change. Until now the post 9/11 generation had hardly featured in this central role in building the country. It took me as the first of that generation who became an NDS director to make the shift necessary. I used my full authority, connections, and influence to make sure I brought reforms and empowered this new generation. As I brought in intensive training courses the complaints began to die down. Then the CIA guys came back, the professor carrying a box of cigars for me. "How the fuck did you do that," he said, laughing and relieved I was still alive.

While the department was getting trained, I traveled round the country to take the temperature. One of our roles was engaging tribal leaders. That brought sniping from the old communist faction that I did not know the job of a director. I should be in my office, not running around "like a street spy." But I knew there was no way I could do my job without knowing what people were feeling on the ground, and besides, I was exhausted by the confrontations with other NDS directors. I needed fresh air, fresh ideas. We wanted to encourage tribal leaders and mullahs—Afghanistan's traditional influencers—to speak out against the Taliban. They would ask for support, with simple requests like, "If I had a gun, if I had a car, then I could go after the Taliban." And we would give them what we could. I encouraged them but accepted their reservations about speaking out. They would be putting their lives on the line, and they lacked protection in remote villages.

I set up a scheme to give them mobile phones so we could keep in contact, and we loaded up the phones with patriotic songs, stories from Afghan history, and poetry about national unity and love. These were popular and gave us access across wider areas.

COVERT ACTION

Once I had made the structural changes I wanted, putting in place reforms which would outlast me if I was killed, I could focus on the task I really cared about, which was using our influence capabilities to disrupt the Taliban ideological expansion. I hired smart young agents with language skills, including Arabic, so we could directly engage religious fundamentalists on their own terms. Our agents played roles on Facebook, pretending to be sympathetic and befriending Taliban fighters in order to really understand them and get inside their networks. This was the start of the internet interception program for the NDS.

The CIA did not support me in this work. They thought it would interfere with our overt engagement with the media and tribal elders. But German intelligence was willing to help. They set up VPNs through software so our IP addresses were not traced back to the NDS. I gave the new agents smartphones and laptops so they could work from home. If they were only online during the working day that might arouse suspicion.

From that we developed a full role-play operation where our agents had phone conversations as well as text exchanges, all the time acting as sympathizers with the Taliban. At the time the Taliban did not have a lot of social media accounts. But the Islamic State group was just beginning in Afghanistan, and we had more success in the early days of the program talking to militants from their franchise in this region, Islamic State Khorasan Province, ISKP.

As conversations progressed, inevitably after a couple of months there were requests to meet. Clearly our young urban agents would never be able to pass in real life as the personas they had created online. I contacted the head of counterterrorism in the NDS, and asked if he could provide an older agent who might pass as an uncle of one of our agents.

One Thursday afternoon, a fifty-year-old man arrived, bearded, with long hair and wearing Afghan clothes. He looked like a villager anywhere in the country. In Afghanistan, Thursdays are casual Friday, and I encouraged this approach among my staff, so when I met him I was wearing jeans, sneakers, and a short-sleeve shirt. He was visibly nervous.

I said, "Are you up for the job?" This was the first time we were trying such a risky operation, and I thought there was a very good chance of him dying.

"Yes, I'm up for it. So what do you want me to do?" And I introduced him to the agents who were working the source, including the one whose "uncle" he would be playing. I asked the uncle what he would need, and his eyes widened when I signed off the purchase of two phones, a laptop, and a cash advance without a pause. In the NDS people did not usually have the capacity to spend like this. But unlike some other directors I was not taking the money for myself or my friends, so there was more to spend on the work.

For the next five days he sat with the team who had been cultivating the source. He needed to know everything about the persona our agent had created, and everything about the other person who'd been on the end of the line for two months. At the end of that he returned and was far more comfortable than in his first meeting. He was very happy and respectful. "Are you ready?" I asked.

"Yeah, I'm ready," he said. He admitted that he had been nervous when he came the week before, and he told me why.

"My boss told me that I can only meet the director of 76 Directorate, not any other officers. And you were wearing jeans and sneakers while everyone here has a suit and tie. I asked myself, why is the director not meeting me? I had no idea that you are the director."

I laughed and said, "Times are changing in the NDS. We would never have done this program in the times when everyone wore a suit and tie."

"I love this program. I want to be involved with it," he said.

This "uncle" turned out to be one of the most successful agents in post-Taliban Afghanistan. He went deep inside ISKP. He helped us map their transport and facilitation across the north of the country. He named a network of people inside the Afghan government and business community who had been in touch with them and gave us lists of names of ISKP recruits.

Based on that information we conducted dozens of counterterrorism operations, making arrests and seizing cash and weapons. We arrested some of their recruiting agents and local leaders, in Baghlan, Charikar, Kabul, Jalalabad University, and even down to some in high school.

And while we were inflicting damage on them, our "uncle" was promoted through the ranks, becoming head of recruitment. They never suspected him. Everybody in the country who was recruiting new people would call him and ask how to transport new recruits and where to house them. He would say "we have friends here or here," and those places were NDS safe houses. The uncle was just the beginning. We succeeded in putting other people inside these networks through the work of the roleplay team.

Since ISKP was an international operation, our infiltration of their network meant we had reach abroad. One of our first hits was against a famous early member of the organization, known as Yusuf al-Khorasani, whose *nom de guerre* gave him away, as he had taken the name of the organization. We tracked him to Australia where he was arrested.

ISKP were avid users of media and modern communications, with groups on Facebook, WhatsApp, Telegram, Snapchat, and so on, that enabled them to connect globally—but also made them vulnerable. Recruits could reach out to each other, saying, for example, that they were in Australia and wanted to go to Syria. And they would ask for where to stay in countries along the way and who to meet. We would be in those groups and could share the information.

One of our best agents infiltrated ISKP so successfully that he became the courier whose job was to take Afghans to join the main organization in Syria. He took two people, a man and a woman, and they flew from Kabul to Istanbul on a Turkish visa. They then drove to Gaziantep on the Syrian border, crossed into the country, and were picked up and taken to other Islamic State hubs. Our agent returned to Afghanistan with a gold mine of information about the way the organization worked as well as the names of individuals all the way along the route. We discovered that some of the facilitators in Afghanistan were police officers. When we rolled up that operation there was no American involvement; all of the arrests were carried out by the NDS. And we were able to pass on useful information to other agencies. ISKP wanted our agent to do another trip, but of course he disappeared off their radar.

Unlike the Taliban, some of ISKP's key members were women, so our female agents could also infiltrate the networks with fake identities. One of them built a social media friendship with the ISKP commander for Nangarhar province in the east, and she built up his profile, the phone number, address where he was staying, and the address of their headquarters in Nangarhar, which was close to a school. We developed a target package and gave it to the US forces, who successfully carried out an airstrike.

One of our near misses was a senior Taliban figure, Qari Fasihuddin, at the time their shadow governor for Badakhshan, in the northeast. Through an agent who had befriended his aide, we discovered that Fasihuddin was injured in an operation and was being taken to hospital across the frontier to Peshawar in Pakistan. We had his phone number, details of his car, the location of the hospital, and the route he would take. We made a target package and then passed it on to Deputy Director Andarabi. But he could not line up what he needed in time, and we missed him on the way to the hospital.

We kept on the case, and twice more provided accurate coordinates to make a target package for Fasihuddin. I warned that if he successfully returned to Badakhshan, he would tip the balance of the war against us. Throughout the spring and early summer of 2015, the cat and mouse game went on, but the NDS system could never respond in time to get him.

Fasihuddin would go on to play a key role in the Taliban seizure of Afghanistan in 2021 and was named as their chief of army staff and head of the army. They even crowned him "Conqueror of Panjshir," a title with powerful resonance for the Taliban because they succeeded in 2021 in taking this beautiful valley to the northeast of Kabul, which they had failed to do when last in power in the late 1990s.

We came as close as we did to Fasihuddin because our agent pretended to be a figure of similar seniority in the Taliban hierarchy, Qari Sattar, the shadow governor of another province, Logar. We used the right name, calculating correctly that Fasihuddin had never met Sattar. The Taliban was like a franchise of small battle groups, whose commanders did not know all of the network. One ruling shura in Peshawar, Pakistan, may have had a grip on all of the network in the east but did not know what was happening in the south. And similarly, the other main shura in Quetta, Pakistan, had no idea of people like Fasihuddin up in the northeast, where they had their own smaller network, as did the Uzbek Taliban in the northwest.

Provided our list of the names was up to date, our agents would assume the name of a real Taliban commander.

Then we would build a detailed target package based on as much information as we had: photos, people around the target, weapons and other defense systems he had available, and so on. Depending on the location this target package would be actioned by our own NDS forces or the US and Afghan Air Force. At the time we could operate freely in Pakistan through hired hitmen. One of the leading members of the Haqqani family, a key Taliban ally, was killed by an NDS-contracted hitman near Islamabad.

We achieved more in a few days with these roleplaying deceptions than might have taken many months by traditional methods. And there was a great atmosphere in the office. My coffee machine provided fuel for the young agents who were doing so much for our country, sitting behind their laptops and acting their parts.

HOW TO SPEND $38 MILLION

Once we started having real success word spread across the headquarters of the coalition forces. An American general came to see me with an extraordinary proposal. At the time my budget was around $1 million a year. He had $38 million available to spend on psychological warfare in the next twelve months. He had already been to the ministry of defense and the ministry of interior. I gave him a tour of our operation, showing him the deception programs, and explained how we were getting deep inside the Taliban and ISKP as well as conducting overt influence operations.

He gestured at the modern, brightly lit office full of young people. "I came here this morning with a prejudice, Mister Sadat, and I want to apologize for that," he said. "I thought this would be another MOD or MOI. But you are ten years ahead of them."

We went upstairs to my office. "I have a proposition," he said. "I want to develop the psychological warfare capability of the Afghan army. Can you design me a program to do that?" We talked for a while about what he meant and how we could help.

But while I was designing his program, the CIA went to him behind my back. I wrote his proposal, but it did not go any further. The American general called me to say that Karen had warned him off, saying that what he was offering me was like crack heroin. "Sami will get so high he'll never talk to us again." The CIA feared that if the US army became my main partner, their programs, particularly the very successful deception operation, would be damaged. This was ironic, because I had developed the roleplaying operation only with German help because the CIA had never wanted to go that far. Now that the programs were successful, of course the CIA claimed ownership.

The general with the big wad of cash wanted me to make the choice, so I arranged a meeting between him and the CIA professor in my office. As I sat behind my work desk they sat in two chairs in front of me. It began well enough with a discussion about how best to help the general spend his $38 million so it could really make a difference in Afghanistan. If it was not going through my department, he asked where he could work that would be most effective. The general was adamant that I should lead his project.

"I've seen the alternatives. No one else in Afghanistan could do this. And I already have a sign-off to go with Sami. This is a directive from the Pentagon."

There had obviously been some tension before they arrived in my office, because voices were raised early in the conversation as the general basically told the professor to fuck off. "I do what my chain of command tells me to do. And then I will fight you in Congress."

"My chief of station in Afghanistan is second only to God," said the professor. "Take this to Congress and I guarantee you'll lose. There's nothing you can do. If this money comes to NDS there are bound to be leaks, because there'll be so many people involved."

He had such confidence in the primacy of the CIA. "There's no way we could let you come to NDS and jeopardize our mission." Clearly the idea of me having a choice was for the birds, but at this point he turned to me and said, "So, what do you want to do, Sami?"

It was a binary choice. I turned down the chance to spend $38 million in order to remain with the CIA, our key partner. That seemed to be the only option. I would be jeopardizing the most successful operation I had in order to build some psyops capability of frankly doubtful value. I knew that. But I had been shocked by the arrogance of the CIA. The professor had zero respect for the man in uniform on the other side of the table.

The general went on to blow away that huge pile of cash on bizarre American-made anti-Taliban TV ads that ran for years. People hated them because they were so depressing. They had images of people blown up in explosions and painted a map of the country in black with snakes and blood all over it. People did not need to see explosions to know that they were bad. If anything, they turned people away from the government.

Another part of their work was to build online platforms with really anodyne messaging to the Taliban saying things like "Let's join together for peace." The campaigns were designed by agencies in the United States who lacked any sense of the Afghan context, in such stark contrast to our own overt operations, which drew on local sensitivity to craft messages, articles, and hold gatherings. We knew we could help shape the information space only if we understood how people felt.

We opened our regional offices to the media so people could see the public face of the NDS. I spent hours on the phone persuading local directors who were stuck in the old mindset that everything should be secret. And we held large tribal gatherings, particularly in the east along the Pakistan frontier, where we took aside individuals we thought were pro-Taliban and tried to turn them to our side. If we succeeded we gave these low-level sources mobile phones and around $200 for each meeting with our agent, twice the monthly salary for a soldier.

And rather than making TV ads that depressed the population, I facilitated access to free media to show the reality of Taliban action. A major bomb explosion in a government compound in Ghazni destroyed an Islamic Heritage museum. I took the media there to show the Taliban did not care about things precious to our faith. When this appeared on the news it did far more than any government advert because people trusted an independent broadcaster. We built an open access program taking journalists, including from international agencies, to border clashes with Pakistan and a major car bomb in a bazaar a couple of days before the Eid holiday, when people were shopping for this important Islamic festival. Again it revealed the Taliban's contempt for normal Islamic family life.

We opened a series of closed doors for the media, showing them special forces training, and briefed them on how the army was operating. Every week I held an off-the- record briefing for senior editors to give them a full brief on the security situation across the country. I did not hide anything, and I would not lie. If things were bad I said so. It meant they could report the news with an understanding of the wider context.

WAZIRISTAN

In 2014 an unusual opportunity arrived to find new sources. The Pakistani army began a huge operation to clear militants in the mountainous border region between our two countries. Operation *Zarb-e Azb* meaning "cutting strike," engaged tens of thousands of soldiers. Around a million people were displaced from their homes, and tens of thousands of civilians were driven across the frontier into Afghanistan. The Americans were concerned that al-Qaeda and Taliban militants would be among them, but I saw it as a great opportunity to cultivate new sources. I was appointed to coordinate nine NDS directors to manage the inflow. We set up camps for people from different regions, with the largest for people from Waziristan, just across the border in Pakistan, which had been a hotbed of militant activity for many decades. We immediately started working with Waziri tribal leaders to identify international terrorists among them.

The Waziris had the strangest ideas about Afghanistan. They had been told that Afghanistan had been taken over and Islam crushed. We were led by infidels, nobody was allowed to pray or do anything they wanted because the Americans had total control of the country. They had destroyed the mosques and killed all the Muslim mullahs and scholars.

To counter this mindset, I identified twelve Waziri tribal leaders, and after giving them $200,000 in immediate refugee support (given by Governor Atta Noor of Balkh province), I sent them on a tour to the rest of Afghanistan. They met religious scholars and saw mosques open and functioning in Mazar in the north as well as in Kabul, cities they had been told were hotbeds of infidel atheism.

Back in the refugee camp in the east they were far more receptive to talking to us. They had completely changed. They saw that we were the same as them, and there was no truth in the Pakistani state narrative that there was no Islam in Afghanistan. I wanted to use them to pass a message back to people across the border that if they were contributing to collections for terrorists or sending their young men to fight or become suicide bombers for the Pakistani Taliban, the TTP, then they should know that they were killing Muslims. There are no infidels in Afghan cities or the countryside. There are Americans in their bases, but they are not stopping people from prayer.

Among the refugees I met one educated man with a degree in international relations from Peshawar. He told me an intriguing story.

"In June when we were coming to Afghanistan, the weather was very hot. I was walking with a family of nine people, including an elderly woman. We walked for hours in the sunshine. It was during the month of Ramadan, so we were fasting. When we got close to the Afghan border, this elderly woman fainted, and I had to carry her on my back. When we arrived at an Afghan frontier post, the police stopped us and asked, 'Who are you carrying?' And I said, 'It's a woman who's fainted.' They helped me carry the woman into their post and revived her with cold water. And they brought us water and biscuits for the children."

The man went on, "The police said 'There are civilian cars waiting. So you can jump into a car and they will take you to their homes where they will host you and give you refuge.' When she had revived, the elderly woman said, 'My son, I wish you were a Muslim, so I could pray for you. But thank you for your kindness.' And the Afghan police officer soldier was so mad. He took his hat, threw it on the ground, and said, 'Mama, what are you talking about? Of course, I'm a Muslim.' And he recited the *Kalima*, our declaration of faith. The woman started crying and said, 'We were told you are not Muslims, especially the military.' And the police officer said, 'No, ma'am. We're Muslims. We're like your own sons.' When we came down the hill, there were around fifty Corolla station wagons and vans driven by civilians offering their homes. They said you don't need pay rent or anything, you get two rooms, three rooms. And then they kept giving us food for a month in the evenings through Ramadan."

The problem was that there was such mistrust between our countries, with opinions formed by malign actors. I asked this man how he could have been deceived when he was educated. He looked down at his shoes. "The problem is that if people push the same narrative for ten years, then even if you're educated, you'll be influenced."

IMITATIVE DECEPTION

In July 2015 the Taliban could no longer keep secret something that had been suspected for some time—their founding leader, Mullah Omar, had died two years before. After a rapid reassessment of all the messages that had gone out in his name during the previous two years, we had the best opportunity yet to sow dissent in their ranks during the months of the power struggle that followed the announcement. For some time we had been developing a program to confuse the Taliban by inserting our own messages into their correspondence. The Taliban communicated with hand-written letters, fearing Afghan and US interception capability in the digital space, and through our infiltration of their networks we knew a lot about how this operated.

What we called our "imitative deception" program was designed to create rifts, misunderstandings and mistrust in their minds. Sometimes we had agents deep inside the Taliban who could write their own letters. In one, for example, my team developed a letter supposedly from Mullah Manan, the brother of the dead leader Mullah Omar, to the leader of a splinter faction, Mullah Mansoor Dadullah. The letter implied Manan's support for Dadullah suggesting he would back him against the likely successor to Omar, Mullah Akhtar Mansour.

If the letter had reached Dadullah, he would have immediately connected with Manan and discovered the truth. But this was a complex deception where the aim was not for the letter to get to Dadullah. Instead we hoped it would be intercepted along the way by someone close to Mullah Mansour, so he would see this "treachery." It worked a treat. From then on Mansour was planning to kill Manan.

As well as these deliberately disruptive actions, we would intercept real letters and replace them with our own imitated letters with changes in the substance to send on to the intended recipient. We were trying to create chaos, rifts, and misunderstandings and encourage splits in the Taliban ranks.

Another part of imitative deception was to publish harsh orders that purported to come from them. And there was no way that senior Taliban figures could come out and deny it because they were all in hiding. So we provoked public anger against tough Taliban decrees that did not actually come from them.

By now I had been on a two-week leadership course at Langley and was confident that what we were doing would achieve the best results. While the CIA did not share much about how they operated, the one difference I discovered was that they were far more attached to technology than us. The best assets we had were through traditional and local networks. I felt that what we were doing was more adaptive and flexible in our context. We had a very broad strategy in Department 76, not wanting to be pinned down to a narrow definition of what we did.

THE COFFEE MACHINE PLOT

We were facing a more determined enemy. Things moved in the Taliban's favor when President Ashraf Ghani took over in 2014 and failed to engage the traditional religious or tribal leadership. He had no Afghan roots after spending most of his life abroad, and sought refuge in his Pashtun ethnicity, but did not play the ethnic card with any skill, leading to worsening divisions across the country. The Taliban assassination campaign weakened the capacity of the government. Anyone suspected of working with the government was fair game. The NDS estimated that twelve thousand judges, rural religious scholars, and tribal elders were murdered across the south. And as the Taliban maneuvered themselves into positions of influence in remote areas, the removal of these people made their task far easier. Rather than trying to restore the equilibrium of traditional power, they disrupted it. With rural networks disrupted by the targeted assassination campaign, the Taliban successfully mobilized opinion against the Ghani presidency, calling it corrupt and Westernized. As religious clerics railed against the mismanagement of the state, tribal leaders hedged their bets, supporting neither the president nor the Taliban.

In my first meeting with President Ghani after he came to power in the 2014 election, I found myself in a different world from what I had experienced with President Karzai. Karzai had always used a small inner office for meetings, but Ghani decorated the large outer office and worked there. He saw his government as the successor to the 1920s reformist King Amanullah. When he was elected he found Amanullah's old desk, dusty and forgotten in a shed, and had it restored. This was the last time there had been an attempt at reform in the country, and in a mirror image of what happened to the republic in 2021, Amanullah was brought down by rural conservative mullahs, the sort of people who later supported the Taliban.

Ghani was a keen student of Afghan history, and as well as channeling the spirit of Amanullah, he had a painting commissioned of an eighteenth-century founding myth of Afghan history when one warring tribal leader in the south crowned his opponent as king with a wreath made from a wheat sheaf. The symbol is part of our national flag.

Sitting at Amanullah's desk, in front of the painting of the wheat sheaf coronation, Ghani thought he represented that spirit of reconciliation. In his mind, his interests and those of the country were identical, and so all of the institutions of the state, including intelligence, were bound to support him. It was false logic, and when he directly told me that I should use my operations, including covert action and psychological warfare, to support him, I was adamant about my responsibilities.

"I can't support politics," I told him. "My job is to support the Constitution."

"But you are supporting Nabil, your director, politically," he said.

And I said, "That's incorrect. I'm not. We're putting everything behind the security operation of the Afghan state. We're not supporting individuals, including you or Hanif Atmar."

He had heard of my animosity to Atmar. "Hanif Atmar is a patriot like you. He's a good guy, Sami." Ghani had appointed Atmar as his national security adviser.

"I don't know, Mister President, if he is or he is not. But I can't support him politically, because if the NDS gets involved in the politics, it will become very, very dangerous."

My relations with Hanif Atmar worsened by the day. When Ashraf Ghani replaced Hamid Karzai as president after a long dispute over the 2014 election result, Atmar became the national security adviser. I had come a long way in the few years since I had worked as his adviser in the MOI. We wanted to keep the NDS independent, but he had very clear ideas of how to conduct intelligence. He thought he knew it all, but he trampled all over doctrine and wanted to run his own policy. He had contacts with foreign intelligence agencies, including in Russia and Pakistan, and would never share the outcomes with the NDS. He opposed the idea of a daily brief from the NDS, wanting to be the only conduit to the president himself. Things spiraled downwards the day Atmar called me in to ask me to spy on Nabil for him.

"Sami, you know that the director general is out of control," he said. "He's not listening to us anymore. I want you to report on him to me. Tell me what he's thinking, who he meets."

"Sir, I can't do that," I said. "This is treason. I can't report to you. I'm an intelligence director. You're not in my chain of command."

"Sami, be careful of what you're saying."

We were outside in the large garden of the presidential palace, where he was walking towards the president's office when I met him. He began to raise his voice, as he limped along with his artificial leg, leaning on an elegant silver-topped cane.

"Listen to me very carefully. Do you want to destroy your future, undo everything you've done and go back to zero? If you want to advance, you join me."

"Minister Atmar," I said. "My future belongs to Almighty God, not you."

"I made you and I can destroy you," he said, as he limped up the steps into the presidential office suite. I was left stunned by this brief, intense, angry exchange. Nabil knew I had been to see Atmar, and now he, too, was suspicious of me.

Former communist that he was, Atmar pushed ideas left behind from the 1980s, with more directives to the media. He wanted total control of information, including tight restrictions on what could and could not be said. He was also keen on using our information capability to support the Ghani government, in contrast to my own duty to serve the constitution and the wider state beyond the government of the day.

Atmar and Ghani wanted to promote their own interests, but I served only the flag, and the sense of a united country where Islamic virtue and our traditional Afghan values like hospitality would be protected. That was my mission, and it was informed by my heritage as a Sadat.

The name means that I am a "Syed," a direct descendant of the Holy Prophet Muhammad. Those of us who can trace that descent are spread across the world, including the Hashemite dynasty who rule Jordan, and, I am sorry to say, the founder of Islamic State, Abu Bakr al-Baghdadi. In Afghanistan there are some 1.4 million people with this heritage, and it gives me the advantage of standing aside from ethnic identity—not Tajik, Pashtun, or any other tribe, but a Syed. Some Syeds are Sunni Muslims, some Shia, and some from the Ismaili sect. And all share a tradition reaching back to the beginning of Islam, that we are seen as guardians of the faith and peacemakers. There have not been famous Syed military leaders in Afghanistan before, and sometimes people challenge me with this peacemaking heritage.

But I am a peacemaker, not fighting for its own sake, but to make peace. My family history gives me a destiny of wanting to free oppressed people. I cannot stand by and see people being tortured and imprisoned. And now that the whole nation is a prison, my role is to liberate it and make peace.

In late 2015, a year after he came into office, Ghani wanted to come and see my operation for himself. It had established a reputation as the most powerful and effective organization within the

NDS. He sent a note that he would come with Atmar, his chief of staff, Salam Rahimi, and his spokesperson, Zafar Hashemi. I sent a note back saying that Atmar may be the national security adviser, but he was not cleared at the secrecy level required to be able to see inside my department. I knew it was a confrontational approach, and I was not even sure that I was on safe ground legally, but I did not want Atmar to see what we were doing close up.

The morning of the visit, the president's advance team arrived early, including a butler carrying a coffee machine. I stopped him, saying, "I have a coffee machine and better coffee than this. I am using dark roasted Arabica beans, the best in the world. So take back your machine to the car. The president can enjoy my coffee." As an Afghan I was offended that my hospitality was being snubbed in this way.

The deputy director of the presidential protection service, General Andar, came in a few minutes later.

"Colonel Sadat, we know you have coffee, and we know you want to be the host for the president. But the president has this particular taste and likes this particular person giving him coffee. And it will be better if you allow the coffee machine and the guy to be there."

So I agreed, although the president was acting like some petty monarch. When he arrived, with his coffee machine installed, I introduced the office and described the layers of our overt and covert work. There was one thing I wanted from him and that was to get permission to install radio stations close to the frontier to broadcast into Pakistan. We had seen the ignorance and prejudice about Afghanistan from the refugees who had come over during the fighting a year earlier. If we did the right programming, we could challenge those attitudes, influencing the Pakistan population directly, unmediated by their government. I wanted to broadcast news and cultural programs to give them a different view of our country. The main network would be in Pashto, a language spoken on both sides of the border, and I wanted a Baloch station to broadcast to the south from Kandahar. Ultimately I had a plan to broadcast in the main Pakistani language, Urdu, across the whole country.

My aim was to neutralize the threat coming from Pakistan by influencing their mindset, so the Baluchis would not give refuge to the Taliban, and the Pashtu-speaking population of Pakistan would not send fighting men into Afghanistan. We wanted to convince normal Pakistani citizens that we were not their enemy.

He was sitting there drinking his coffee. I drank my coffee. And he turned down the radio stations.

"You don't have the capacity to do that. And I don't have the budget for it."

I said, "Sir, when you look at what we have already done here, don't doubt my capacity. I don't need more money. We can fund this through existing budgets."

The president may have turned this down but was enthusiastic about everything else, staying for more than four hours when the visit was scheduled for less than half that time. He spoke to everyone in the office and liked to see there were so many young people. Ghani was like a child, enthusiastic about his latest toy. Back at the palace, he told his staff that he had seen something incredible. The NDS had powers he had not suspected.

Hanif Atmar sat listening, boiling in his frustration, as Ghani went on and on about the great Colonel Sadat; how professional the staff were; this is the tool that will neutralize terrorism, preventing young men from becoming sucked in; how they had to invest more in the NDS.

When Ghani had finished, Atmar went back to his office and called in the security team and other staff members who had been on the trip. They said it was all positive, the president was happy, there were no disagreements. He pushed them on the details, and they said, "There was this one incident. Colonel Sadat didn't want our coffee machine. He said he had his own coffee machine. But we ultimately persuaded him to accept the president's coffee machine."

Atmar went straight back to the president's office. "Mister President," he said. "We have neutralized an assassination attempt by Colonel Sadat." The president said, "What do you mean?"

"Did you know that Colonel Sadat planned to kill you by putting poison in your coffee? He tried to stop your coffee machine being brought in. It was one of my staff members who successfully thwarted this plot, and we're so happy that you came back alive."

And like a child throwing his new toy out of the pram, the president now turned 180 degrees against me.

A week later, I was called into his office. I did not know about Atmar's wild claims and was expecting some kind of a medal or a raise, or at least some words of appreciation. I could not have been more wrong. Two armed members of the presidential security team stood by the door. This was unusual. The president usually met NDS directors alone. It was very intimidating.

"Colonel Sadat."

"Yes sir."

"A very trusted colleague of mine has informed me that you attempted to kill me. In my meeting in your office."

I was paralyzed for a brief moment. My tongue felt heavy, as if I could not respond. And the whole scene hit me all at once. It was a plot against me, and the armed guards were there to arrest me because of whatever made-up story the president had believed.

After what seemed like an age, I found I could speak and said, "Mister President, that's not true. Who told you that?"

"Sami, someone told me that I trust a lot. And he's a friend."

"Mister President, whoever told you is your number one enemy," I said. "I would never act against you. I understand that the lack of a president for this country could mean chaos—or civil war. It has national security implications of such magnitude that we should avoid it by all means. What lies have you been told about me?"

"I heard that you were trying to poison me with coffee," and he repeated the nonsense he had been told by Atmar.

"Oh, that." If I had not been in such a bad situation I might have just laughed this off. "Mister President, I don't need to tell you that in our culture guests are treated as if a member of your own family. Guests do not bring their food with them. And by the way, I have the best coffee in the entire city. I was trying to ensure you had a good experience. There was no poison. I drank my coffee all day. I'm an intelligence officer. If I'm going to plot an assassination, be sure that I have the skill to avoid that assassination in my own office. I'm not that incompetent."

It was clear that he preferred to believe Atmar and any other conspiracy theorist who came his way. He changed tack. "You also told people that I have brain cancer," he said. "And when I die of that soon, the NDS will support Marshal Dostum to take over."

Dostum was the first vice president. He was a powerful northern 1980s warlord who had changed sides more often than any other, and it was a crowded field. Ghani had compromised his democratic credentials in putting Dostum on his presidential ticket in 2014 in a cynical move to win votes in Dostum's heartland in the north. Dostum had proved a disaster, spending much of the time since the election in exile in Turkey, escaping charges for the kidnap and rape of a political rival. In a complex deal brokered by the US secretary of state, John Kerry, to resolve a dispute over the 2014 election result, the losing candidate, Abdullah Abdullah, also had a role in government as "CEO," although no such role existed in the Afghan constitution, setting him against Dostum.

"If you died there would be acute national security consequences, sir," I said. "Doctor Abdullah and Marshal Dostum would take up arms and fight each other over who should become the president, and that would translate very quickly to a wider civil war along ethnic lines. I do not support that."

I spoke clearly, but very firmly. "And there's no truth in any claim that I've been spreading rumors about your health, Mister President."

He would not be stopped. When he was angry his voice raised in pitch. A young comedian had a big following on TV imitating it. The squeaky voice cut across me.

"But all the media is talking about it," he said.

"Mister President, I'm aware the social media is talking about it. But the mass media had not made that claim, and I have certainly not repeated it."

"What are you going to do to stop the social media when they're talking about my brain cancer, and I don't have brain cancer. Could a person with brain cancer spend four hours in your office and talk to you coherently?"

I was beginning to think that the real purpose of his visit to our office was to show that he was healthy, competent, and capable of holding onto his job. He expected political support from the NDS, exactly as the communists had. He seemed to think it was there to support his political campaigning and eliminate his enemies. In a democratic, modern society we were not willing to do that. Afghanistan was not just President Ghani. Everything we did was for greater Afghanistan, not for a sitting president. He misunderstood our indifference, thinking we were out to get him.

Sitting and listening to the claims against me in the squeaky voice at the other side of the table was not a good experience. I went through my mind what I thought would happen next. An arrest by the armed guards, paraded in front of the in-house palace TV team; then fake charges and a show trial, and I would forever be known as a traitor, the man who tried to kill the president. Then the president changed tack. I had come with General Jalil Gulistani, the director of Signals Intelligence.

"I hear that you and Jalil, the gentleman sitting in front of me, have been listening to my calls," the president said. "And you are trying to arrest my team members who are talking with other people."

So that's why Jalil was there with me. Ghani wanted the wider NDS implicated in the conspiracy he was weaving that existed nowhere but in his mind.

Jalil spoke for the first time. "Sir, there's been one incident when Hamdullah Mohib, your policy adviser, was talking to a member of the Haqqani network in Pakistan. We traced the call, and respectfully asked him to explain why he was talking to the Haqqanis."

"I told him to talk to the Haqqanis," the president shouted. "As you know, we're trying to establish a way to negotiate with the Taliban, and my team members are working on that." Then he pivoted again, jumping to a new subject, speaking quickly in his high voice and breathing shallowly. I had never seen a man so out of control of his own emotions.

"What are politicians saying about my mental health?"

"I don't understand, Mister President." Jalil had no idea what he was talking about.

"What is Doctor Abdullah saying about my mental health?"

"Sir, we're not listening to the conversations of our politicians. It's against the rules of the NDS. We only intercept matters of national security related to terrorism, drugs, and espionage. Even if you ordered me to do it, I could not listen to anyone, especially a senior government member, without the approval of the chief justice."

The president punched Amanullah's desk. "But you are listening to my team members, like Hamdullah Mohib, you're listening to Atmar?"

Jalil rocked back on his heels, answering the tirade as evenly as he could.

"Sir, whoever is talking to the enemy, we will listen to that phone, we will track it and trace it. And once we find out that this is a senior government member that has been trying to do a hostage deal or national negotiation, then we drop the call."

The president had had enough of this exchange and turned back to me.

"You see, the media is talking about my mental health, but you do nothing. You have this powerful machine to influence and to turn things upside down, but you're not using anything in my favor in my support. So from now on, you will do what you can to support me, you will support Atmar."

As the yelling went on, I stood up, took my badge from my front jacket pocket, and put it in front of him.

"Mister President, I give up. I resign, I no longer want to work for you. This is the third time we are meeting, and every time you're insulting me and now you're yelling at me. I don't want to work for somebody who's not happy with me. This is my resignation. As long as you're sitting president, I will not work for the NDS."

His change of mood was pathetic. He immediately stood up, kissed me on both cheeks, and laughed this weird laugh.

"Sami. I trust you. And I didn't fire you. I wanted to see you, to hear your explanation. And as president and commander in chief, I refuse your resignation. You will resign when I say you resign. Take back your badge."

And then he turned to Jalil. "Mister Gulistani, you see, our young officers are very, very impatient. You know, they don't listen to their seniors. And sometimes they lose their temper. What would I do without you guys? You're the cadre of officers I need. You're the cadre of officers Afghanistan needs. Rarely do I find people like you to who are so capable, with good leadership, who have created successful programs for the security of Afghanistan. But I need you to support me and my policies. This will bring incredible change to Afghanistan."

And then we both left his office, not under arrest. We had been on a rollercoaster in there. I was sad and angry at the same time. Jalil had a blood pressure problem, and his face looked so swollen that we sat on the large lawn in front of Ghani's office so he could recover.

"I swear, I will never come back to the president with you," he said, when he got back his power of speech. "I don't think that next time we'll walk out free, but in chains. How can you talk to the president like that? You were almost yelling at him. And this guy is crazy, he's dangerous. He could put us in jail forever."

I laughed at Jalil. "Look, we are in the right and he is in the wrong. I raised my voice to tell him that. We are officers of the law. We are not breaking the law. We're not against him. We're actually all he's got. And we will do anything for national security and the national interest of Afghanistan. So you know, there is no problem with that."

That was the last encounter I had with President Ghani before he made a phone call two weeks later to Nabil, who told me the exact words of the president: "Get rid of Colonel Sadat and don't give me an excuse. Get rid of him today and call me when you've done it." It was insane. He called Nabil three times that day to make sure I had left the office.

The professor and Karen called me and said there was no way the CIA would let this happen. They would talk to the president and bring me back. I told them I didn't have the motivation to work anymore. Even if I came back, it would be bad for the organization. It would be bad for the president, because from then on, I didn't think I could work with a clear mind after what he said.

My ambition to put something in place that would survive me proved futile. When I left a number of my more important programs stopped. There was no more engagement with the refugees from Waziristan, a program that had given a rich intelligence harvest of new sources. The relationships with tribal leaders and religious scholars were downgraded. Worse, the covert operations became a tool for Ghani and Atmar. Instead of deception operations disrupting the Taliban, they became more focused on media and social media. Two new civilians were appointed from outside the security services as political appointments, answerable only to Atmar, to oversee the changes. As the focus turned inward and was less effective, the CIA cut their support, so Department 76 was on its own, delivering only to its political masters, and I think that continued until the end of the Afghan Republic in 2021.

Chapter Five

"KISSING THE KING'S RING" (2016–2018)

"Are you now, or have you ever been, part of any group planning, or financing an attack on the United States of America?"

"No."

"Are you reliable?"

"Yes."

"Do you support the Taliban?"

"No."

"Have you ever met with or contributed to any terrorist organisation?"

I went silent. The other questions in the CIA polygraph test were standard stuff. But I had been recruiting and paying sources among the Afghan and Pakistani Taliban.

"What's the problem?" The woman asking the questions looked up from her tablet.

"You know my background. I have sources in the TTP and Haqqani network."

"So the answer's yes?"

"I guess so."

"Have you ever used a terrorist organisation against the United States or Afghanistan?"

That was an easier way to put the question. I answered a clear "No."

"Would you kill President Ashraf Ghani if you had the power to do it?"

"You mean if I had the ability?" I asked.

"Yes," she said. "If the opportunity arose."

I laughed. I got it now. "Oh, you mean the coffee machine plot?" I could not believe they had taken this claim seriously.

The woman on the other side of the desk did not smile but carried on looking at the waves on her screen measuring my heart rate, breathing, and blood pressure.

"Answer the question."

"No, if I had the ability and the opportunity..." I started. She cut me off. She wanted yes or no answers. I would have gone on to say that I would always protect Dr. Ashraf Ghani. I am not a man for elimination, especially not friendly forces. I believe in democracy, and he was elected by the people. I had every reason not to like him personally, because he fired me after believing wild claims. I did not like the way he governed the country or dealt with Pakistan, but I would protect the president of the republic with my life.

She removed the tubes attached to my head and chest, blood pressure cuff from my arm, and clips off my fingers. I had passed the test.

The CIA had moved quickly when they heard of my troubles with the president and the national security adviser, Hanif Atmar, offering me a new role in a secret counterterrorism unit. Its role was to track down international terrorism, including al-Qaeda and Islamic State Khorasan Province (ISKP), both of which were growing stronger in the east of the country. I was joining an elite fraternity of the most highly skilled CIA case officers and the cream of the

NDS—Team Alpha. It was the first time that I worked closely with Khoshal Sadat, who would become my closest friend in the Afghan forces. He is one of the bravest and best, who trained both at the UK military officer school at Sandhurst and the US Army graduate college at Leavenworth. In the CIA/NDS counterterrorism unit he was my second-in-command, while Hashmat Khesrow, also a Sandhurst graduate, headed operations. We trusted each other like brothers.

Before I started the role I went for two weeks' leave in London, and while I was there a series of government plots against me emerged, orchestrated by Ghani and Atmar. A story appeared on the most prominent news website, Pajhwok, that the security team protecting my home in Kabul were beating women, harassing people, and stopping access to the street. The president responded by demanding the NDS disarm my men. It showed how incompetent he was as a leader that when he should have been focusing on winning the war he was conducting a personal campaign against me. The next day a journalist arrested by the NDS held a press conference to say he had been detained and tortured in "Sami Sadat's personal prison."

It was true that a journalist had been arrested by the NDS, but it was nothing to do with me. I did not have that power. I discovered senior politicians were working with the journalist, paying him and others to work against national unity for their own ethnic interest.

Ghani then ordered my arrest on a series of charges including running an illegal detention center, torture, and running operations for personal gain. These were serious allegations. I shortened my trip, and back in Kabul I called the editor of the Pajhwok agency, who now he thought he had been misused and took down the original story. And the case against me fell apart when the journalist who had been making the torture allegations lost courage and fled the country. I had no intention of harming him, but he heard that I had powerful friends.

Atmar's campaign to destroy me backfired as the cases collapsed. It raised my profile and strengthened my position as the police and prosecutors would not move against me on what it was clear were politically motivated charges. Before the news stories appeared nobody knew who I was because I had been operating in the secret world. Now I became better known, and powerful men across the country called me to offer support. General Raziq, the police chief in Kandahar, one of the most effective fighters against the Taliban, was among them, and would be a close friend until he was killed in 2018. He offered me protection in Kandahar, or to send a new protection team to Kabul. But I turned it down. I had my own loyal guards and plenty of support from inside the NDS as well.

I decided that being as public as possible was my best protection. Prosecutors had been calling me for an interview to answer the series of trumped-up charges, and I sent them my address and dared them to come and get me. Wearing a Ralph Lauren blazer, with waistcoat and smart casual pants, I drove around in a convoy of three armored vehicles, would step out with fifteen armed bodyguards, and sit outside pavement cafés smoking a cigar. I was sending a signal that I was ready to fight. No one tried to arrest me.

I went to America for six weeks around the time of the 2016 election on an advanced leadership training course in the name of the former secretary of defense, Donald Rumsfeld. I met highly influential players, including Rumsfeld himself and the former vice president, Dick Cheney. I had a lengthy discussion trying to persuade the former head of Central Command, General Jim Mattis, who would be appointed as secretary of defense in the incoming Trump administration two weeks after our meeting, that Pakistan was a greater threat than Iran,. Mattis had argued that Iran had global reach, while Pakistan was only a regional player. I pointed out that it was Pakistan who harbored al-Qaeda.

Ever since the creation of the state of Pakistan in 1947, it has been wanting to control Afghanistan. The border between the two countries, called the Durand line after the British colonial officer who drew it up, remains disputed. It cuts through Pashtun mountain tribes who have never acknowledged it. Pakistan's principal security preoccupation is its giant neighbor to the east, India, and the Pakistani military have long justified interference in our country under the concept of "strategic depth," that it should not be stabbed in the back if there were a conflict with India.

Of all the designated terrorist groups in the world, one fifth are in Afghanistan and the border region with Pakistan. This is the epicenter of global jihadism, destabilizing not just Afghanistan, but the wider world.

I may not have persuaded Mattis, but I got further with the former head of Homeland Security, Tom Ridge. After making the pitch to him about the threat from Pakistan, an unstable nuclear-armed state that was the crucible of international terrorism, he invited me to a breakfast of influential Republican Party figures who were close to the new president. I sent a separate note warning, "The extremely dangerous vulnerability of Pakistan's strategic nuclear installations provides an excellent opportunity for al-Qaeda-type groups and ISIS to use it for their benefit." I like to believe this had some effect in what became a far harder line from the Trump administration against Pakistan.

MR. HASHEMI

Once I started my new role in the counterterrorism unit I was struck by the scale of the task and the lack of basic information on the people we were trying to track down. We were not chasing the Taliban but were focused solely on al-Qaeda and other international terrorists. I was taken into a control center with a big map on the wall.

The CIA briefer waved his arm in an expansive way. "The al-Qaeda leadership in this region could potentially be in eastern Afghanistan, southeastern Afghanistan, Pakistan, to include tribal regions, the city of Karachi, or Iran."

"That's a big area. Give me some start points."

"The place we think you should best focus on to start is P2K." It was American shorthand for Paktika, Paktia, and Khost, three provinces bordering Pakistan in the east. On the other side of the porous frontier snaking through the mountains lay North and South Waziristan, for many decades a notorious hotbed of Islamic militancy, which Pakistan had not pacified, even after the major Zarb-e Azb operation in 2014.

I had a good contact there in General Wazir Shaheen. I had started working with him in 2014 to help identify terrorists among the thousands of refugees fleeing the Pakistani army operation on the other side of the border. Nobody had a better network of sources among the terrorist groups in the region. His unit had originally been set up by the CIA as a strike force against the Taliban and had now been handed over to the NDS to interdict named individuals.

My new role was to cultivate sources which I would hand over to other case workers. I was known as "Mr. Hashemi," and when I delivered a source willing to share information we called it "kissing the king's ring," like out of a fairy story. Kissing the king's ring was the turning point for a source, meaning he had agreed to share information of value. Sometimes I would need to go back later if things did not work out, but mostly I was on to the next case, leaving the team to work the new source.

The main insurgent group in this region was the Pakistani Taliban, the TTP, formed originally as an insurgent movement against the democratic government in their own country, but often fighting on our side of the frontier, allied with the Afghan Taliban to fight against international troops and Afghan government forces. I put together a plan that we would offer the TTP a deal. If they gave us information on the international terrorists in their midst and stopped operations inside Afghanistan, we would ensure that American and Afghan attacks on them stopped.

I outlined the plan at a meeting in Ariana. I knew it would be tough to persuade the CIA. The TTP had carried out major attacks against Americans in the past and were responsible for some of the biggest suicide attacks against civilians, working alongside the Haqqani network.

"Why don't we stop killing the TTP and talk to them instead?" I said. "See what information they can give us."

I had immediate pushback. "They are terrorists. Why would they tell us anything?"

"It's worth a try. Nothing else has worked. And I may have some influence in the TTP."

"Why am I not surprised," Karen said with a smile. "So how would this work?"

"I know people who can build a relationship with them, and we can try for a deal with the whole organization not to attack Afghan or American targets," I said. "If we deal only with individuals, we will never cut the knot. But if our aim is to end the attacks, then we need to give amnesty to the whole TTP: recruit them, protect them, and see what they tell us."

"This would be the first time in Afghanistan that a whole organization has been taken off the hit list. How do we trust them?"

"We will never trust them, but we have a clear if brutal test of whether this works," I said. "If the attacks keep coming then you go back to targeting them."

By 2016, under President Obama's strict rules of engagement, American forces were very limited as to what they could do to target terrorists. And Afghan forces were not yet good enough to protect themselves. We were taking a lot of casualties, and large-scale suicide attacks were causing mayhem in Kabul. The CIA were willing to try anything.

Even I did not believe it would be 100 percent successful, but it was the best I could come up with. If we could stop the Haqqani assault on Afghanistan at the same time as unlocking knowledge on al-Qaeda for the price of letting some bad men live a little longer, I thought it worth a try.

The NDS approved the deal, but I do not know if President Ghani was told. He never understood the subtlety of intelligence operations, of infiltrating the enemy to turn things in your favor.

THE PAKISTANI TALIBAN

The TTP, Tehrik-i-Taliban Pakistan, (literally Pakistan Taliban movement), was inspired by Mullah Nek Muhammad as an umbrella group of jihadi terrorist organizations to fight against the government of Pakistan. A religious fanatic and once a key facilitator for al-Qaeda in Afghanistan, Nek Muhammad came from the Waziristan border district of Pakistan and fought alongside the Taliban in Afghanistan in the 1990s.

When the border was artificially imposed on Afghanistan when Britain ruled India a century before, it cut through Pashtun tribes, leaving some on one side and some on the other, and there were strong links between people along tracks through the mountains. Traditional leaders still ruled small fiefdoms in this area, one of the most heavily armed communities in the world, with small weapons foundries turning out guns in every village, and since the days of

British India a haven for criminals. After 9/11 it sheltered thousands of fighters ousted from Afghanistan when America defeated the Taliban. Al-Qaeda, the Haqqani Network, as well as insurgents from Central Asia trained in a region out of the control of either Islamabad or Kabul. Nek Muhammad worked to unite them.

The Pakistani government played a double game during Afghanistan's long wars, pretending to be a good American ally in the war on terror while backing the Afghan Taliban. Where their interests aligned, they would share intelligence, as they did in successfully calling in an American drone strike in 2004 against Nek Muhammad. The TTP was set up after his death to mirror the Taliban's resurgence in Afghanistan, with the aim of uniting tribal militias up and down the frontier under the flag of the TTP to take control of Pakistan.

The first leader of TTP, Baitullah Mehsud, carried out attacks against the Pakistani military and police. He developed strong links with Sirajuddin Haqqani, who was now under increasing pressure from American drone attacks and wanted a wider terrorist base to protect his operations in the frontier region. This new alliance led to several high-profile attacks on foreigners, including the destruction of the luxury Marriott Hotel in Islamabad, killing more than fifty people.

Through these closer relations between their two leaders, the TTP now sent more fighters into Afghanistan, both to fight conventional operations alongside the Afghan Taliban and as suicide bombers. There is clear evidence that Pakistan's military establishment facilitated these bomb attacks. They opposed the American-backed government in Kabul and had close relations with Sirajuddin Haqqani. So it had become a really dirty war, with the TTP as the foot soldiers for Haqqani in attacks against foreigners in Pakistan and the Afghan government in Afghanistan. Pakistan was playing such a dangerous game that while the Haqqani network were protected by Pakistani intelligence, their allies, the TTP, carried out attacks against Pakistani soldiers. The Pakistani military did not care about the death of their own citizens. What they did was brutal, morally bankrupt, and condemned their country into a never-ending cycle of violence with a bad effect on the economy.

In the summer of 2009, the TTP leader, Baitullah Mehsud, was killed in his turn by a drone strike, and six months later the TTP responded with the most devastating attack on the CIA during the war, when seven CIA staff and contractors were killed and six injured in a suicide bomb attack at Camp Chapman in Khost province. This was the largest CIA base in the region, which had close links with our NDS strike forces who would carry out operations across the frontier deep into Pakistan. The suicide bomb was carried by a Jordanian doctor, sent by al-Qaeda and the TTP, who the CIA thought had been persuaded to defect. America's response was to increase drone strikes, which hardened the Haqqani/al-Qaeda/TTP nexus even further.

Pakistan wanted to end the TTP attacks, and that led to the 2014 Zarb-e Azb offensive by thousands of troops into the frontier region, pushing refugees onto our side of the border in Afghanistan, including many terrorists among them, as described in Chapter Four. But Pakistani military intelligence protected their Haqqani friends, who were proving so useful to them in their double game in Afghanistan, pretending good relations with America while sending Haqqani suicide bombers to damage our government. We had intelligence that Haqqani leaders were spirited out of the region during the military push to the frontier, crossing through Pakistani army lines in SUVs with tinted windows to safe houses in the cities, so they could return to the frontier once the fighting had died down.

The success of the Pakistani military operation broke the TTP into several different factions. The main group was reformed under Mullah Fazlullah, who became known as "Mullah Radio" because he sought popularity by broadcasting his sermons on FM radio. Not all of the TTP remained with him. One part of the Mehsud tribe was co-opted by the Pakistani military. Another Mehsud faction went into Afghanistan. And as the frontier tribes looked to new ways to protect themselves against the Pakistani military presence among them, the Orakzai tribe, in the mountains south of the Khyber Pass, went for the most ruthless option. They were the first to raise the black flag of the Islamic State, pledging allegiance to ISIS in Iraq and founding the Islamic State Khorasan Province, ISKP. Their first leader was Abu Saad Orakzai.

DEAL WITH THE DEVIL

My aim was to cut into the rotten meat of this complex nexus of jihadi groups and focus on what mattered to us—stopping attacks in Afghanistan by offering a no-strike deal to the TTP in exchange for information on al-Qaeda, ISKP, and the Haqqani network. The TTP's most high-profile senior leader at the time was Shahbaz Muhammad, also known as al Khorasani. He had a public face as their main spokesperson. But we could not strike a deal on the phone; I needed to meet him. After some negotiations through intermediaries known to my friend General Wazir Shaheen, I met him in an agreed spot just on our side of the border—a remote hilltop in the desert. Al Khorasani was a tall, energetic man with very long full hair, a beard, and full dark eyebrows, dressed in traditional clothing, with a shawl round his shoulders and wearing a white *pakhool*, the rolled woolen hat common in that region. When he approached he refused to let go of his AK-47. Wazir tried to take it off him, but he held it tight. Our first conversation was difficult. He was a religious fanatic and did not trust us at all. He had no sense of humor, spoke very softly, and was rigid in all his dealings with us.

But I knew they needed a pause in the fighting. The continuous US bombardment and Afghan operations had them on their knees. And on the Pakistani side the continuous push from the Pakistani military had exhausted their resources. As the group splintered they had lost the support of the tribes. I did not tell him, but we were desperate too. Most of the suicide bombers at the time causing mayhem in Kabul and other cities were his men, working on behalf of the Haqqanis. We wanted to stop them.

After talking for a while on the hilltop, I said, "There are more strategic matters that we need to discuss. Why don't you come into the base and we can talk there."

He was understandably hesitant. He had a price on his head and had no reason to trust us. When we persuaded him to come, he insisted on driving in his own car. We escorted him down the dusty mountain track.

In the base, we went into a room without windows, just me and him. He still held his rifle close.

"Khorasani," I said, "You don't need your rifle. I know you are a courageous man. You have the courage to come in here. If I wanted to kill you, it would be no protection."

He had nothing to say to that, wrapping himself more tightly in his shawl, which he used like a mask. His eyes went round the room all the time, concerned we had set a trap. A cup of Indian masala tea lay in front of him, but he did not touch it.

"So what does the TTP want?" I asked.

"We want freedom for Pakistan from the occupation of foreigners and the Punjabi elite," he said.

"So why kill innocent Afghan citizens, who share your Islamic faith and have nothing to do with Pakistan? You're not fighting for your freedom here, you're killing thousands of Afghans every year with no reason."

"We come across the border to Afghanistan for refuge."

"So what's that got to do with a campaign of terrorism and murder?"

"The Taliban offer us protection," he said, "in return we join them for attacks on Afghan forces."

The discussion went on for three hours. After the second hour, he briefly lowered his shawl down his face a little as he made the key ask.

"If you offer us protection on this side of the border, then we might be able to stop supporting the Taliban."

I had been waiting for this. "I can give you and your families protection in Afghanistan," I said. "In return I need three things. First, TTP fighters will not attack Afghan and American forces, or any Afghan citizen. Second, the TTP will not operate as an armed group inside Afghanistan; when you are here you remain peaceful. Third, we need you to report on all al-Qaeda activity, on both sides of the border."

The al-Qaeda question surprised him. "There is no al-Qaeda."

"Come on. I know there is al-Qaeda and you guys are providing some security for them here and in Pakistan."

It was difficult to convince him to work for us against al-Qaeda as well, but finally he agreed. "I will report only to you. I don't want to talk to anyone else and I don't want anyone else to know about the deal." For this important case I said I would continue as his controller. The deal did not extend beyond the Haqqani network and al-Qaeda. "I can't report against the Afghan Taliban," he said. "They are my brothers,"

It was enough. In return for the information he provided, Afghan and US forces would cease operations against their key leaders, such as al Khorasani himself and the overall head of the TTP, Mullah Fazlullah, a.k.a. "Mullah Radio."

Once we had the deal we recruited al Khorasani as our source. CIA skeptics were won over when, based on the information we received from him and other sources we soon recruited in the TTP, we were able to prevent many Taliban major assaults on our border check posts and stop several suicide and truck bombs heading for Kabul. We did not stop them all, and the Pakistani government continued to facilitate some terrible random attacks on our citizens. But during the next two years there were no security incidents in Afghanistan that could be tracked back to the TTP. And Afghan military casualties were reduced in all the places where the TTP were strong, particularly in the eastern provinces along the border.

For them, the deal was that we would not arrest and prosecute them in Afghanistan because of their affiliation with TTP. They could come across, bring their families, and get protection and a wage. We encouraged them to go back to North and South Waziristan every two or three weeks to collect information. This released a constant flow of actionable intelligence against Al-Qaeda facilitators and members of Central Asian and Chinese insurgent groups. We built a map with names, locations, and phone numbers.

On one clear moonlit night I was driving across the desert to meet a source close to the frontier in Paktika. The whole bowl of the stars was lit up overhead in a beautiful display. These operations needed a large but discreet security backup. The road was secured by NDS strike forces, and we traveled in a convoy with some thirty vehicles full of troops from the Afghan special forces. They spread out, and by the time I arrived at the meet-and-greet point they could not be seen, but I knew there were snipers on every hilltop all around me, with night vision capability, pointing their weapons down into this gully in case of an ambush.

They kept me in touch with the progress of the source by radio. About a mile before his arrival his three-vehicle convoy was hit by a drone strike. Wazir and his deputy were with me. We all knew what this could mean. This man had not been targeted before. He was only hit when he started talking to me. One of the vehicles in the convoy survived the attack, turned round, and managed to leave unscathed.

"What the fuck are you doing?" I shouted at my contact in the CIA. "I thought you had this all coordinated."

"We can't tell the air force everything," he said. This was not reassuring.

"So what do I do?" I asked. "Will they hit me as well?"

"You're traveling with Afghan special forces. They know where they are."

Around four in the morning Wazir got a call from the potential source who had been on his way to meet us. He was alive.

"I was in the front vehicle, it was the back one that was hit. We have two casualties," he said.

"You know we had nothing to do with this," Wazir said. "It was a bad mistake."

"What about Mister Hashemi," he said. "Is he involved?"

I took the phone from Wazir. "No, I'm not involved. I think somebody from your side must be spying for the Americans. And this is why they let you get hit."

"I was told you speak on behalf of the Americans now," he said.

"I do when we have a deal. Until we have a deal you'll continued to be hunted and there's nothing I can do for you."

"I trust you," he said, "although I don't know why I should. I lost two dead, but we have two wounded men. Can you treat them?"

We took care of his wounded men and slept during the day. The next night I called the man again. This time I wanted to meet him without the Americans knowing. I had no idea what had caused the drone strike, and my imagination ran wild. Perhaps President Ghani had ordered it, or the Americans had some reason to kill me on that moonlit night in the desert or were firing a warning shot in case I stepped out of line. I knew that the world of espionage and terrorism was full of danger.

"So what's the deal?" he asked.

I said, "I'm a person who keeps my word. I said we will meet, and we will meet. The reason you could be identified last night was from your phone. So leave it behind." I gave him the coordinates of a hilltop where we could meet.

"Don't bring any electronics with you, don't use the same vehicle you've been driving. And I won't carry a phone."

I gave my phone, which the Americans could track, to Wazir's deputy, Kamal, and told him to go to another location as if he were waiting for somebody to arrive there. So if anyone were tracking me they would follow him there. I told Kamal, "My friend, you are the tethered goat." He left the base an hour before me with a large convoy of special forces like the one I would use, so that US drones would follow him and not me.

I went to the hilltop with Wazir to wait. Shortly before the source was due to arrive we had a panicked call on the radio that the men were armed.

"No problem," I said. "Check them for explosives."

"I have, sir. They say that four of them are wearing suicide vests."

We told our men to walk away from the car and let the TTP commander talk on the radio.

Wazir yelled at him. "Are you crazy? Why would you bring suicide bombers?"

"Remember what happened last night? I don't trust you guys," he said.

"So how are we supposed to trust you if you come with suicide bombers?" said Wazir. "Are you trying to kill Mister Hashemi?"

"No, I don't want to do that, but we have to be sure you're not going to arrest me."

We let him wait at the checkpoint for two hours while we talked. Wazir wanted to kill them all and be done with it. And that was tempting. We did not even know if we had the right man. Maybe they were doing the same thing we did, putting in decoys who assumed other identities. The Americans had tried to kill him the previous night; he had a reason to be mad at us. But if he *was* the real thing I wanted to meet him. I said, "Wazir, we have been driving for three hours today and six yesterday on this terrible road. I can't drive here again. Let's finish it tonight." He had a ton of intelligence that could give us a breakthrough in the fight. We knew he was opposed to al-Qaeda, and we had two of his wounded aides in our base. Besides, I wanted to see the man who had the guts to travel with suicide bombers in his vehicle. We put blankets on the ground on a hilltop as a meeting place. Wazir was brave enough to stay with me, and some of his best snipers were on their knees surrounding the site, keeping the suicide bombers under constant watch.

Their car drove up the hill, we flashed three lights as the signal to go forward, and the five men walked out onto the hilltop. The commander was a big fat man, who smelt terrible. It was summer and hot even at night. After greeting in the elaborate Afghan fashion with a hug and kiss on both cheeks, the only time I needed to go close, we gave them tea and began the meeting. I had to admire the nerve of the stinking commander. Our allies had tried to kill him only twenty-four hours before.

The suicide bombers sat in a protective ring behind him. Three of them were alert enough. But the fourth looked as if he might fall asleep any time. I kept an eye on him throughout. My biggest fear was that he would nod off and detonate his vest by accident.

For a first meeting, it went well enough. He told me his life story and why he had joined the TTP, because the Pakistani state had killed his father. And he told me what kind of information he could get. Being a first meeting I did not expect any real secrets, but we did recruit him as a source, and I believed he could deliver. He would have been kissing the king's ring—if he had not brought suicide bombers.

When he left I gave him a phone. "This is your protection. Turn it on at noon tomorrow, and if you turn it off I can't protect you from being identified and killed by our forces. Keep it on you at all times. I don't care where you are. You're walking in the bazaar? You have the phone. You're sleeping with your wife? You have the phone."

He laughed and agreed. "So are you listening to this phone?"

"No, I'm not listening. But we know where you are. It's like a reverse of last night. I will feed information into the system so no drone can hit you if you are carrying it. Turn it on at noon, and then after that, if you turn it off you are not protected."

I gave him money to compensate for the loss of his men. He said he had not buried them yet and had to borrow money for fuel to come and see me, and I gave him more than I was allowed to do. Back at base, I immediately inputted what I needed to request removal of his name from the hitlist. The next morning they got back to me. Everything was good. They said they would remove him as long as he continued to share intelligence with us. On the stroke of noon I called him and his phone was on. That was a good sign; he was following orders. It's very important that your source follows orders. I told him he was off the list and asked if we could meet that night.

"No, not tonight. Make it tomorrow, because we have the funeral for the men killed two nights ago."

The attack that nearly killed this source was a problem that kept repeating during the war. There were so many moving parts in the American military machine that operations were sometimes not deconflicted. The counterterrorism unit worked in the shadows, officially deniable. If anybody asked me what I was doing, I never admitted my role. We had a full team of lawyers and analysts as well as access to transport and safe houses, but our work did not appear in any official reports. This meant we had to be agile on the ground. We never wanted to be seen by conventional Afghan forces meeting sources in case that fed conspiracy theories that we were supporting the Taliban. After so many years of a complex war Afghans were prone to believing conspiracies. And we had difficult calls to make if sources were arrested by conventional troops, who had good reason to go after them for what they had previously done.

There were other challenges in strike operations against what we called "pop-up targets" across the frontier where a wanted individual suddenly came onto our radar, and the NDS knew that if they did not act immediately they might lose him. In our culture, when there was gunfire at night, people would immediately come out armed to see what was going on. In the dark their status as civilians was not immediately recognized and there were many casualties that way. My friend General Wazir Shaheen avoided these casualties by recruiting only from local tribesmen, who could read the situation better than outsiders.

When the stinking TTP commander first came to our base, he was armed with an AK-47 assault rifle with the largest magazine of bullets I had ever seen. I picked him up in a tactical pickup truck and we bonded over the fact that we had both taken a risk to meet on the hilltop. He had come although American forces had tried to kill him, and I had faced down his suicide bombers.

"I like that you took the risk," he said. "You can never trust any of us. Every one of us will be trying to kill you, every one of us will be trying to kidnap you. So don't give us that opportunity." Looking with a meaningful stare, he said, "You have to remember that the name of our tribe, 'Mehsud,' derives from the Arabic word for 'jealous.'"

He gave me really good information. I took a picture of us together, and when I sent it back to our office it shocked everyone. He had been high on the kill-or-capture list for years. And now we were drinking tea as he shared information about al-Qaeda and the Haqqani Network. That is kissing the king's ring. He continued to work for us and provided vital information, based on which we avoided many terrorist attacks and were able to move more freely around P2K as he would tell us where the Haqqani network laid landmines.

THE TRIPLE AGENT

For the TTP, the motivation for sharing information on al-Qaeda and other terrorists was that it gave them a breathing space as they no longer faced American attacks. We also recruited sources inside the Taliban in Afghanistan, and other motives came into play. Shal Akhunzada, the Taliban shadow governor for Nawa district in Ghazni province in the center of the country, worked for us for money. We wanted to recruit him because we knew that the al-Qaeda leader, Ayman al-Zawahiri, had been seen in his district. Getting to people like this required meticulous planning, cultivation of sources, and luck. We found a source in Kandahar who traveled around collecting raisins from small farmers and bringing them to market. We heard that he was a friend of Shal Akhunzada and through him made a deal to meet our target when he would be coming to Shahjoy district in

Zabul, not far from the border with Pakistan in the southeast for a doctor's appointment. As always the first meeting had to be face-to-face. I had planned to fly to Kandahar, take vehicles from my friend General Raziq, and drive to the meeting place. Soon after the flight began, the pilot of the light aircraft from the special mission air wing came on the radio and said that the oxygen had failed and he would not be able to make the journey. The flight would cross some high peaks, and we could not make it without oxygen. We returned and picked up another light plane. But now time was running out for me to make the meeting. I asked the pilot, who was called Zakaria, if he could drop us off in the desert to shorten the journey.

"I've never done that before," Zakaria said on the radio. "But it seems this is very important."

"It's a matter of national security," I said. Shal Akhunzada was the highest-level source we had attempted to reach in the Taliban, and we knew he had direct links with al-Qaeda.

He looked at his map. "There's an old airstrip from the Russian war in Zabul province not far from where you need to go. It's not been maintained, but if I can find it I can try to land there."

The airstrip was in the desert close to an army base. It was covered with rocks and sand, with goats and sheep eating scrub along it. Zakaria did one low pass to scatter the animals and take a good look at the ground, then landed well, although there was a huge clatter of stones thrown upwards that damaged the fuselage and wings.

"You see that column of dust," I said. "You need to take off before they arrive." Our unscheduled appearance had provoked the base to send out a team to have a look. As the plane flew away I was connected by radio on an army truck to the local head of the NDS.

"I need two civilian vehicles to go to Shahjoy district," I said. There was a pause as the radio went silent. When it squawked into life again I could hear he was shocked.

"That's about eighty kilometers from here, and there are Taliban all along the route. You'll need an escort." The NDS did not have enough firepower locally, and he said it would take days to put together an army convoy.

I said, "I have to be there this afternoon. I will go in just the two civilian vehicles."

"You'll never make it there alive."

I called the director general of the NDS, Massoud Andarabi, in Kabul, who put pressure on, so I was given two vehicles. The NDS commander of a Quick Reaction Force heard about the trip and said he was willing to come with me, and when the police heard I was there, they sent a unit on the trip.

As well as my two vehicles, we finally set out with four police Humvees and two NDS tactical pickups, full of hand grenades and rocket-propelled-grenade rounds. But on a day when everything was working against me, none of the police vehicles went the whole way.

Five minutes after we left town, one of the Humvees crashed against an incoming truck, and we had to send another back taking two injured police officers. Half an hour later the last two police Humvees crashed into each other. I left them to sort themselves out and drove on. With the NDS escort we made it to Shahjoy without being attacked. We did have an American drone keeping an eye on us all the way, although I did not have any direct communication with it.

The town of Shahjoy was quiet. We arrived at a small clinic. When I called I saw a man sitting outside answer his mobile, and I knew at once that this was Shal Akhunzada. He was an undistinguished man, wearing traditional clothing and a turban. He had tired eyes. I jumped out of the vehicle in full body armor, grabbed him by his hand, and said, "Come with me." He had a little girl with him, and she would not let him go. He said her name was Salasa, which in Arabic means number three. A woman started to cry.

"Who's this?" I asked Shal.

"It's my sister."

"You know, sister. I'm his friend. We're not going to hurt him. We'll bring him back."

We left his sister behind crying in the street, but he would not let go of the hand of his daughter. She was his security cover. He calculated that we would not harm him if she was there. We drove him to a nearby school and heard his full biography. And in a surprisingly rich harvest for a first meeting, he gave us information about al-Qaeda movements. We paid him money for the information, and as a goodwill gesture, I gave him a Rado watch worth around $1,000. We let him go and he walked off still holding his daughter by the hand.

Shal Akhunzada was a good source for some time, meeting us in safe houses in Kabul several times. His only motivation was money. We paid him close to our ceiling of $3000 a month. We did not want our sources to be too rich, as they might be compromised flashing their money around or not care enough to give us material. We later discovered that he was a triple agent. As well as us, he was paid by the Pakistan Intelligence Service, the ISI, and his principal client, al-Qaeda.

He gave us high quality information which enabled us to map the al-Qaeda network in Ghazni province. Through his information we carried out a series of airstrikes and night raids through October 2017 severely disrupting the al-Qaeda network, killing many leaders and hundreds of foreign fighters. One of the people killed was Qari Saifullah Akhtar, also known as Bukhari, a Pakistani citizen who had been a jihadi fighter in Afghanistan, Pakistan, and Kashmir since the 1980s and led more than twenty thousand Pakistani fighters who supported the Taliban in the late 1990s. Bukhari was one of the masterminds of the operation that killed the legendary Afghan commander Ahmad Shah Massoud two days before 9/11 in 2001, working with the al-Qaeda commander Ayman al-Zawahiri, who was then at Bagram airbase. Bukhari hired the two Arab suicide bombers, posing as journalists, who killed Massoud with a bomb in a TV camera.

Bukhari also conspired against the democratic government in Pakistan and commanded the operation that killed the former prime minister Benazir Bhutto in 2007. In her posthumous memoir she accused him of trying to kill her. He was arrested several times in Pakistan but always released in unexplained circumstances, suggesting he had close links with Pakistani intelligence.

Bukhari was a key broker between Pakistani recruits and the Afghan Taliban and a guiding light for fighters coming to Afghanistan. His death was one undoubted success of the joint NDS/CIA counterterrorism operation. But it did not stop Pakistan's attempts to play their dirty games in our country. In one operation we discovered the whereabouts in Afghanistan of Haider Gillani, the son of a former Pakistani prime minister, who had been kidnapped with two other high-value Pakistani citizens by an anti-Pakistan group, Lashkar-e Jhangvi. Through our TTP sources, we tracked them down to a hideout in Paktika, close to the frontier, and they were freed in a joint US/Afghan special forces operation.

Shal Akhunzada's triple agent status became complicated when we discovered a target, Qasim Kayani, living in his house. Qasim was trying to develop al-Qaeda in the Indian subcontinent, AQIS, as a separate organization, recruiting hundreds of Indians and Pakistanis into his ranks. He was the main link in al-Qaeda's banking operations, bringing cash in from Pakistan to fund al-Qaeda fighters and their families. In an illustration of how messed up Pakistan had become, Qasim Kayani, a key al-Qaeda asset, was a distant cousin of the chief of army staff in Pakistan, General Ashfaq Parvez Kayani. We had credible reports that the cash coming in to fund the AQIS was actually coming from the Pakistani military.

AQIS were becoming a security problem for us, specializing in attacks on remote police posts. We asked Shal for help to find Qasim Kayani. He would give us accurate information for other people in the movement but kept giving us bogus locations for Qasim himself. It turned out that all the time he worked for us, Shal was staying in Qasim's house, which we discovered when we started to watch it. We could not hit him there because of our no-strike deal with Shal.

We finally killed Qasim when we followed his car as it left the house to a neighboring district where we conducted an air strike.

It was an intense period. My two closest comrades in the unit, Khoshal Sadat (Kosh), and Hashmat Khesrow (Hash), joined me on a lot of the operations against targets. We would get information, jump in the helicopter, and carry out attacks, sometimes with as few as six people, against American and Afghan rules of engagement which demanded more planning and more people. The CIA would say, "You're crazy and you'll get yourself and your guys killed." But they loved it because we got results.

One of our best early sources was Haji Abbas, who helped us to track down Faruq al-Qahtani, the head of al-Qaeda in Afghanistan, a Qatari citizen who spoke good Pashto. Qahtani was smart and traveled between villages only when there was cloud cover to avoid detection from above. He never used a mobile phone and communicated through letters or meetings, moving cash around by hand. He never moved in a big convoy but just one vehicle, or even on horseback. This made him a difficult target. But we finally pinpointed him, and when we hit, his deputy, Bilal al-Tayebi, a Saudi citizen, was there as well, so we severely disrupted the capacity of the leadership to operate.

Qahtani was replaced as al-Qaeda leader by Hamza bin Laden, Osama's son, who was also soon targeted and killed. Our source, Haji Abbas, was identified in Kunar as an informer and executed, the only time our unit's source was exposed and killed. I fired the case officer for Abbas as he should have trained him better to avoid detection.

NEAR MISSES

We were not successful all the time, and the biggest fish that escaped the net during my time in the counterterrorist unit was the al-Qaeda leader himself, Ayman al-Zawahiri. We had learnt a lot about al-Zawahiri since he had taken over from Osama bin Laden. We knew that he had been living in South Waziristan on the Pakistan side of the frontier since around 2002, and he had moved across to our side, along with the mass movement of people caused by the Pakistani operation in 2014.

For a while we were tracking his deputy, Abd al-Rahman al-Maghrebi, a Moroccan terrorist who was also his son-in-law. We first noticed him when we heard reports of Pampers diapers being left outside a house. He had a newborn child, and these were signs of a foreigner in the area as they were never bought by local people. We began a series of operations to close in on him, but he disappeared again, and we heard that Pakistan had again given him safe haven.

For a while we were following al-Zawahiri himself across Afghanistan. We discovered that when he traveled he and his wife would both be covered up in *burqas*, the powder-blue all-covering garment demanded by the most traditional Islamic practice.

These two "women" would always insist on being left alone when they stayed in Afghan houses. They kept apart from the rest of the household, and staff were told to put food outside the door, knock, and walk away. No one was allowed into their rooms. Our agents would hear these stories, but always after al-Zawahiri had moved on. We followed him as far as the Iranian border where the trail went cold.

In late 2016 we had a breakthrough in operations against al-Qaeda following intelligence from our TTP sources. In one raid US and Afghan special forces discovered al-Qaeda's propaganda arm, the Al Sahaf media operation. The raid delivered files of information about the leadership and led to the arrest of a key facilitator for al-Zawahiri was arrested. His name was Ilyas al-Swati, and after interrogation, he gave us information that both helped our understanding of AQIS and built our knowledge of al-Zawahiri himself. He told us of secret underground bunkers with air conditioning that were dug in tunnels some fifty yards long where the leadership could hide. Above ground there would be only a simple mud hut, but al-Zawahiri could live in the bunker for weeks on end. For a while we were tracking one of the gatekeepers for this operation, Usama Mahmood, also known as Abuzar. As well as providing protection, support and transport for the overall leadership, we believed he was the main leader of AQIS. We were within a couple of hours of getting him in Ghazni in 2018, but he got away. Ilyas al-Swati was released after the Taliban takeover and today he is the head of intelligence for AQIS.

HUNTER BECOMES THE HUNTED

In October 2017, the same month that we had our biggest successes in effectively destroying the capacity of AQIS in Ghazni province, President Ghani and Hanif Atmar once again moved against me. The NDS director general, Andarabi, called me and said, "You have to give away all your guns, from either the NDS or your own guards."

"You and I both know," I said, "that if I do that I'll be killed. Very, very quickly."

"I don't care. That is an order, and you have to do it."

We were friends and I thought he was joking.

"I'm the director general of the NDS. I would not joke about this. We have a lot of people like you, and they don't get killed. We have one hundred eighty colonels in the NDS, and none of them has the protection you have."

"Boss, you have zero colonels like me. I'm involved in some really serious counterterrorism operations."

The next morning Andarabi sent men to my house and disarmed all the guards. My CIA contact called to ask what had happened and immediately responded by sending a Delta Force unit. Nine very tall, bearded special operators arrived to do a quick survey and recommend measures for protection.

"There must be something behind this," she said. "We need to relocate you to Bagram Airbase while we find out what is going on."

I refused the offer and stayed in Kabul. I had weapons sent by friends and I bought more on the black market. I felt like a player in a very dark comedy: a colonel in the country's most important security service reduced to buying weapons in the bazaar to protect myself—from our own president.

Ghani then upped the ante. He called the CIA chief of station to his office and told him that I was out of control, a rogue element.

"I don't trust him with the country's most important secrets, and anything he is doing for you is illegal. He should be fired now."

"It's not illegal," said the chief of station. "It's sanctioned by the US government. He's our employee."

"No, he's an NDS colonel," shouted the president. "We fired him, and he is still facing serious charges. He needs to be arrested and go to jail."

"Mister President, let me remind you that you're not my president. You have no right to yell at me. If you have any beef with Sami Sadat, you have to call Washington. They contracted him." And he added, because he knew I was now in extreme danger and needed heavyweight protection, "If anything happens to Colonel Sadat, it'll be catastrophic for your administration."

He called me straight away to advise me to leave the country for a while.

"You're a young guy. What did you do to piss off President Ghani so much?"

I would not leave the country. If I did that I would risk losing everything I had built up. But the threats went on. A week later, my friend General Rahman, the deputy minister of Interior, called me to his office at night.

"Sami, there's a risk to your life," he said. "I can't tell you what it is, but I want you to leave. I can buy you tickets for Turkey. Take your family for a couple of weeks while we sort this out."

I smiled. "I think I know what the threat is, and I'm not leaving for anywhere."

He pulled open his drawer and put a file on his desk. He opened the file and turned it round so I could read it. I recognized it immediately. I had seen similar files dozens of times, but not with my picture at the front. It was a target package: instructions for agents to kill me, with details of my house, my office, my cars, everything.

"I've been told to make this happen."

Rahman paused to let that sink in.

"I was in the meeting with Andarabi when Minister Atmar gave the order to kill you. I told the minister that you were a reasonable guy, and we should talk to you, why did we need to kill you. But Atmar interrupted. 'The time for talking is over,' he said. 'The only talking Sami Sadat should be doing is with God. Blow him to the sky.'"

Andarabi refused to take the package because of my deep connections with the NDS. He said that I would be bound to find out and the assassination would fail. General Rahman readily agreed to take on the target package when Atmar told him he should.

"So, are you going to assassinate me?"

He laughed for the first time in our meeting. "Fuck no! Fuck these guys. I want to shove all my ranks up Atmar's ass. I will never do that to you, Sami."

I said, "If you don't want to do it and the NDS doesn't want to do it, I'm not worried."

"What's your problem with Atmar?" he asked. "You should make your peace with him."

"I don't make peace with traitors."

"You should be careful, Sami. Don't underestimate Atmar. He could hurt you. He could turn your friends or even use the Haqqani Network against you. The reason I took this on was to make sure that nobody carried it out."

Then he came round to my side of the desk to sit alongside me.

"You're awfully calm for someone who has just been told that the most powerful man in the country wants to kill you. Who's backing you? How are you so calm?"

"Every day every Afghan citizen faces a threat to life as soon as they open the front door," I said. "It's no worse for me. We're trying to stop those threats, and I won't run away from the fight."

Even as I left his office he was pleading with me to take a plane out of the country.

I picked up the target package and heard his words as I walked down the corridor. "Atmar is reckless. He issued his threats in front of Andarabi and Defense Minister Stanekzai. Everyone knows he wants to kill you."

I did not doubt it was true. Atmar was capable of anything. There was a rumor that he had even tried to engineer a Taliban ambush against the vice president, General Abdul Rashid Dostum. Atmar saw Ghani as mentally ill. If he could have him removed for incapacity to govern, and destroy other potential successors such as Dostum, then as national security adviser he could take power without the inconvenience of an election.

Just like the last time the president had threatened my life, I decided that going as public as possible was the best response. I had just bought a new-model black Range Rover Sport, the only one in Kabul. It was not armored, and sometimes I would drive it myself with one of my friends and just go and sit, having a coffee downtown again. I wanted to brazen out the threats, but it was a tough time. In my working life I was on the frontier, meeting potential sources who might want to kill me and avoiding suicide bombers. And then when I came home, I would get a call from someone like General Rahman to say, "Hey, by the way, we want to kill you too."

Atmar continued to act against me, removing the security license for my company and blocking my brother from bidding for government contracts. The family had to move our business to Dubai in order to keep going. He went after my friends too, making a case against my deputy Kosh, in an attempt to turn him to his side. Kosh had been tracking a Haqqani network planner, Qari Ajmal, who was conducting surveillance on a suicide bomber. Kosh had alerted an NDS Quick Reaction Force unit, but when they could not make it in time, he took matters into his own hands, arresting the Haqqani planner and shooting the potential suicide bomber, as he feared he was wearing an explosive vest. Atmar claimed he had acted rashly. But the accusation went nowhere. He misunderstood the close bonds of loyalty that those of us working in the front line of the secret world had for each other.

The deal we had for the TTP to share information that would help us win in Afghanistan came to an abrupt end in 2018. It followed a new momentum in the war signaled in a speech by President

Trump in August 2017. For several years before that American troops were severely limited in what they could hit in Afghanistan, a policy imposed by President Obama, who wanted to wind down the war. When Trump came into office at the beginning of 2017 his instinct was to pull out. He could see that he had inherited a failing war. But he was persuaded by two generals who had served in Afghanistan, his secretary of defense, Jim Mattis, and national security adviser, H. R. McMaster, to give American forces one last chance to go after the Taliban. He changed policy in a way that turned the war in our favor for the first time in years. He took the gloves off, allowing American planes to aggressively pursue the Taliban again, as they had not been allowed to do under Obama. "We're not nation-building again, Trump said. "We're killing terrorists." Things were going to change. "Retribution will be fast and powerful, as we lift restrictions and expand authorities in the field." The drift stopped for a while and we began to regain the initiative. More robust American air power raised morale in Afghan forces.

It took a few months for the impact of this to affect my work, but by early 2018 there was an abrupt change in counterterrorism policy. There were no longer to be "good" and "bad" terrorists, a useful shorthand for the policies we had adopted to give a free pass to TTP as long as they gave us information on al-Qaeda and ISKP. The CIA told me that they were now going after every terrorist, and even asked me for my TTP contacts so they could kill them.

I refused and left my job. I had no sympathy for the TTP, but I had made a deal as an Afghan and did not want to break my word. I told all my contacts that the deal was off, and they should throw away any phones we had given them. Mr. Hashemi was retiring.

I thought the change in policy a bad mistake. I did not want to start a new war, and our deal had brought great results. We already had our hands full with the Taliban; the argument was really one of sequencing. I wanted to fight the TTP at a later stage, but first I wanted to focus on the existential threat to my country—the Afghan Taliban and their al-Qaeda backers. There were also growing threats to the republic from former mujahidin commanders, who had grown stronger in recent years. Taking on the TTP as well lost us a stream of intelligence and opened a new front.

A few days later, a US drone strike killed Mullah Fazlullah, the leader of the TTP. It was so stupid to kill the enemy of Pakistan while that country was doing everything in its power to support the enemies of America and Afghanistan. The Pakistani military supported groups who wanted to kill Afghan and American soldiers. By killing their enemies, all America was doing was giving them more time and resources to kill our people.

I left Afghanistan to live in Dubai for a while, where I took over our family business. Since 2001, my father and brothers had become wealthy, initially with an oil import franchise and later with other contracting for the American forces, including for security services. Having the business behind me meant that I was never tempted by corruption. And my role in government provided cover for the family. Business owners without those links were exposed to demands for cash. But I had been in government service one way or another since I was eighteen years old and needed time out to put money in the bank for myself.

Chapter Six

"NEW AND DIFFERENT" (2019)

By 2019, five years after President Obama declared combat operations "over" and limited American offensive capacity, the Taliban were stronger than they had been at any time since the start of the war. They were no longer fighting as guerrillas, but massing in large groups, and their Red Unit special forces had secured sophisticated equipment, including night vision goggles taken from our side. Every night we became weaker, and every night they became stronger, as they destroyed isolated police and army outposts and seized vehicles and weapons supplied by America. They had their own shadow governance system and were now set on taking major cities.

The increased American bombing during the previous year, since President Trump had taken the gloves off and licensed his forces to go hard against the Taliban, would not change the dial on the war unless Afghan forces could follow up the raids on the ground. And despite nearly two decades of training and support our armed forces were still not capable of holding territory on their own.

Eighteen years in and with no sign of victory, there was a lot of pressure from the Trump administration to pull all troops out. But General Scott Miller had other ideas. He wanted to stop the slide and help Afghanistan win the war. He was the best American commander of them all, with the possible exception of General Stan McChrystal a decade before, who also had a will to win.

Miller's immediate predecessor, General John "Mick" Nicholson Jr., was more interested in the political lane, too often seen in dress uniform with the Afghan president and not enough on the ground with Afghan or even American troops. During his long period of command we lost twenty districts. General Nicholson presided over a war effort so ineffectual that when he relinquished command, I tweeted that he left "many shortfalls, failures and strategic mistakes in the Afghan theatre." The Taliban had the initiative on the battlefield, while political interference meant some of the most incompetent people were promoted as generals. There were low-grade generals in the US military too, and I often wondered how such people rose as high as they did.

Morale went even lower when my friend General Abdul Raziq was shot and killed by an infiltrator while walking with Miller inside the governor's compound in Kandahar. He had previously been targeted by twenty-eight suicide attacks, and injured four times, only to be shot by a cowardly insider attack.

Raziq had fought an aggressive war against the Taliban in their southern heartland, and I felt his loss deeply.

Miller's trip to Kandahar was typical. He liked to meet Afghans, get to know the country, and understand the training, motivation, and capacity of the Afghan army at all levels. He knew they were taking heavy casualties and blamed the senior leadership of the Afghan military for the continued failure. They were mostly incapable and corrupt, their ranks stuffed with old communists and mujahidin left over from previous wars—and now supplemented by Ghani loyalists. They did not trust Americans and were not honest with them as a result.

Under rules of engagement since 2014 American forces were now supporting Afghan partners, mentoring their progress on operations rather than leading in the field. It meant that in practice unless Afghan forces took the initiative, Americans were not fighting at all. And since Afghan commanders did not have a clear strategic objective, or capacity to coordinate an offensive war against the Taliban, until Miller took over, most of our highly-trained special operators were effectively locked up alongside American mentors doing nothing.

From the start Miller talked of the need to be "new and different." He sought out my generation—Afghan military leaders whose talents were not being properly used. He did not want to impose his own ideas but find out what worked on the Afghan side and employ those tactics more widely. I saw him constantly telling his team to listen to Afghans, work with Afghans. And not listen to be polite, but listen because we may have the right answers. It was an attitude that bred trust. The Afghan military respected General Miller because he was not afraid to walk into a frontline position or an isolated checkpoint in Uruzgan or Ghazni or jump out of his vehicle in the city of Kabul and say hello to people. Soldiers recognized a fellow soldier. He was a kind leader: friendly, formidable, with a character that could inspire men in battle, and he wanted to win the war. I liked him a lot.

Miller's whole career had been in special forces. He was wounded twice—when ground commander in the Black Hawk Down firefight in Mogadishu in 1993, and in Fallujah in Iraq. Inevitably much of his service since 9/11 had been spent in Afghanistan, where he was one of the first special operators on the ground in 2001. When working in the Pentagon in 2009 he created the "Afghan Hands" program, designed to turn out American officers who spoke our languages and knew our culture. At the time of his promotion to the Kabul command in 2018 he had been the commander of US Joint Special

Operations Command for two years, which meant he had been in Afghanistan on many occasions.

Miller's son, Lieutenant Austin Miller Jr., four months out of West Point, was at his confirmation hearing in the Senate. Acknowledging "this young guy sitting behind me," Miller called the Afghan conflict "generational." He said, "I never anticipated that his cohort would be in a position to deploy as I sat there in 2001." He knew he did not have another generation to win, and from the moment he arrived in Kabul he was looking for ways to change the course of the war.

I had first met Miller during the months I was out of government in Dubai in October 2018 few days before his trip to Kandahar. Hearing of my service he called me in for a one-on-one meeting soon after his appointment. I flew back to Kabul and did not look like a military commander as I drove into the American base in my Range Rover Sport wearing Ralph Lauren blazer and slacks.

We sat in his private dining room at the back of the headquarters eating burgers and drinking army coffee in a one-on-one meeting while I talked to him about how Afghans and Americans could work together. He listened intently and took few notes. He asked me first about my assessment of the Taliban. I said that he would need to know about al-Qaeda as well, as you could not see one in isolation from the other. I explained their composition, strengths, weaknesses. I said that the Quetta Shura in southwest Pakistan was their strategic center of gravity and connection with Pakistan's intelligence service, the ISI.

"Center of gravity" is a useful military way of analyzing conflict that goes back to Clausewitz and refers to the hub that allows for the freedom, ability, and will to fight. I told him that Helmand province in the southwest of Afghanistan was the Taliban's operational center of gravity.

"So how do we fight them?" he asked. "What else do we need?"

"You need far better integration into what Afghan forces are doing," I said. "You are now supporting Afghan operations, not leading from the front, but that change has not been understood by some of your forces. There should be more coordination between us. Sometimes there's an American bombing raid and Afghan forces don't even know it's happening until it's over. If we knew, we could follow up on the ground."

I mentioned a number of Afghans I thought he ought to meet. Some were obvious, such as the Jamiat leader, Salahuddin Rabbani, who I had worked with on the High Peace Council, and former president Hamid Karzai, who would ground him in the political atmospherics. But I extended the advice to meet some other Afghans who I knew would not have been on any list he had seen so far. And to really understand the Taliban's operational center of gravity, I even included Sher Muhammad Akhunzada, one of the key powerbrokers in Helmand, who was opposed to the Taliban. He had been previously been *persona non grata* at the headquarters because of alleged links to drugs and crime, but Miller was curious to meet him.

"These people could be allies," I told him. "If you don't work with them they'll be against you, so it's better to listen to them and keep them at least neutral. They are not against the US. They have their own Afghan political problems, and could be friend or enemy, depending how you treat them." I got the impression that he had not heard some of this before.

I warned him that Al-Qaeda was starting to build combat strength in Afghanistan, with bases in Ghazni and Paktika provinces. Then I talked politics. "President Ghani is now basically breaking the fabric of unity inside the Afghan military, politicizing the intelligence agency and misusing the police." Miller did not show emotion but was surprised by the vehemence of my analysis. "Reforms in the

Afghan security forces are politically driven," I said, "not led by challenges on the ground."

We talked a lot, too, about communications and the need for him to keep in touch with the Afghan people. I said, "You need to explain your intent. They will listen to you as commander of coalition forces. Tell them what you are doing—and why. And then if there are civilian casualties, you'll have people on your side." Every time there was a civilian death, rumors spread that this was what the Americans intended to do. He needed to get out ahead of that.

"If you signal your intentions in advance," I said, "people will understand better, not of course for specific operations, but the general focus of your actions. Afghans are patient and respect honesty."

Miller called me back two weeks later to talk to his command staff. "I want you to brief them exactly as you briefed me and put solutions on the table," he said. "We need to know how Afghans and Americans can work together."

I met them in an Italian restaurant on the base, and when they arrived they were courteous and initially showed little interest as we shared pizzas. I was just another Afghan intelligence voice the boss had called in. But as I spoke they began to take notes, and I could see that I was getting a hearing. Proof that Miller was listening came when later his entire program was based on what he called "reliable leaders," wanting to make sure there was space for the younger generation of Afghans to be promoted on merit.

DARK FORCES

In 2019, the last year of his first term in office, President Ashraf Ghani had a shakeup at the top across the security sector, promoting people who had made their names in the secret intelligence agency, the NDS. My old colleague Massoud Andarabi moved to head the ministry of interior, and another former NDS chief, Asadullah Khalid, took over at the ministry of defense.

Khalid was a good friend of mine, an intellectual with a passion for poetry unequalled in our nation of poetry lovers. He had been on the mujahidin side in our previous conflicts, and in the 1990s spent time in America on a CIA training course. He still suffered from wounds received when he was hit by a suicide bomber in 2012 by a fake peace intermediary, a similar attack to the one that had killed my mentor and friend Professor Burhanuddin Rabbani.

Soon after taking over at the MOD, Khalid called me in Dubai.

"I need you to come back and work as my adviser, Sami."

I knew I would not be able to turn down the call to serve, although I had a good life in Dubai with lots of friends, and on the weekend we would drive into the dunes of the desert in an avalanche truck. My business in Dubai was going well. I had an office downtown, and I had secured a patent on a system to track military vehicles by GPS, disabling them if they were stolen.

"There is one problem," Khalid went on. "Why does President Ghani hate you so much?" I explained about the absurd coffee-machine plot and how Hanif Atmar had tried to have me killed.

"Atmar is no longer in the government, and I can talk to the president. You are working for me and not him."

I was still wary of what Atmar might do. During the year I worked in Dubai, Atmar had tried once again to get the NDS to mount an attack on me when I made a trip to Kabul. The claim then was that I was sheltering terrorists in a guest house I owned. I mounted guards and stayed up all night. We stopped one car in the street and took away NDS identity cards from the two people in it as well as phones that showed they had been contacting NDS Unit 600, which carried out raids in Kabul. I called the NDS to say we would burn the next car they sent. Then I called my main CIA contact, who called the director general of the NDS, now Masoom Stanekzai.

"We've heard that some unit in NDS is going to raid Sami Sadat's house," he said. "This is an abuse and shows why the NDS doesn't need a strike force. You only use it for your political purposes. If there's a raid, we'll cut our funding." There were no further incidents during that tense night.

At dawn I went to Stanekzai's home. He was the man whose life I had saved the night Rabbani was killed. But he was an indecisive head of the NDS. When counterterrorist units wanted kill orders against suspects, he would delay approval, preferring to try to negotiate. He meddled in politics and was more loyal to President Ghani than to Afghanistan. Like Atmar, he saw the country's intelligence agency as a political tool and used his position and bags of cash to buy off opposition to the president, weakening other centers of power such as the country's chief executive officer, Abdullah Abdullah. He encouraged ethnic division, promoting presidential loyalists. And he hated the new generation of Afghan officials and soldiers—my generation.

Stanekzai was angry at my early morning intrusion, and I was apprehensive. I was about to threaten the director general of the most powerful spy agency in the country, a man with the power to make me disappear.

"Why are you calling the Americans and giving them false information about a house raid?" he ranted. "None of this is true."

I did not say anything but pulled out the phone from one of the guys I had arrested and played the WhatsApp message he had sent reporting on the number of my guards to NDS Unit 600.

Stanekzai immediately changed tack. "Son of a bitch. I don't know who ordered this. Maybe the NDS director did it independently. I had no idea, Sami, I don't know anything about this."

"Sir, I'm not here to listen to excuses," I said. "I'm here to tell you something."

"OK." He was listening now.

"Remember the night of September 21, 2011, when Professor Rabbani was killed? I came and rescued you and put you in the car and saved your life, took you to Bagram Hospital?"

"Yes, thank you," he said uncertainly.

"I've not come to hear that. I am a key witness to the assassination of Professor Rabbani, and that file is still open. And as a key witness, I could go to the media and tell them that you were involved in the plot. I don't know if you were involved or not, and I don't give a shit. I will tell them you brought the suicide bomber and *you* caused the assassination of Professor Rabbani in favor of Pakistan."

"You wouldn't dare do that. It's not true."

"It was also not true to charge me with having terrorists in my house."

I paused to let it sink in. But I had not finished.

"I know you were being paid by the British Embassy when you headed the High Peace Council. And I also know that many Taliban who contacted us at that time to reconcile with the Afghan Government disappeared. When I go public with this it will be up to you to explain yourself to the people of Afghanistan and, indeed, to the Taliban."

"For God's sake, Sami. I know your father. Your father and I have been friends for thirty years, and you're not going to do that. You're not thinking straight. These are dangerous allegations that will set light to the country, especially the assassination of Professor Rabbani."

"Well, that's up to you to handle. You mess with me one more time, and this is exactly what will happen to you and President Ghani," I said. "In my eyes, you are all traitors, and for traitors I have no mercy. So what do you want to do?"

"Sami, I am ready to listen," he said.

"I want the NDS to back off and do their real job. I know you are only doing this because of Minister Atmar."

"Yes, he is literally asking us in every single NDS meeting to go after you and a couple of other people," he admitted. "So I needed to do something for him. But from now on the NDS will have nothing to do with you."

He had a soft voice and manner, and this kind of menace did not really suit him. He still walked with a stick from injuries he received in the bomb blast. "You are an honorable man," he told me. "I should look to you more for advice on NDS matters."

"And there is another thing. I want you to appoint Colonel Mustafa Wardak as commander of the NDS special strike force. I am sure that under his command no one will be coming to my house again."

"Done. It's a deal," he said.

And that was it. After that, the NDS did not bother me or threaten any of my property. And true to his word, Mustafa Wardak was appointed as commander of the NDS special strike force.

Shortly after that attempt by Atmar to arrest me in 2018, he resigned. He had turned his role as the national security adviser into an alternative power base in the Afghan palace, securing the loyalty of thousands of members of the security services. When President Ghani heard that Atmar was now patron even to senior members of the presidential protection service he forced him out. The public account was that they had clashed when Ghazni fell to the Taliban, and the president blamed his national security adviser. But the truth was a bitter battle for power at the heart of government.

I witnessed the threat of the dark forces that Atmar had at his disposal on the night he resigned from government. I was with two close friends, Ajmal Abidy and Matin Bek, both deputies at the NDS and in the group of young reformers who backed President Ghani. I had been warning them for months that Atmar was a threat, and I saw them working the phones all that evening, trying to ensure adequate security preparations in case he mounted a coup. It was well known that Atmar had links with a number of countries hostile to Afghanistan, including Iran, Russia, and, worst of all, Pakistan.

MINISTRY OF DEFENSE

I arrived at my new job as the adviser to the minister of defense, Asadullah Khalid, in the depths of winter. The corridors outside the minister's office were clogged with generals wrapped in coats against the cold, carrying large bundles of paper. They would sit for days, not really waiting for a decision, but competing for influence, a word in the minister's ear. It was such a waste of resources. They were obsessed with pushing advantage for their ethnic group. The ministry suffered from a policy of balanced recruitment between the tribes. It was designed to produce harmony, but instead became a game that encouraged patronage, corruption, and cronyism. The old generals with their badly dyed hair and mustaches were just the same lost generation I had cleared out of the NDS.

Khalid wanted to reform the organization, promoting a new generation on merit, rather than being stuck with ethnically based appointments. He saw the old guard as incapable of reform. Their only ambition was to stay in the job. He tasked me to reorganize the MOD to streamline decision-making. I began with military intelligence, until then run by a cousin of the president and delivering very little for its large resources. Across the country there were 3,800 agents on the books who produced less than one hundred reports a day. It was a pathetic return, and I soon discovered that all but 200 of the agents were dead or ineffective, while other people were still taking their salaries. On my recommendation Khalid replaced the military intelligence chief with a younger officer who was not corrupt.

There was another strategic intelligence department looking at open source material and foreign information that did not coordinate with the military intelligence stream. It was an easy fix to create a fusion cell to manage both streams. But the problems went deeper than that. I discovered that we had warehouses full of unused high-tech equipment, including Boeing ScanEagle drones and Wolfhound radios. The drones could stay in the sky all day providing streams of information. And the Wolfhounds could intercept enemy communications, fixing a precise location for the caller, a ten-digit grid reference. If a Taliban commander was talking on the radio our interception team quickly could provide the location to the nearest foot, not only fixing a target inside a house or compound but the exact corner of a room.

These were powerful capabilities we had been given by America but never properly used. And even where some of the equipment had gotten into the field to send information, it was not being acted on. Because of interagency rivalries, intelligence agents would not tell the army locally what they knew but report to Kabul, who would report across to the chief of army staff. It would take several days for actionable intelligence to come back down the chain of command from this process, by which time it was dangerously out of date.

As well as unused equipment, we had under-utilized specialists. I discovered that there were around two hundred highly trained air-to-ground attack coordinators sitting in Kabul. We immediately sent them out to the army corps headquarters across the country. Through a combined arms concept, we paired them up with the Wolfhound radio operators to find targets so they could call in strikes in real time, coordinating with commando and conventional forces—pushing decision-making down to a lower level.

I was not the only new face at a senior level in the MOD. Khalid brought in Lieutenant General Fahim Ramin to head the air force, and we developed a close relationship, setting up a new air strike policy and better intelligence management, which shortened the time from collection to action in the battlefield. We set up a national operation intelligence center to speed up decision-making and coordinate attacks.

Fahim is tall for a pilot, with a ready smile, and real leadership qualities. He had previously commanded 777 Brigade, the special mission air wing, that supported night raids and surveillance missions for Afghan special forces. It was only when he took over the whole operation that the air force began to fulfill its potential. He reformed it from top to bottom, bringing in young professional officers who could integrate with the rest of the Afghan army.

Our troops desperately needed air support they could rely on. We now had had US-supplied Black Hawk transport helicopters, a fleet of Super Tucano A-29 light attack aircraft, and some Russian-made MI-24 helicopters gifted by India. In addition we had attack variants of aircraft that could otherwise be seen at any civilian weekend airfield. The Attack Cessna 208 fixed-wing plane and the tiny MD-530 helicopter were popular sights to frontline troops when armed with missiles. And for the first time under Fahim, Afghan pilots began to be able to fly at night, an awesome extension of our capability.

There were limitations to our ability to use the air force, and some were imposed by the US. Our fleet of Black Hawk helicopters, headquartered at Kandahar, was confined to the south, when we would have preferred to deploy them nationwide. And different NATO allies had responsibility for different regions, partnering with MOD with their own role of engagement. There were foreign advisers in offices across the MOD all with their own programs to push, mostly Americans but some from NATO countries as well. But most of our problems were self-imposed—interagency rivalries, cronyism, and corruption that kept good kit and well-trained operators out of the fight. We needed to change the way we fought to take on the renewed Taliban threat, and this was just the beginning.

Our American allies backed the changes we made to reform the MOD. Khalid was close to them, and it made a difference that they could now communicate quickly in English across the top of the main security ministries, which had not always been the case. Khalid brought in women at senior levels, including as a deputy minister. He did not like political games and did not attend cabinet meetings, but only the National Security Council, and he held one-on-one meetings with the president. He was a patriot who would put Afghan interests ahead of anything demanded by the president or his American backers if he thought it necessary. And he was strongly opposed to Pakistan—a position that was now possible to take since President Ghani's policy of appeasement had failed.

THE BATTLE OF BADAKHSHAN

It would not be long before I got into the fight. But the day it happened I was not expecting it. I was dressed casually in my trademark Ralph Lauren blazer and chinos and having lunch with Khalid when he took a call on his cell phone from Brigadier General Yazdani, the commander of 217 Corps in the northeast, who reported that they had failed to recapture a mountainous district close to Fayzabad, the capital of Badakhshan province, which had fallen to the Taliban. This was strategically important. The province had stayed out of Taliban hands during their last period in power in the 1990s. It was the gateway to the Tajik border in the north and one of the main recruiting grounds for Afghan soldiers.

Khalid talked briefly to the general, who said that they had tried everything but had to admit defeat. Putting down his phone on the table, Khalid said calmly to me, "Sami, I want you to go to Badakhshan and take command of that brigade for two weeks or however long it takes."

"Yes sir. I can do that."

"Your objective is to coordinate the operation for retaking the district center. Find out what you need, and I'll send it."

"When do you want me to go?"

"As soon as you can. It's a worsening situation."

Pausing at home only to collect my body armor, boots, and a compact Czech-made Škorpion submachine gun, I was off that afternoon. I did not even have a combat uniform, so I picked one up from Fahim's office at the air force terminal.

When I arrived night had fallen and things were in a desperate situation. The local head of the NDS had been my deputy in the covert action department, so I trusted what he had to say. The Taliban, believed to be around three hundred strong, were local recruits who knew the area and held strategic positions including caves on mountain passes up to fifteen thousand feet above sea level, threatening a district center. There was disarray between the civilian and military leadership, with no good intelligence. I went to a meeting where the director of the NDS, the chief of police, and a senior army officer argued over tactics in front of the provincial governor, who could only look from one to the other without any resolution of how to act. I learned that there were some 1100 Afghan forces available, about half of them combat soldiers. They were concentrated in a valley, and above them all the high ground was in the hands of the Taliban. To reach the district center would involve a major combat operation across some of the toughest terrain in the country. Before the meeting ended, the governor turned to me.

"What did you bring from Kabul to support the operations?"

"Governor, sir. I have nothing."

"I heard that you were bringing commandos in here."

"No, it's me, I'm alone, I've been sent to provide an assessment and understanding and also help the brigade to sustain itself and see what they need for this operation."

The governor looked at me with dismay and said nothing.

It was clear that as they were configured the forces available were quite incapable of retaking the district, especially as the local commanders were all blaming each other for the failure. I felt bad; we had all these forces, but we could not defeat the Taliban in one district. I needed to find out why.

The situation on the ground was changing so quickly that anything other than an assessment from the front line had no value. Taking the executive officer of the brigade, Lieutenant Colonel Sharif, and one other officer, I drove to the valley where the main force was based. Around midnight we woke the brigade commander, who tried to persuade me not to go any further.

"There's nothing to see on the front line, just a couple of ditches and holes, and the enemy is firing down at it so you might get hit."

Ignoring his advice, Sharif and I went up to the front line with escort, walking up slippery ground into the snow line. I arrived to find hundreds of men trying to sleep in shallow trenches, with sporadic firing between them and the Taliban in the mountain peaks above. Because it was night it was easy to see enemy positions when they fired, so I called air force headquarters in Kabul and they sent an Afghan surveillance manned aircraft. When the aircraft arrived at around 2:00 a.m., I linked to it by computer, and once I had accurate locations for the Taliban I ordered artillery fire from down in the valley behind us. My order was simple: "Don't let them sleep."

Once the artillery began I told the small force of Afghan soldiers pinned down in trenches on the mountainside that we needed around thirty men to move up behind the Taliban, but their officer refused to comply, calling it a suicide mission, saying it would take six hundred men to mount a decisive offensive.

I called my friend, General Haibatullah Alizai, the director of operations in Kabul. Such was the intensity of the conflict at that stage that he was still in his office in the middle of the night.

"Do we have any commandos in Badakhshan?"

"Yes," he said. "I sent a fresh unit up there two days ago to support this operation."

Shortly afterwards their commander, Captain Mohib, called me, and by 5:00 a.m. I had my thirty commandos.

We stripped down so we were carrying only weapons and ammunition. While my aide, Humayun, took some of the conventional soldiers to cover our right flank and distract the Taliban with suppressing fire, we began to move up into the mountain area. I left with the words of General Alizai in my ears.

"Brother, you are on a suicide mission. I don't have any air support for you. The best thing I have is the manned surveillance aircraft, which is not enough."

"General Alizai," I said. "If I remember anything from what I studied in military schools, the best operation in the mountains is by foot with a small force. The larger the force, the more casualties we will have. The only way to clear these positions is to walk up." But while small forces had agility, I knew, too, that the textbooks would demand a larger force than I had at my disposal. The odds were brutal and suggested we would fail.

We had two guides from the Afghan Local Police who knew the area well. We were trying to get behind the Taliban, so they would not see us until we were close. But we lost the element of surprise as the first sunshine of the day reflected from the snow, and we could see distant figures on the peaks above watching us through binoculars.

After more than two hours walking, at around 8:00 a.m., we came into the range of a Taliban ambush, firing from both sides of the path. We ran back down, quickly losing the height that had been so hard to gain. As I reorganized my small force, dividing them to try other routes for a second attempt, Alizai called with very welcome news.

"The US will provide one armed drone to support the operation." We headed back up the mountain with renewed morale, our artillery still pounding the heights above us.

The American drone soon identified the two heavy machine guns that had caused us such trouble on our first attempt and successfully destroyed them. Then I looked back down the valley and saw hundreds of conventional combat soldiers following our path, looking like columns of ants against the snow. Khalid had called the brigade commander and was shocked to hear I had only thirty men with me. He ordered the full mobilization of the force to follow me.

"Get your ass over there," he told the brigade commander. "And call back when you are with Sami."

When the force reached me it even included the fifty-year-old commander of the artillery detachment who had been supporting my advance.

"You shouldn't be here," I shouted.

"There is no way I am sitting on my ass while I watch a young man like you heading into battle," he yelled back.

I told the troops who had arrived to stay behind us. I wanted to go on with commandos and clear the first Taliban positions so they could hold ground as we took it. But they had slept and were fresh, and being headstrong Afghans and mountain-fit so they could breathe at altitude, they ignored my orders and went ahead of us. Most were not wearing body armor so they could go much faster than us. By 3:00 p.m. we had reached the top of the first mountain and then had to head down the other side for an assault on the main Taliban positions on the higher peak beyond.

We were spread out across the ridge when the second Taliban ambush began, with firing that seemed to come at us from every mountain peak. The commandos and I took what cover we could and began to return fire, but the conventional soldiers were so poorly trained that they broke under fire and ran back as fast as they could, heading down the mountain. As we tried to regroup, the commando leader, Captain Mohib, said that he had lost touch with half of his force who were on the other side of the valley, and he had to send other troops down carrying two injured ANA soldiers.

We were left with four commandos; Mohib; my driver, who was called Khalid; and myself—seven altogether. And now we were stuck. If we went down the Taliban snipers would pick us off one by one. If we stayed where we were, the Taliban could literally walk down and finish us off. We were lying in the snow in narrow drainage trenches, and if we so much as stood up the snipers would have us. We still had the drone, but it could not find any Taliban positions as they were inside the mountain caves. Lying down with cold snow to my hips, I asked myself, "What have I done? If I go back down defeated, it's the end of my army career, and if I push forward I might get killed, along with six others who are depending on me." I was very hungry as well, short of energy after hours of walking. We were now high enough in the mountains for the phones to find a signal.

When my phone rang, the minister was on the other end of the line. "Hey, Sami, where are you?"

"I'm actually very close to this Taliban position."

"I heard about it. So you are trapped, and there is no way they can send you reinforcements."

He exploded when I told him I had only six men with me. I said, "Sir, the only way to survive is actually to go and take the district."

"Sami, this is suicide. I regret sending you to Badakhshan," he said. "Come back. I'm sending helicopters to pick you up from wherever you are and bring you back to Kabul because you're going to get yourself killed."

As the argument went on, I found I gained inspiration from his mood. I did not want to let him down.

I took off all my gear, including body armor and ammunition. The American drone could use its sensor to identify the snipers only while they were firing. Leaving even my weapon behind, I started running upwards. The snipers started shooting at me, and I could hear bullets close by. All the time I was holding a phone, and on the other end of the call, Major Ali Ahmadi, the 10th Special Operations Kandak commander in Kunduz, was watching the drone feed with his American counterpart. When I heard they had pinpointed the Taliban's firing positions I dropped to the ground

Ten seconds later a rocket hit the top of the mountain on a spot which to us had looked like snow.

I slowly stood up again to test the result, and there were no more shots. I walked back to my position, picked up my gear and said little to the guys. We walked up past the destroyed Taliban position, a well-camouflaged bunker, linked underground to two others. The sniper who had caused us such trouble was lying dead on a blanket on top of the snow, with a white cloth covering him and a white cotton sheath to cover the barrel of his Russian-made Dragunov sniper rifle.

Khalid called to say he was sending two Mi-17 helicopters to take us out. We could see them flying up the valley, and one landed, but it was some distance away. They could not have landed on the steep slopes where we were and did not have our precise location. It would have been more useful if they had brought us some food, but they left without finding us. I turned off my phone to focus on the mission.

The Taliban continued to fire down from the caves they occupied high up the mountain, but we came close enough to be concealed by rocks. Then we assaulted the caves one by one, the sound of our firing echoing across the mountains as we ran in. It took three hours to clear all four caves, and we were continuously under fire. There was no way back now; it was kill or be killed.

As evening fell, we still had two caves to clear, and after a tactical pause until it was fully dark, we put on our night vision goggles and finished off the Taliban resistance. We were exhausted and expended our last energy to clear the final positions.

Company Sergeant Major Arif kept calling on me to take cover, but I was so tired that I just walked into the last cave, and after throwing a hand grenade, I collapsed onto the ground.

That was the vital position to control the district center. Now that we held the mountain I was confident of victory. We lost the drone as the night fell, but we had the advantage of night vision.

My small team had prevailed, leaving behind a trail of destruction, with a lot of weapons and ammunition to gather in. They would all play big roles in the fights that were to come. Captain Mohib, Sergeant Arif, and Private Murtaza all later joined my Joint Special Operations Command. Murtaza moved quickly through the ranks, training for special forces and taking command of my guard force. He never left my side and was injured twice. I cherished his loyalty. My driver, Khalid, who was not even in the special forces, but a very tough guy, had also played a part in our victory.

I turned on my phone again to call the brigade to send forces to hold our position. "And bring warm kit because there is a strong wind, and it goes through your bones." Then we slowly made our way down the mountain. Walking in the dark with night vision goggles is difficult and dangerous as the ground looks as if it is flat. We all kept falling and carried each other's backpacks through the snow. I arrived at the commando outpost at around 3:00 a.m. and slept the deepest sleep until woken by my aide to say that the minister was on the line. He was mad at me.

"We have dozens of districts under the control of the Taliban," he said. "We need to get back all of them. And if you die there is no way we could ever take those districts back." But I could feel the sense of pride in his voice. The police, army, and NDS had moved back to their headquarters in the district and were clearing the land mines as he spoke.

"Next time I'll be more careful," I said. Khalid he saw the value of what had happened. If the Afghan army coordinated all its assets under clear leadership, it could take on the Taliban and retake lost ground. I had become more than an adviser.

Sami Sadat alongside LTG Christopher Donahue and G Haibatullah Alizai, Regional Targeting Team RTT North in Afghanistan, 2020. These newly established teams became the most effective firepower controllers that support corps operations as well as conduct high value targeting utilizing Afghan Special operation community and Afghan Air Force.

AUF leadership engaged in a pivotal discussion with Congressman Michael McCaul, Chairman of the House Foreign Affairs Committee, outlining our vision for a liberated Afghanistan, 2022. Mr. McCaul is leading the Afghanistan investigation on withdrawal and is a key ally to the people of Afghanistan.

Moment captured by Sami—stunning view of the Badakhshan mountains amidst Arghanjkha district retaking operation, April 1st, 2019

Coordination with ANDSF leaders in Kandahar province before launching the significant Ops BABA during the Battle of Arghandab, October 2020.

In-action shot of the intense clearance operations during the Battle of Farah, December 17th, 2019.

Moments captured during the Battle of Nimrooz, showcasing the clearance operation in Chakhansoor district, July 15th, 2021.

With Dr. David Kilcullen at the New York Unions Club, part of the AUF's tour across the United States, 2023. The tour was named Hopeful Afghanistan. It was aimed to remind US citizens and leaders that all is not lost and we must write the next chapter in our favor.

Combined NDS and Afghan Army Special Forces during the first deployment of the Mobile Targeting Team in Ghazni province, April 25th, 2019. This operation became the baseline for building Regional Targeting Teams RTTs and was also the foundation of how the younger generation of ANDSF should be empowered and work jointly in order to achieve the military objectives.

Engaging with the community in Lashkargah during an Eid ceremony, fostering solidarity and hope, July 22nd, 2021.

The official launch of AUF, Governor Qayoum Rahimi, a key figure on the AUF leadership council, October 2023.

Captured in Shorabak, Helmand, Sami Sadat with LTC Salahudin Daud, Deputy Commander of JSOC, Corps Advisor Reza Sarvari, and Captain Asem Shukuri aide decamp to General Sadat, January 13th, 2021.

215th Corps personnel preparing for Maiwand Operation, April 12th, 2021.

Greeting an elder resident of Nimroz province, July 11th, 2021.

Captured during a night clearance operation in Nimroz on the border with Iran to stop the incoming Taliban from Iranian side, July 2021.

After a meeting with General Scott Miller following the successful closure of operation Raziq Qalat, Zabul, October 20th, 2019.

Soldiers Day event honoring ANDSF sacrifices—held by AUF political office in Virginia US 2024.

At the US Navy SEALs Base, Garmsir district southern Helmand right across the border from Pakistan to its east and Iran to its south.

With Minister Asadullah Khalid during his visit to Lashkargah, Helmand amidst the Taliban major offensive that overrun over 160 ANDSF checkpoints in two weeks of intense fighting. This was one of the key Taliban operations after the Doha agreement where they agreed not to attack cities, October 14th, 2020.

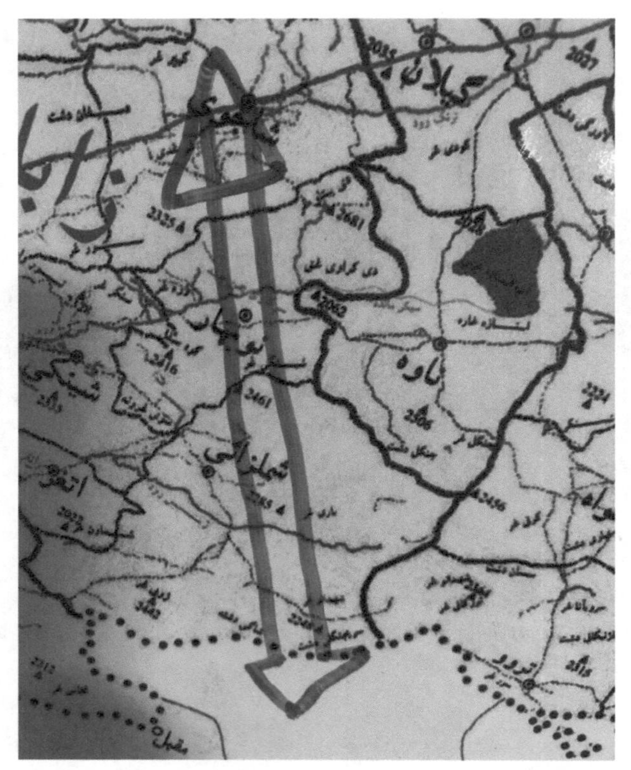

Map of three districts in southern Zabul province where American Professor Kevin King and Australian Timothy Weeks were exchanged with Anas Haqqani, the brother of Serajudin Haqqani and two other senior Taliban leaders. The Exchange happened in Naw Bahar district and the Taliban party needed a corridor to enter Afghanistan from Pakistan via Shamalzai district. This corridor was announced as safe from November 16th to 19th, 2019.

Retaking operation of Arghanjkha district during the Battle of Badakhshan, 2019.

ANA Graduation ceremony, 215th Corps HQ, Helmand, 2021.

Visiting the front lines in Eastern Lashkargah during the Battle of Lashkargah, May 25th, 2021.

Command Center during the Battle of Lashkargah, May 3rd, 2021.

Briefing meeting for the Battle of Lashkargah, May 17th, 2021.

Camp Antony handing over ceremony to the Afghan Army, Shorabak, Helmand, April 29th, 2021. By May 1st, the US soldiers departed and this became the first US camp closed after President Biden's Order of Go-To Zero. In the same day, the Taliban attacks increased by 600 percent as they had been waiting for the right time. Taliban leadership also planned to take Lashkargah as their first city in Afghanistan.

Counter Terrorism Unit (CTU) operations, the party travelled to meet a key source in Shajoy district Shal Akhundzada. Zabul province, May 14th, 2017.

With General Khoshal Saadat and BG Khalid Wardak in Lashkargah during the battle. Khalid was injured twice but refused to leave the battlefield and became one of the bravest soldiers during our fight for defense of Lashkargah, May 17th, 2021.

Alongside MG Mustafa Wardak, LTG Farim Ramin and BG. Abdul Qayum Salari in Lashkargah, January 4th, 2021. They came to a visit to support my new plans for southwestern Afghanistan.

With Reza Sarvari, my key advisor, preparing for Maiwand Operation—Shorabak, Helmand—April 12th, 2021.

JSOC introduction ceremony. From left to right: General Miller, Asad Sadat, and Jamshid Sadat. My brothers who came to attend my new command responsibility, December 2019, Kabul.

Greeting Lashkargah's elders and residents, July 2nd, 2021.

Ops BABA during the Battle of Arghandab, October 31st, 2020.

Chapter Seven

TAKING THE FIGHT TO THEM (2019)

The March operation in Badakhshan and my role as a mobile commander delivered results. And this became the template for a new way of fighting the war. The minister of defense, Asadullah Khalid, divided the country up into four zones for a new spring offensive to take the war to the Taliban. While I took the southern zone, the deputy minister, Yasin Zia, went to the west, Haibatullah Alizai to the north, and Habib Hisari to the northeast.

I went first to Ghazni, one of the most strategically important cities in the country, the gateway to Kabul from the south. It was the ancient capital of the eleventh-century Ghaznavid Empire, when Sultan Mahmood had waged war as far as Delhi, and sat on two vital routes—Highway One, the main north/south route from Kabul to Kandahar, and the east/west route used by the Taliban to move from Pakistan into areas further west in Uruzgan province under their control.

Ghazni had fallen to the Taliban before, and the military base inside the city itself was seen as so dangerous that most of the forces were in a headquarters ten miles to the east. Major General Ahmadi—then commander of Afghan army special forces, sent down a week earlier to organize Ghazni's defense—had little imagination. He issued orders from the base outside town and did not engage with the people actually fighting the war. It was one-way communication with Ahmadi; he would issue orders and then sit in his room and watch TV.

I was not going to join Ahmadi ten miles from the action. Instead I immediately set up in the base in the center of town, under constant rocket attack. As in Badakhshan, we faced a major problem of coordination. There were three special forces units spread across the city, and not only were they not in communication, their commanders had never even met. One unit was NDS, another police, and the third army commandos. When I called in the commanders I had to introduce them to each other. The commander of the NDS unit, Colonel Taher, was the first to enter our makeshift conference room in the base.

"I've seen you somewhere before," I said.

"Yes, sir. I was with you in Bermal district in the east when you were trying to meet a source that night the Americans nearly killed him."

"Congratulations on your promotion, Colonel Taher. Good to have you here."

There were four hundred highly trained special operators available across these three units, more than enough to hold Ghazni if they were properly employed. But instead of going after the Taliban they were stuck in static outposts across the city, chasing shadows on ineffective patrols. I quickly gave them new orders.

"I want you to pull out fifty percent of your troops tonight, and the other fifty percent in three days. From now on, I'm in charge. I'm the minister of defense, the minister of interior, the director of intelligence, and the chief of general staff. From now on, you take orders from me."

I could see them thinking, "Who are you?" I was still in my early thirties. They were concerned about the scale of the change and what authority I really had.

Looking deliberately from one to another, I tried to reassure them. "I'm Sami Sadat. I'm the senior military adviser to Asadullah Khalid, and in the next few days Ahmadi will be gone."

They seemed relieved to get new direction. They felt their skills were wasted in being used as conventional police. They were exhausted and did not like the way they were fighting, taking casualties but not moving forward. Taher said, "We want to raid Taliban compounds, but we're just responding to reports of Taliban presence in this street or that street."

That night, when the troops pulled back, Ahmadi called me, terse, angry. "What are you doing?" he demanded.

"I'm giving a rest to our special forces," I replied. "They have not been resting for the last several weeks and I'm putting them on fifty percent manning."

"You can't do that," he said. "It's my job."

"Well, it seems that you were not successful. That's why I'm here. We have two ways to do this: (a) we work together; (b) we oppose each other. I will accept you as a commanding general, the senior commanding general, but not in command of special forces. I will use the Afghan special forces, you command the rest of what is available—the governor, chief of police, conventional forces, the civilian government, and all that, which I'm not interested in. I will work with special forces to make a real difference."

I gave him little choice, so he agreed reluctantly. "But what about tonight?" he said. "The city is falling apart."

"General Ahmadi, please go to sleep, the city is not falling apart; we're here now." That night there was some fighting, with thirty-eight separate incidents, but in the morning we still held Ghazni.

I had successfully liberated our best forces for a more flexible and mobile campaign.

The next key task was intelligence. I had learnt the value of this in my time in the NDS. We needed to know everything about the enemy: where they lived, who backed them, how they moved, thought, prayed.

I was introduced to some of our informants, and one of them— let's call him Nabi— was literally a walking encyclopedia of Ghazni terrorists. We had two MD-530 attack helicopters, brilliantly flexible little aircraft whose military use went back to Vietnam. Nabi quickly learnt how to work the electronic map and provide accurate grids, then we sent the MD-530s to go after targets he provided. I had my own sources too, back from the days I was hunting al-Qaeda for the CIA, who we had often tracked back to Ghazni. I met some of those sources and introduced them to my NDS case officers to start collecting information. In just three days we developed dozens of real-time targets. Nabi was giving us information about the Taliban senior leadership moving around Ghazni, while my other sources were providing us with their network of relationships, radio frequencies, phone numbers, and everything else.

We set up two teams to listen to enemy radio chatter, delivering another stream of intelligence. That turned the course of the campaign in Ghazni. We now went on the offensive, killing hundreds of Taliban fighters. Nabi was in the room with the targeting team, and he would say, "There's a mosque on the left. There's this house. There are trees here. This is how the street looked," so the pilots had a block-by-block visual understanding of their targets before even getting on to the aircraft. It became really effective and had a devastating impact on the Taliban.

A week later Khalid called me. "Sami, I'm flying back from Bagram Air Base, and I want you to talk to their targeting commander." I texted this US colonel, and he replied, "Yeah, I've heard about you. I want you to work with our targeting team in Bagram. We have aircraft; we can support your operation." He put me in touch with Sergeant James Erickson at Bagram airbase, so we could coordinate American as well as Afghan air strikes. We would get multiple targets and I would pass some on to Bagram, who would allot tasks to drones, F-16s, and A-10s, while areas near the city were hit by our MD-530 attack helicopters.

The pace was relentless. Some nights we were conducting up to four special operations, releasing prisoners, killing or capturing senior Taliban leaders. During the three weeks of the campaign, we killed three shadow governors in Ghazni province, one after another, as they were appointed—after that nobody wanted to become the shadow governor of Ghazni.

Once we had rocked them backwards with special forces night raids, we went after them with bigger ground operations. This opened Highway One for military supplies and government vehicles to go between Kabul and Kandahar without any problems in the Ghazni area for the first time in years.

The Taliban had developed hideouts underground in tunnels developed from ancient water networks, in some places half a mile long. We destroyed one tunnel by dumping captured ammunition into it and then pouring petrol into both ends before blowing it up, killing many Taliban who were inside. It was improvised, but it worked. The Americans and Afghan commandos had tried to drop bombs on tunnels before with no success. I just tried it with what I had: ammunition, petrol, and detonation cord with a charger. Now the Taliban knew they were not safe anywhere. And we were getting ahead of them. They had laid hundreds of roadside bombs, especially along Highway One. Instead of just clearing them, which would have taken months, we pursued the teams who had laid them to tell us where they were.

Prior to our arrival, the Taliban were moving in groups of ten, twenty, sixty people, assaulting highway checkpoints with hundreds of fighters. After three weeks they had gone from Ghazni. Our intelligence showed they were traveling only in ones and twos, sometimes disguising themselves among women so it became extremely difficult to hit them. As well as destroying Taliban confidence by killing hundreds of them, including senior leaders, in this key central location, we restored morale in Afghan forces. They had been tired and demoralized and had lost trust in their leaders, taking casualties and not making progress against the enemy. But being properly used as special forces had changed that. Not only that, I often went on operations with the first assault team, and that built confidence that we were *all* special forces, bonded by combat.

Most fighting was at night when we had the advantage. And when they woke in the afternoon, the sergeants and captains would come to my office. Outside the targeting room we had a sitting area where they could have tea, coffee, laugh and joke, smoke a cigar and shisha. It was the first time they had sat with a senior Afghan commander who was letting them smoke, joking with them, and then putting on the same kit as them at night and driving in the first vehicle towards the enemy.

It changed everything they were doing, and now every night more sergeants would show up to try to join the raids. The way it worked is one team would go on assault one night, and the second team would be the quick reaction force, ready to respond if we needed reinforcements. They swapped roles the next night. Now I had volunteers who wanted to go every night. And if they did not go, they wanted to come into the targeting cell to watch how the team was doing.

We constantly needed fresh targets, and the key to our success in Ghazni was intelligence. The glue bonding that intelligence, the air force, the Americans, and our own Afghan commandos was this targeting cell, where intelligence was analyzed and shared with special forces planners and air force controllers in the same room. For the first time, Afghan officers developed their own plans and had confidence to operate on their own. At the same time I tapped my other sources across the country in Kandahar, Helmand, Paktika, and anywhere I had good intelligence.

About two weeks into the mission a team of some fifteen American special operators showed up in giant armored vehicles, all tooled up. One jumped down and said, "We are here to see Colonel Sadat." They had been in the Afghan base outside Ghazni city, and General Miller had told them to meet with me to support whatever I needed on the ground.

I was sitting outside with some of my commando friends smoking a hookah. "Please sit down. I am Sami Sadat." They looked very nervous because this did not look like any operating environment they had been in. They said, "We are here to see how we can work together." Putting down the hookah, I said, "Well, let me show you the targeting room." The room had been the office of the US colonel who ran the Provincial Reconstruction Team for Ghazni, and the bald eagle on top of the flag stand was still in the corner.

I took them round and introduced them to some of the guys. The captain pulled out a notebook and a pen and started to ask me what I needed. And I actually did not need anything.

He asked, "How many forces did you bring from Kabul?"

I gestured round the room. "We are eight guys altogether."

"Did you bring any special forces or commandos?" He wanted to have something to put in his notebook.

"No, we have enough special forces and commandos here."

And he laughed and said, "Yeah, we realized. We can't do operations anymore because we lost all our partners. You're using them all the time." Still with his notebook open he asked me what we needed.

He asked about logistic support, ammunition, fuel. But I said again that we did not need anything. Then I said, "Well, I actually do need something, and I don't know if you have it or not."

"And what's that?"

"I need coffee. Do you have coffee? Because we're running out of coffee."

They looked at each other. "Sir, do you mean like coffee-coffee or drinking coffee?"

"Coffee for a machine. I finished all mine, so the guys don't have any coffee."

The captain closed his notebook with a smile. "Yeah, sure," he said. "If you send someone to our camp, we'll give you some coffee." They also brought information that they had developed, analysis on how they saw the Ghazni situation evolving in favor of the government, and stuff like that. Compared to our information it was not as detailed, not as specific. It was put on nice paper with a map and drawings, so it was cool to have, but we had much deeper knowledge and information about the Taliban in Ghazni province. That's how we could cut so deep into the enemy's throat. They did send over a ten-pound bag of coffee, but it was standard army stuff from the canteen, tasting like goat's piss, not the fresh-ground Arabica I liked.

At the end of our mission, General Miller and Asadullah Khalid came to the city of Ghazni and met with the governor, local elders, and security chiefs. Everyone was happy. The city was safe. Highway One, the main route between Kabul and the south, was safe. The Taliban were defeated by an onslaught they had not faced before. Miller came down and told me that during the operation they had a screen in the control center in Bagram with a label stuck to the bottom which read simply *Sami* with our live feed, including WhatsApp messages, requests, and the videos we sent after operations, for battle damage assessment: BDA.

"You send us pictures more quickly than anyone," said Miller. "Walk me through the method of your operation."

So I explained how we put together the air force and special assault forces and who we had killed.

"Sami, I'm not interested in who you killed. I'm interested in how you managed intelligence, the air force, the special forces, Americans, all together."

"I have a team."

"Who's on your team?"

And I told him how we put all the people we needed into the same room: air force, intelligence, police, planners, and mapping. "A source reports a potential target to their case officer, who reports it to me. I give it to JTAC [the Joint Terminal Attack Controller], and JTAC calls in the air strike."

"How long does it take?"

"It can be as little as five minutes, never more than thirty."

"This is the first time troops are using intelligence from an open commercial site like WhatsApp," Miller said.

"Yes, sir. It's difficult to bring Americans and Afghans into the same physical room, but easy to put them in the same chatroom. It's as if everyone is together."

"So, explain to me your team composition."

"We have JTACs, intelligence case officers, commando liaison, police liaison, and a media guy for information operation. And then we have sources connected to them, and that's how it works." It sounded so simple to me—it was just about coordination of assets so we could strike quickly as soon as we had identified a target. But it seemed it had not been done before.

"Can you put that on paper?"

"Sure, I can put it on paper. The key is coordinating intelligence in real time so that it can be relevant and acted on quickly. That means having all of the key elements in the same room. The missing element is the presence of an American with the team. But I have an idea on that. If we can create this team virtually on the internet and then connect the Americans as we connected to Bagram, I think that will solve the problem. We don't need an American sitting with us all day long; we just need to be connected to an American center so we can coordinate our efforts all together."

I wrote this concept on how we operated in Ghazni: what worked, what did not work. And that became the blueprint for a new combined situational awareness room, CSAR, cochaired by an Afghan general and an American general, with American and Afghan operators sitting side by side—air forces and special forces with shared access to intelligence feeds.

Before we set up the CSAR, it could take up to four hours to call in an American airstrike. We brought this down to twenty minutes by giving authority to young Afghan controllers in the room. Previously there had been three layers of approval, sometimes going up to the Pentagon. But now planes could be retasked quickly.

The effect was immediate. The Taliban had eighteen commando Red Units. With our improved air strike capacity we destroyed more than half of them in 2019. If the Taliban attacked a district, we could quickly divert an American F-16, and that changed the direction of the war. Ninety-four Taliban Red Unit members were killed in one operation and one hundred sixty in another, including a shadow governor. It was the first time for many years that they had been pushed back like this.

We still needed ways of making the attacks more precise. We would get calls saying, "Hey, I need an aircraft; we're under attack in Alishing district of Laghman." We would say, "Do you have coordinates, do you know where your forces are?" And there would be silence, because most conventional Afghan units did not have the ability to report their positions accurately enough to call in a strike. To plug this gap we set up mobile targeting teams to improve that capacity, replicating what I had done in Ghazni, with all of the relevant skills in the room as a package that could move around the country.

By the fall of 2019, every zone had a regional targeting team, which would also feed back intelligence, supporting ground operations and not just responding to emergencies. It was like a "mini-CSAR" in the field, a concept of operations that was one of the most successful applied to the Afghan battlefield. We could now fly complex operations with four or five levels of planes in the sky. US drones sat at the top with F-16s underneath them, then the Afghan ScanEagle drones, and closest to the ground were our planes and helicopters. Coordination was a complex task, deconflicting flight plans so there were no accidents. The technical skills to do this were rapidly spreading among our young officers in the Afghan air force.

Inevitably we faced pushback. Some Americans were worried about the potential security breaches using WhatsApp, but they realized they were being left out of a fast-moving campaign, and Miller signed a waiver to allow its use. We could conduct up to thirty or forty strikes, ground operations, raids, clearances, or arrests in the same time in the same battle space in a province like Ghazni. When Miller had his daily summary in the evening, everyone would report, and some of the officers who were not on WhatsApp realized what they were missing.

The minister called me in to ask, "What's this concept that General Miller has asked you to write?" And I explained about coordinating intelligence and making better and more effective use of resources. And he said, "You know, the Americans like a lot of writing, and you can make them happy with it. But I want more action instead of writing." And we laughed and he sent me to Faryab in the northwest where the Taliban were massing troops to attack the provincial capital, Maimana. They were supported by extremist fighters in the Islamic Movement of Uzbekistan.

Battle of Maimana

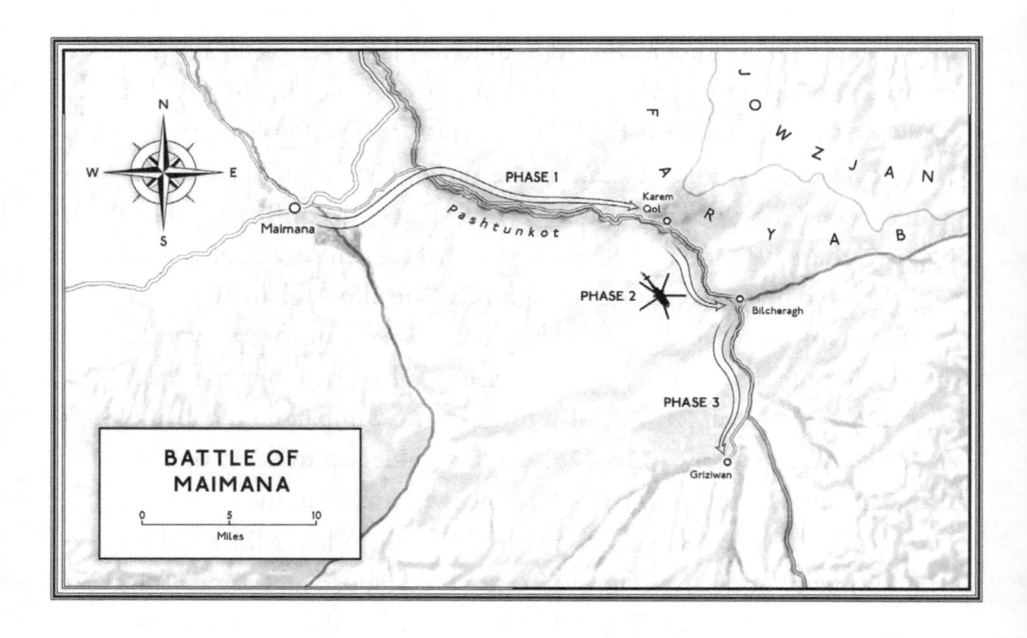

BATTLE OF MAIMANA

I went to Maimana with a team including two senior generals. It was odd to travel with them, and I asked Khalid if it would make it harder for me to command the operation. "How can I be in charge with these guys there?" But the way he explained it they were little more than ethnic window-dressing—providing the public face of a diverse leadership while I fought the war. There were tensions in Faryab between three different ethnic groups, and he did not want the Taliban to be able to say that the army was biased.

When I arrived I walked to the American side of the base at the airport. They complained that the Afghan brigade commander was drunk and incompetent; they had been threatened by his bodyguards and not been allowed to work with him for three months. The region was at the western end of a large area commanded from Mazar, the main city in the north, where the corps commander was General Ahmadzai, one of the worst officers in the army, who then moved onto Helmand leaving another trail of incompetence. He never met me during the whole operation.

I had a separate briefing with US special forces and there was a young man, suntanned with a long beard, who their commander introduced as "my guy."

I broke into the introductions to ask him if he was Afghan, and he nodded.

"Well, then you are *my* guy." I gestured to him to move round before we sat down. "Get your ass to this side of the table."

He grinned and stood his ground. "But this is my team."

"Not anymore. These guys are not going on combat operations. I need you over here." He was commanding one of the four special operations units in the region—highly trained global tier-one-level special forces sitting idle. It was a clear demonstration of a system designed to fail. If Afghan commanders did not have the capacity to deploy their forces against the Taliban, American mentoring had no value. Since the Americans could not themselves engage in combat operations, if there was no Afghan lead, then the Afghan special forces teams were just sitting in the base, effectively doing meet and greet every day. It was time to tell the Americans that we were going to take their partner force into the battlefield. The American captain objected.

"We came together from Shindand in Herat. We want to work together."

And I said, "Excellent. I'll give you target packages, and I want you both to conduct operations in the next few nights."

"Sir, I don't want to make this difficult. I didn't mean these are our forces. We need to be a partner."

"Brother, the Taliban are about to break into this fucking base, and you're not doing anything. You're keeping some of the best forces we have in your base, referring to them as 'your guys.' What do you think is the solution? If you're not going out of the base to conduct operations, I'm going to take away Afghan forces and use them for the operation to save the province."

And the American officer said, "There are things we could do. We could provide air support, and when my guys, the Afghan guys go on an operation, we can coordinate air support and provide air cover, close air support, because we have Apache attack helicopters." This had all been available, but the drunken brigade commander did not have the ability or sense to use it.

"Here's the deal," I said. "We will develop the intelligence package," and pointing to their Afghan special forces commander, "he will shoot it to you. You're a partner, so you guys can still work together. You will get the air support schedule. Then from our side, I will prepare the assault forces for conducting the operation. I will give you one guy to sit beside you in your mission control room, so you know what's going on on the ground, and then you can speak to the pilots and the guys on the ground, the forward controllers to actually conduct strikes."

"Yessir, that's exactly what we will do."

So we had a solution. The partnership spirit was very real, strong, and bound by respect and love for each other. Both sides wanted to get into the action and do operations and become an effective team.

After months of wasted inaction, we had an opportunity if we worked creatively. The Americans were still here and could provide air support to Afghan special forces, Afghan commandos, and also local forces like the Afghan police.

The Faryab operation was the first time I would command such a large conventional force. The Taliban had taken three valleys threatening the capital, Maimana, in an area with steeply wooded hillsides. We planned to retake the valleys one at a time, extending ground communications all the time as we moved further up. It was an ambitious plan with a lot of moving parts since we needed to hold ground and not just conduct raids. As well as the police and the army, there were also some locally recruited Afghans in training for a new territorial force. The ministry of defense had never liked the concept, which sounded too much like the creation of a militia, historically prone to being manipulated by warlords. But we fast-tracked their training by the Afghan special forces, who had been sitting doing nothing with their American partners until now.

Commander Shamal, a local leader from Pashtunkot, the first valley in our plan, barreled into our command center ordering people about. He was a giant of a man with a big belly. When he came in there were a number of territorial force guys round the table, and he told them what they could do or not do. I interrupted him. "Why do you think you own Faryab?"

Shamal talked about his status as a commander under the main northern Uzbek powerbroker, General Abdul Rashid Dostum, now vice president. Although facing charges for the kidnap and rape of a rival, Dostum remained a feared figure in Maimana. Shamal was demanding vehicles and ammunition ahead of the Pashtunkot operation. But he did not offer any real support.

"Why should I give you anything if you don't have troops?" I said.

He was unused to being contradicted. He scratched his belly and continued to make demands until I became impatient and threw him out. "I don't care who supports you, and I don't give a shit what you think," I told him. "The Taliban are about to come into this city, and I'm going to defend it. And if you get in my way, I will shoot you first." Everyone in the room—the brigade commander, chief of police, director of intelligence—was silent, as if afraid of him. It was a visible demonstration of the continuing power of old warlords, but I was not cowed. I banned Shamal from any military premises.

Ten days after I arrived, we tried our first move into Pashtunkot valley and faced immediate heavy resistance from the Taliban. It was the heat of summer, and heavy flooding made the going tough. We had expected to take the valley in two days, but six days later we were bogged down. The Afghan air force were finding targets difficult to spot. Strict rules of engagement to avoid civilian casualties meant they could not bomb compounds, and they could not identify targets from the air that we could see on the ground because of the trees. American planes were even more reluctant to drop bombs.

Then we had a break. Our first territorial force recruits finished their training, and their commander brought them straight to the valley. Using local knowledge, they showed the commandos how to move under the disguise of the tree lines. Exactly as the Taliban used the tree lines as disguise, so we would do the same. That night the Afghan commandos and territorial forces moved in the dark and captured some of the high ground the Taliban had been using to keep us pinned down. The commandos had night vision capability, the territorial forces knew the ground, and the minister had now given new orders to allow air strikes on buildings. So we started hitting some of the Taliban headquarters.

The first building we hit belonged to Commander Shamal, the man I'd had thrown off the base for making demands. He had identified it after calling me to apologize. It seemed that he had complained about me to some other politicians and nobody backed him. They knew that, unlike some commanders, I would not listen to appeals not to hit a property if we had good intelligence that it was a target. We took few prisoners. They did not want to get on the wrong side of me. Shamal claimed to have good intelligence, and when he came into our targeting cell he was shocked to see Afghans operating advanced computer programs.

The targets he identified included two of his own houses, which he said were now in the hands of senior Taliban. When I pointed this out, he said, "I don't care. Bomb my houses. I just want to go back to my village. I can rebuild my houses."

We moved up into the next valley with the largest all-Afghan helicopter dismount operation since the war began—320 troops dropped in waves overnight. I was in the lead assault team because I had seen hesitancy when I proposed the plan. Both the commandos and territorial force guys thought it potential suicide. But with the element of surprise we took the second valley quickly and continued the momentum towards our third and final target.

I had been hearing growing concern from our American partners about the risks I was taking. Rumors were circulating around the military that Sami Sadat was putting seven hundred men into danger, bogged down in Pashtunkot. Before we had taken the second valley, I got a call from an American major who said, "I want you to shut down the operation." I shot back, "Excuse me?"

"I want you to shut down the operation," he repeated, "because you'll get these people slaughtered, and if we lose then that will give the Taliban a chance to overrun the city."

"Remember I'm commanding the operation, not you. And I think you need to understand your position. You're an American major talking to an Afghan colonel. And this is my country. I take orders from the MOD, not from you."

"Well, you might get other phone calls."

Just minutes later I got a call from General Miller's deputy for intelligence. She had just arrived in Afghanistan.

She said, "We can't commit our air force all the time if there is no progress."

"Your air force is shit. They are not dropping any bombs. How can I make progress if they're not shooting people under the trees? Look, I'm trying to be polite here, but my chain of command is different. I can't listen to you guys as well."

"You'll get a call from your own chain of command too," she said. "The initial request for shutting down the operation came from them, from General Ahmadi, the commander of the Afghan special operations corps." He was the same commander I had side-stepped in Ghazni, who liked to issue orders from his office and had no contact with troops on the ground.

"That's strange. His deputy is sitting beside me. Why is he telling the Americans? Don't you think he's trying to use you guys?"

"Well, Sami, if you continue to be stubborn like this, we can no longer support you."

"What do you mean? What is the support you are giving me exactly?"

"The air force."

"Well, you know what? Take away your air force, because they're not doing anything for us."

When we cut off the call I was mad, boiling over. I had promised the minister a success to take to a meeting in Brussels, so the stakes were high. Major General Randy George, the director of operations under General Miller, called to ask what was going on. He was a great guy who always wanted to make sure Afghans were supported. And I explained that I had been told we would no longer have any air support.

"Well, Sami, whatever you want—you call me. I do prioritization of US assets. And I will allocate whatever resources you want."

"Thank you, sir, I am OK with what I have for now."

I went on to capture the final district as planned with no US air support. I wanted to show the Americans that Afghans could do these complex operations. If they wanted to be part of our success, they were welcome, but we could operate alone.

Just after we had taken the third valley I got a call that two senior Afghan generals and Major General Chris Donahue were coming to visit. Donahue was a special forces commander who had achieved success in Syria. He would later have a moment of history as the last American soldier to leave Afghanistan at the end of the evacuation effort in 2021. Miller had appointed him as commander of NSOC-Alpha (NATO Special Operation Command-Afghanistan) and CSAR, but we had not yet met.

I had prepared some slides and invited all of my senior team as well as the civilian governor. Before I began Donahue looked at me and said, "How long are you planning to bang on with this failed plan?" He had clearly not heard of our progress in the previous two days. I looked back at him evenly and said, "As long as it needs." And I went on through the slides—showing the move up Pashtunkot, the helicopter drop into the next valley, how we'd successfully stormed the third valley.

Donahue just looked at the American commander in the north. "How do I not know all this?" All of the anger he had been directing at me now shifted towards his own staff.

"Sir, there've been some recent developments," one aide stammered.

In the middle of all these Afghans and Americans, Donahue said, "You're feeding me shit. I've never seen anything like this." And Donahue looked at Sergeant Craig, who Miller had sent to stay alongside me, and said, "You'll email me directly every day with progress of the campaign, Sergeant." Craig said, "Yessir."

I was told that before boarding the plane that morning, Donahue had asked, "Who the fuck is this Sami guy? We should go to Faryab, get him back in the airport, handcuff him, and drop him in Kabul. I heard he has no military experience, he's incompetent, and has no mercy on his own Afghan forces. He's just a colonel who's leading these hundreds and hundreds of men to their deaths. We have to stop him."

At the end of the meeting, Donahue asked to speak with me alone.

I replied evenly, "General, I have nothing to say to you alone. If you want to meet, I want my team present."

"Let's go to the US base, then."

"No, I'm not going to the US base. This was an Afghan operation, and we'll discuss it on an Afghan base."

He could see my mood was tense and said, "Wherever is comfortable for you." And we walked into the brigade commander's office, with him and four other Afghan generals present.

Donahue said, "Sami, I was misinformed about this operation by both Afghans and the Americans." He confirmed my guess that it was General Ahmadi who had tried to blacken my name. "Ahmadi told me that you were losing dozens of commandos for an operation heading for failure. And my team also informed me that the leadership of the operation was very weak, and the forces didn't listen to you. For that I apologize. This is a huge success, and congratulations." And then we moved on to talk about operations in the neighboring province of Badghis. He was offering to divide air support, giving us some backup.

"Sir, you can keep all your assets for Badghis," I told him. I was confident that with the right coordination Afghan air power was now enough. And I guess I was making a point that we had succeeded in the complex moves up the valley at Maimana without them. "We are happy with what we have, and I don't think we need US air support here anymore."

I liked Donahue's directness and obvious ability. At one point General Ahmadi was doing other work and clearly not engaged. Donahue called to him, "Hey, are you listening?" It was just the tone we needed to change things and only his second week in the job.

BABY KILLERS

In September we were shocked by a huge truck bomb at a maternity hospital in Zabul province, killing many women and children. Later that night we were tracking the mastermind of the attack as he headed into neighboring Ghazni province. I had two ground operations going on there, already stretching our resources to the limit. I called the company commander of the commandos on the ground, Lieutenant Kabir Noorzai. "How many guys do you have with you?" I asked.

"Only a handful, and they are sleeping the sleep of the dead as they were on an operation last night," he said. I told him to wake them and rouse some of the Afghan special police at the same time. And he called me back with eleven of his men and ten police available.

"What's our mission?" he said. I told him we had eyes on the mastermind of the maternity hospital bomb.

"You have air support, but there is no time to check for explosives on the road at the target." The suspect was sleeping in what we called a *serai*, which was like a motel. They surrounded it and grabbed thirteen people.

Kabir quickly identified the bomber, who was neatly dressed and had a trimmed beard, unusually for a Taliban fighter. His phone had the number the Americans had given us. Back at headquarters we needed to interrogate everyone from the serai to see if they were connected. While I was interrogating them I had a call from the Bagram air controller.

"Sir, I think your guys are killing the suspects outside your office." They were watching pictures from a drone which showed the special forces troops beating them up. My troops were mad at these baby-killers and wanted to take the law into their own hands. I ordered them to back off several feet. But emotions overcame them again. Before the situation spiraled out of control I put the prisoners onto helicopters and took them to Kabul for their own protection.

We continued to have successes, and later that month General Miller went to see the president to appeal for him to clear out the incompetent officers from the MOD and replace them with a new generation. And the president said, "Do you have anyone in mind?" When Miller pulled out a list with my name on top of it Ghani lost his temper, his voice rising as he shouted that if I was in the army he would resign as president. Miller did not know what he had said. Minister Khalid called me in to warn me that the president had still not forgiven me. I was deeply upset. Even as I'd dedicated my life towards being a professional officer and a patriot, my efforts were still not fully recognized.

The minister sent me to Zabul to try to improve security along Highway One. I was on the verge of resignation instead of going. But I also knew that the momentum we had built would be lost if I left. I was building relationships in several provinces, and that work was not yet done. I decided that even if the president hated me, I would continue to fight for my country.

Before going to Zabul, Khalid wanted me to fly down to Kandahar with senior US officers to improve coordination. When we arrived I stood on the margins of a meeting for a while, before asking my friend Major General Taylor, the deputy commander of the training and mentoring team, for a flight to Zabul. Brigadier General Brown turned and asked, "Who are you?"

Both he and the Afghan corps commander, General Murad, had thought I was a translator because I was on my own and carrying my bag.

Murad said, "So you're Sami Sadat. But you're so young."

I shrugged. "I'm old enough."

I went to the flight line, where I could see around twenty Afghan Black Hawks. I was told they only flew if Brown had signed them out. The Afghan controller said I could not fly that night because flight orders were written in the morning. "What if there's an emergency?" I asked.

"Then we can ask for another flight, but permission usually takes a couple of hours."

I went back to Brown. "I need to fly tonight," I said, "because Zabul is falling apart." He said the pilots had already gone and he would not call them back.

"Who are you to give them permission?" I asked him. "You gave these Black Hawks to Afghanistan. They are under the MOD. They are my Black Hawks." He was genuinely surprised; it was the first time anyone had said that. He had not caught up with the fact that America was no longer leading operations in Afghanistan. It was just like the conversation about the Afghan commander, "my guy," in Faryab. He was acting as if he could overrule the Afghan corps commander.

I insisted and was given helicopters to take me and about fifteen other people who were waiting to go the next day. All this bureaucracy was so incompetent. The Taliban were at the gates of Kandahar, and Brown was effectively handing them victory with rules and regulations to prevent flexible use of assets.

When we landed, the local brigade commander came out to the helicopter landing zone. As we walked together to the targeting cell, he said to my aide, Humayun, "Well, it seems Mister Adviser did not come tonight." Humayan smiled and pointed to me, saying, "This is him." He did a double take, and said, "I'm sorry. As you were carrying your own bag and an M-4 rifle, I thought you were just a soldier."

In the makeshift targeting room where my team had set up, they gave me a briefing. Things were not good. After our successful operation in neighboring Ghazni, the Taliban had moved to Zabul and were preventing our convoys from moving up and down Highway One, at the same time securing their route from Pakistan to the mountains of Uruzgan in the west. The Afghan army locally was about 70 percent undermanned. Their commander, whose eyes were dead and had no fight left in him, complained that nobody wanted to come to Zabul.

An hour later the local governor, Yarmal, arrived in civilian clothes, no older than me. "Mister Adviser, did you bring special forces with you?" he asked.

"No, how bad are things?"

"The Taliban are everywhere in the district," he explained. "But there is one pro-government village called Chino that has still not fallen."

Two hundred local police were surrounded by the Taliban. We sent a message to them to hold out until the morning when we would relieve them. There was no way we could go by road because of the intensity of the Taliban presence.

By midnight we had a plan. We had no helicopters of our own in Zabul, but I ordered two Black Hawks and two MD-530 attack helicopters to arrive by 7:00 a.m. It might not have happened so easily if I had not insisted that these were *our* helicopters to use for *our* operations. The Kandahar air wing had gotten the message.

It was a cold night and Governor Yarmal warmed himself at a makeshift fire outside. "I've been trying so hard, but things are still falling apart," he said. He cared more than the army commander did and really wanted us to save the stranded police chief and his men. I took his hand and told him it would be all right. I asked him if he knew Chino, and when he said he did, I said, "Great—we have our guide."

The next morning the governor was brave enough to join us as we flew in with no backup, not knowing where we would land. After circling the village we landed in the middle of the largest compound. There was dust flying everywhere and a loose horse panicking. I was worried it would get tangled up in the propeller, but it stayed away. As the helicopter dropped us and took off, we saw men running towards us, not in uniform and carrying weapons. We did not know at first if they were police or Taliban. Nobody fired, and we warned them with our hands to stay away as the second helicopter landed.

Once my small force was on the ground, a young man with a beard wearing an army coat covered in dust walked towards us. The governor identified him as Bakht Muhammad, the police chief. I said, "I am Sami Sadat. I sent you the message last night."

He froze and could not talk for what seemed like minutes. Then he said, "Why would you come here?"

"Because I promised I would support you."

"You know, sir, men will fight to their deaths now for you. We have never been supported like this before." He had faced the influx of Taliban displaced from Ghazni by my previous operation, and he could tell us where they were. He could not read a map, but I had my four-man targeting team with me and he could point things out to them. I ordered the Wolfhound radio interceptor to be brought to Chino on the next helicopter flight. The Taliban were not using phones as they cut the network every night when they attacked the mobile towers. But the Wolfhound would give us a precise location for every fighter who used a radio. I flew back to base with the governor by lunchtime, leaving my satellite phone with Bakht Muhammad. And that afternoon our attack helicopters were hitting locations he provided. Two days later we had broken the siege of Chino village and stalled Taliban momentum in Zabul.

I flew back to the corps headquarters at Kandahar for a debrief, and when we arrived American and Romanian soldiers blocked our path and told us to hand over our weapons and be searched, saying it was General Brown's orders. I had already confronted Brown over use of our Black Hawks, and I said, "Fuck off. You can't search me or any of us." The captain went into the office and came out five minutes later to say that Brown knew who we were but was still insisting on the search.

I could see this was not going to end well. With me were the governor and the chiefs of police and intelligence, who were unarmed. I told them to walk in and said to the captain, "If anyone touches these guys, you'll regret it." They walked in without being searched.

Then we argued for a while. This mattered to me because I was a senior Afghan commander entering an Afghan headquarters. On another occasion I might have left my weapon in the vehicle, but I happened to have brought it and an American search implied they did not trust us and thought this was not really our base. I suggested none of us go in armed, that the Americans should leave their weapons outside along with ours, but the captain did not accept that. At one point it became so heated that the Americans and Romanians took up firing positions, and so did my bodyguards.

An Afghan general came out and he said, "It's OK. You can give your weapons to me and not the Americans."

And I swore at him and threatened to shoot him too. "This is an Afghan army HQ, not American army. You are asking me to hand over my weapons in my own base."

And then Brown arrived, red in the face and shouting, "What do you think you are doing?" He was the kind of American officer who saw "partnering" as making decisions for Afghans, not working with us. There had been too many of his sort over the years.

"What are you doing, General Brown," I replied calmly.

"What is the deal?" he said.

"I will give you five minutes to get out the way, and then I am walking in."

"Is this how you want to play it?"

"This is exactly how I want to play it," I told him. "I don't need you in the meeting. In fact, the meeting is now only between Afghans."

Brown knew he was beaten. "I need to be in the meeting," he said weakly.

I walked in with all my combat gear on, carrying my M-4 rifle. I hated myself for being so rude, but we needed to make the point. This was our war. America was a supporting partner. We made a plan for the operation, dividing tasks between us, and called it Operation Raziq after my close friend, the Kandahar police chief, shot in 2018.

These were not just symbolic arguments. Brown's attitude was about more than body searches or signing off helicopters. It had impact on our capacity to fight. He had a command-and-control node with feeds from US units, and when he refused to share the information with our new regional targeting team, I used my direct access to US special forces and the air force, the only American assets I needed, and cut him out. I discovered that both the special forces team leader in the south and Donahue himself did not like Brown, who had a separate command center, not for the use of special operators. It was unbelievable that some four hundred Americans had two command centers in the same camp. From that moment I did not take Brown's calls. Symbols mattered.

OPERATION RAZIQ

Operation Raziq, the major assault to retake Zabul province, started with a morale-boosting military parade, with dozens of armored vehicles and the whole of 4th Brigade of 205 Corps standing for inspection. Smoke from flares in red, green, and black, the colors of our national flag, billowed between the troops. Helicopters flew overhead, and we sang the national anthem before I made a rallying speech, ending with the roars of the troops in the Afghan battle cry—"Jouand, Jouand, Jouand," (Life, Life, Life). The operation was a textbook military success, and we significantly weakened the Taliban in this strategically placed province on the southeastern frontier.

During the Zabul operation I did one thing that I knew would make President Ghani happy by bringing security to an area where an eighteenth-century monarch, Mirwaiz Hotak, had lived. Knowing of Ghani's appreciation of Afghan history, I brought together elders from the district with the governor to lay plans for the rebuilding of Hotak's house.

Soon afterwards, when we were wanting to press home our advantage in Zabul and push west to Kandahar, I had unwelcome news that America wanted to hand over one of their most prized prisoners, Anas Haqqani, the brother of the leader of the Haqqani network, the Pakistani-sponsored terrorist group allied to the Taliban. With his uncle and another militant, he was to be released and flown to Doha, while at the same time two Kabul university professors, one American and one Australian, were being released from a Haqqani jail in Pakistan. This directly impacted my operations because with no notice, I was ordered to halt operations in three frontier districts in Zabul for a corridor so the professors could be brought safely into the country and handed over. I did not like it one bit. I was not involved in any of the preparations although it was my war zone. I sent over a drone to keep watch, but I was told to shift it because it was interfering with American drones. I had spies on the ground who saw three vehicles come in from Pakistan, and Mullah Yaqoob, the son of the founder of the Taliban, and himself now a senior leader, was in one of them.

During the three-day window that we had been told to allow for the handover, one of our convoys that had come down from Ghazni was fired on in the area where there was supposed to be a ceasefire. When the attacks continued I ordered our forces to return fire and killed a number of Taliban fighters. I was sending a clear signal both to the Taliban and our American partners that we would not be pushed around. There may have been a Taliban/US deal, but if we were attacked we were going to respond with force.

The video of the rally of troops before Operation Raziq went viral, and I was immediately called by Asadullah Khalid as I was supposed to keep out of the media because the president still hated me.

Khalid could see that this situation was unsustainable, and soon after the operation he visited the president in his house on a Friday before prayers, appealing to him to forgive me and appoint me as a brigadier general.

Until then, throughout this year of commanding Afghan troops I had no formal role; I was still just a reserve colonel from the NDS with no contract. Questions were being asked everywhere I went, my unofficial status a constant reminder that I did not have the support of the president. This undermined my authority as people asked, "Who is this guy? He is not backed by the president." Khalid told me that he was beginning to feel guilty, worried about what he would say if I died, and I did not even have an army rank.

By making a personal appeal in Ghani's house Khalid was directly referencing our Pashtun honor code on hospitality, which bound Ghani to accept the request, and he did so reluctantly. Ghani said, "I know Sami is a patriot. He's brave, he's capable, but sometimes he is a rogue and not polite enough." I saw it as a reconciliation of necessity, but he never really trusted me. We met only once during the three years I served as a senior army officer.

2019 Winter Campaign

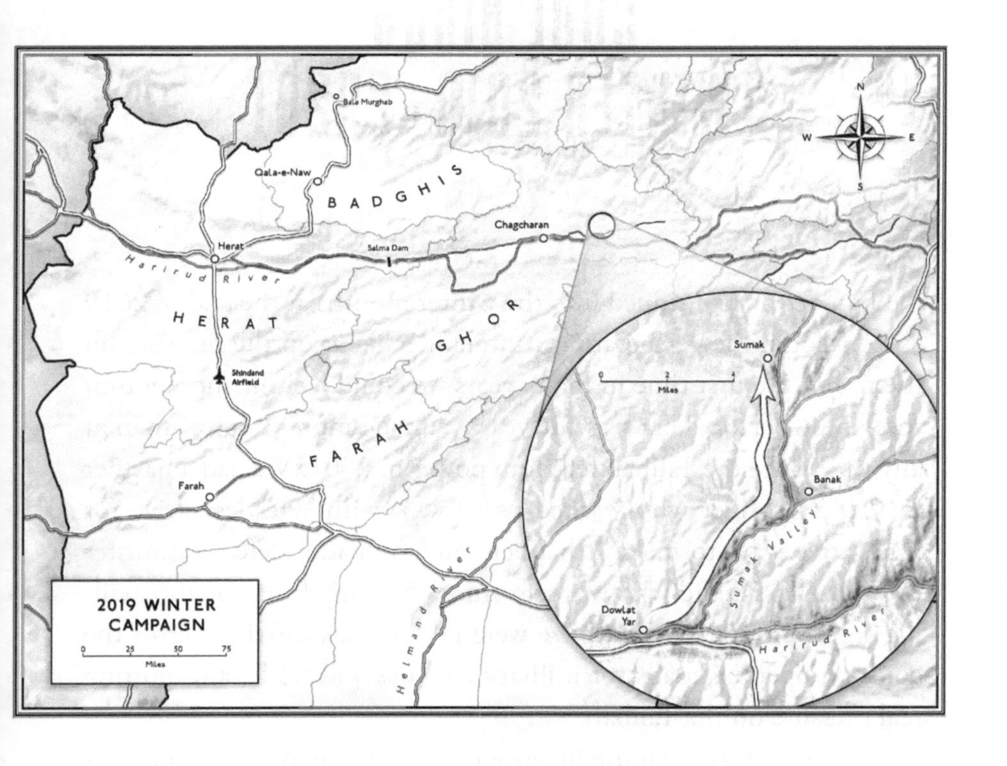

Chapter Eight

COOL BIRDS (WINTER 2019–2020)

Taliban defeats continued into the winter months at the end of 2019 as I and other new generation commanders kept up the pressure on them. For the first time in many years we could feel the momentum shift in our favor. That was the year we made more progress than at any time since the Taliban fell from power in 2001. We had a partner in General Miller who wanted us to win, with a restless drive for innovative ways to make it happen, and we had a defense minister in Asadullah Khalid who was reforming the army from the top, willing to promote new talent. We were taking back districts across the country, opening roads for military convoys and trade, and putting real pressure on the Taliban.

A joint US/Afghan intelligence report estimated that 40 percent of Taliban fighting capability was destroyed that year, with twenty-seven thousand dead. The Taliban had the capacity to replace fighters with their endless production line in Pakistani *madrassas*, the religious schools that had so harmed the minds of our young. But we were killing their best, battle-hardened commanders, with experience that was not easy to replace.

As their backers in Pakistan continued to send reinforcements, they were hard to destroy completely. There was a danger of Taliban whack-a-mole: we hit them in one place and that just moved the problem elsewhere. When I was sent to stabilize the west of the country towards the end of the year, I wanted to change the narrative. I now commanded operations across four provinces in one of the most dangerous locations in Afghanistan in the middle of winter, and I needed a plan for a coordinated campaign to hit the Taliban and leave them nowhere to run.

When I arrived I traveled from north to south of the region to make an assessment. The corps commander, Major General Junbish, who went with me, was one of those remarkable survivors of Afghanistan's wars, a man for all seasons. He first trained as a tank officer during the communist era in the 1980s, then crossed over to the mujahidin, and when the Taliban took over in the late 1990s he became the head of their maintenance workshops. Since 2001 he had moved up the army of the Afghan republic to this command position in the west. The region he commanded was similarly hard to define as being for one side or the other. Alliances here were fluid: groups allied with the Taliban one week were opposed to them the next. I hated that. I would rather have a clear enemy than a reluctant ally. I always had respect for my sworn enemy who at least had the courage to stand up to me: I know their position and they know mine. We needed to change the narrative to make it clear to people here which side they should be on.

First we went to the northwest of the region to the troubled district of Bala Murghab, a patchwork of villages hard against the Turkmenistan border with many different tribal backgrounds. For centuries it had been a notorious haven for criminals, who hid in its beautiful rolling green hills and sparkling river valleys. We had a military base there but all the countryside around was under the control of the Taliban, and they used it as a hideout to hit the ring road, preventing trade between the north and the west of Afghanistan.

Further to the east lay the poor mountainous province of Ghor, under severe threat from the Taliban and with no resources to fight back. The day I arrived in the provincial capital to assess the situation there was a crowd outside protesting the security situation. We met a skeptical group of elders who had heard it all before. As so often in remote places, their question to us was, "Will you stay?" They knew that if the Taliban were pushed out and they were seen to have sided with government forces, they would face retribution on the Taliban's inevitable return, because the government had never been strong enough to hold ground.

One old man was blunt in his criticisms when I promised I could improve security and keep the Taliban out.

"I have heard lies and lies and lies. People like you come here all the time making promises and then you disappear."

"I have never been here before," I protested, shocked by his vehemence. He said that the protests would get worse with plans to surround our headquarters the next day.

"Will you do one thing for me?" I asked.

"What's that?"

"Ask your people to stop protesting for one week. Give me one week and I'll secure Ghor."

He was unsure, but I went close to him, took his hand, and said, "I'm not a liar. I know you have heard promises before. This time it will be different. Give me one week."

And he agreed that the protests would stop while we carried out our offensive. My first target was the Sumak valley, which the Taliban used to move between their stronghold in Bala Murghab to Ghor. It was already winter and even when not snowing, the temperature had dropped to minus twenty. The Taliban would expect us to pause the fighting at this time of year because of the weather. That made it even more tempting to launch an offensive. In our first meeting, the local commanders were hard to convince.

"Ghor is one of the coldest places in Afghanistan, the roads are bad, and this is the coldest time of year."

"I am here to conduct operations," I said. "I have not been sent to take a defensive stance. Tell me what you need, and I'll make sure you get it. The snow is as bad for the Taliban as it is for us, and we have the advantage of air power."

I wanted to give them the confidence that they could win, which was often lacking in our conventional forces, and I needed to put some fire into them. "You are not coming back to headquarters until you have taken the valley," I said. "So unless you want to spend the winter in the snow, let's get going."

While that operation was being planned I dealt with a chronic problem of supplies across the region. It was as if Afghan conventional forces were already abandoned two years before the eventual American withdrawal. The Afghan police in the west had received no supplies for three years, and the army and NDS for more than a year. I began an airlift of supplies from Kabul to the region, including winter clothing and boots as well as ammunition. I discovered that a convoy of more than a hundred military vehicles destined for the corps in the west had been stuck since the summer on the road through Ghor, unable to go forward because of the Taliban, and unable to return to Kabul because of the snow. If we could clear a road for the convoy it would give us major new capability in the west.

When our troops first headed into the Sumak Valley they were met by a deputation of elders with a blunt message they had been given for us by the Taliban.

"Leave now before we kill you all. Many forces have come and been killed by us in the last six years. None returned alive. And that was not in the winter."

The senior Afghan officer on the ground who heard the message, Colonel Mahmoud Andarabi, (no relation of the NDS director Massoud Andarabi) was troubled by it. He called me to ask what to do. I was furious and insisted he put his phone on speaker and hand it to the elder.

"Are you the head of this village?"

"Yes, sir. The Taliban message was clear. There are hundreds of them here, sir. They are well equipped, and they know the area."

"Tell them to come down the valley now," I said. "They must throw their weapons away and we'll let them walk out alive."

The guy just laughed at me like a crazy person, as if he had lost his mind.

"Old man," I said, "this negotiation is over."

I told Andarabi to walk away confidently, not let the elders take pictures, and to tell them the Taliban would be the losers. We would not be beaten.

But the battle started badly for us. I watched feeds from drones in the joint Afghan/US special forces base near Herat as our forces came under attack on the first night in the valley, taking casualties, and we could not provide effective air support because of cloud cover. We made no ground and during the day we saw the Taliban digging into fighting positions on the slopes looking down on the valley. We tried again late the next afternoon. The way was impassable to vehicles and the only walking route, a steep path up the valley, was vulnerable to being raked by Taliban gunfire. Andarabi was still faint-hearted.

"If we go that way we'll be slaughtered," he said.

"Don't worry," I said. "This'll be a big success. Keep going. I'm going to send you air support, a lot of air support." That night our US partners sent three drones, two A-10 Thunderbolt attack planes, and there were also F-16s not far away that we could retask for the Sumak battle, but they faced thick cloud cover. During the night there were some opportunities to use air strikes, but as clouds returned in the morning I had a tough call to make. If our forces were deep inside the valley and the enemy was not defeated, they would be sitting ducks.

Andarabi called me to ask if he should push further, and I guess he knew what my response would be.

"Keep moving in."

Our small assault force remained under Taliban fire during the day, but they did not sustain casualties as they had dismounted from their vehicles and broken up into small groups to find cover behind rocks and isolated houses. The next night our troops tried to push further up the valley. We had some successful airstrikes, but the terrain was very difficult, and the Taliban were effectively shielded from sight by good cover. The drone pilots were reluctant to drop munitions without a clear target.

Andarabi called me around 10:00 p.m.

"You promised us air support, but we are not getting enough. We are facing stronger resistance than expected. The number of Taliban is higher than previously reported."

As the A-10s arrived I was more confident in ordering our forces forward again. Their pilots had a more robust approach than the drone operators, especially since the battle was in open countryside, so the risks of civilian casualties were much reduced. Our troops were fighting for a second night in extreme cold and needed persuasion to go forward, but they had to move forward so the planes could accurately pinpoint Taliban firing at them. "Advance to contact." It was the most elementary infantry maneuver, and the close air support provided by the A-10 was the perfect way to take advantage of it.

Once our troops moved, and they were being shot at, within a short time the A-10s had identified four targets and suggested that they make a simultaneous strike, with two missiles from each. That would give the Taliban no time to recover. On the ground our forces heard a huge explosion, and after two follow-up missiles the remaining Taliban ran away down the valley to a big meeting hall. We had broken their resistance.

For a while we watched from a drone as more and more Taliban arrived by foot and motorbike to the compound around the meeting hall. And once I knew our forces were not far away I ordered an air strike. Dozens of Taliban fighters including the commander of the Sumak operation were killed. Our forces now had full control of the valley, counting more than two hundred Taliban bodies, and reclaiming hundreds of weapons. We bought in local government and police to secure the ground.

The following Thursday I went back to the provincial capital and once again met the local elders. The man who had agreed to stop the protests for a week and doubted my resolve was looking at the ground, not catching my eye. Towards the end of the meeting I turned to him and I said, "Sir, you remember my promise, and are you happy?" He looked up, and I thought I saw the beginning of a tear in his eye.

"I am ashamed of what I said to you, young man," he said. "As you were discussing matters for the last hour, I was thinking what kind of a nice word I could find to cover for my mistake last time. You were right and I was wrong."

"No offense taken," I laughed and took his hand just as I had the week before. "I just wanted to make sure I delivered what I promised."

GENERAL WINTER

The success at Sumak had given our forces confidence that they would be able to fight in the harsh conditions of the winter and that there would be air power when they needed it. Just as the Russians had in 1812, defeating Napoleon with the help of "General Winter," so we turned the conditions to our advantage.

It was always cloudy and cold and miserable, and that meant the Taliban had to find shelter. Andarabi developed a plan under which he would first use armored vehicles to clear improvised explosive devices, and then surround an area or a Taliban checkpoint with soldiers and send commandos house to house, mosque to mosque, hill to hill, to clear the Taliban out. There was not much actual fighting, and we took hundreds of prisoners this way, filling warehouses with military materiel they had taken from us.

We would find four Taliban in one house, five in another, ten in the mosque. Some would run into the mountains, but in deep snow with no cover they could not survive. In a few hours they would come back down with frozen hands and feet and surrender to Afghan forces. Success bred success, and confidence in our tactics grew. Colonel Andarabi was acting as brigade commander, and I told him he would be promoted and his deputy become police chief of Ghor.

Because we had destroyed the Taliban's capacity to control the region from their stronghold in Sumak, we could now clear the road from Ghor to Herat to allow the stranded military convoy to bring in new vehicles, and we mounted an operation to defend the Salma Dam. This was one of the biggest infrastructure projects in the country since 9/11, funded by India, designed to provide hydroelectric power and water for agriculture. The dam was unpopular in neighboring Iran, where the government thought it prevented water crossing the border for their farmers, and it was rumored that they paid the Taliban to destroy it. While Andarabi's forces moved from the north, Major General Abed was supposed to push from the south to meet at the dam, but Abed's forces became stuck in a very exposed position, with heavy cloud cover preventing air strikes on the Taliban.

That's when we made the first use in Afghanistan of a weapon which would give us a significant advantage in winter fighting.

Even on a secure line, the CSAR American deputy commander, Major General Mike Martin, would not tell me the name of the plane. "Sami, I can't tell you the type of the aircraft we are employing, but it can bomb accurately through clouds."

"Let's call them Cool Birds," I suggested. So that's what they became in our calls for the time we had them overhead. They turned out to be F-35s, the most sophisticated warplane in the world, invisible to normal radar, whose pilots wore helmets that could see to the ground, whatever the obstacle. Their synthetic thermos-visual capability gave them something like x-ray vision so they could see through the floor of the plane and thick clouds to find targets. F-35s have a glass touch screen cockpit with sensor screens in the eyes of the pilot who could see the information with his helmet glass and use the touch screen cockpit as well.

We were able to link them directly with our commanders on the ground through the CSAR, so they could get authority to release weapons in real time.

It was raining heavily with thick cloud cover all night. No other planes or drones could accurately drop weapons through that. From his makeshift forward headquarters, Abed walked outside and put the phone up so I could hear the rain.

"General, I believe you. The weather is terrible tonight," I said. "But that's when we can win. Trust me, there will be air strikes. Keep your radio on."

Abed's team had Wolfhounds with them and once they had identified Taliban fighters using radios, we plotted them on a map and could literally watch them move.

"The Cool Birds have visual on the targets," the CSAR controller said. "Can we get confirmation from the general on the ground that we have authorization to strike?"

And then we heard the pilot himself.

"Abed, Abed, this is Panther. Can you confirm the enemy locations?"

And once Abed confirmed the grid references, the voice said, "Are we authorized to strike?"

"Yes, go ahead," said the general. But he was confused. He could hear no planes. He had no idea of the capability of the F-35s. A minute later he called me.

"I was looking down the valley. I heard something like an earthquake, and then a huge boom, and I called the troops on the ground. 'Is everything OK?' They said, 'Yes, sir, we had several bombs dropped around us, and we didn't see any Taliban and we didn't see any aircraft.' Abed then asked the commando Wolfhound operators to check again on the Taliban communications, and they were dead.

"Some kind of airplane came and bombed all the Taliban," he told me. "Up to this point I thought you were just giving me false confidence, and I thought that there was no way that there is such a kind of plane that could fly in the wintertime as well."

And so through confident patrolling village after village through the snow, allied with the most sophisticated technology available on any battlefield, we turned the winter to our advantage. I believe it was America's first use of F-35s in Afghanistan, and they were glad of the opportunity to test their capability in real conditions. F-35s are supposed to replace A-10s for the US military in the coming years.

They are in a different league in technical sophistication, but are not designed to fly low, so do not replicate the accurate, timely, and effective close air support of the older plane. Although slow-moving, A-10s are the best close-air-support aircraft in the world. They have a formidable arsenal of different missiles, guns, and bombs, they are maneuverable, and pilots like to keep in good contact with ground forces. F-35s do not have that ability. But they delivered a punch in Ghor through heavy clouds that we have never had available before. The two airplanes can complement each other, but it is not a like-for-like replacement.

We could not process the many hundreds of prisoners we took, so apart from holding a few commanders they were all released. I would have killed the commanders and held the others for at least two years, but we had no capacity.

CLEAR, HOLD...AND BUILD

While we were moving to contain trouble from Bala Murghab and retake Sumak, reopening both the main east-west route to Kabul and north-south round the ring road, we also kept up pressure on Farah, the desert province to the south of the region, so the Taliban would have nowhere left to hide. I brought in fresh supplies to Farah with flights round the clock and used whatever air power was available to keep the Taliban guessing.

The Cool Birds were still heading from Qatar into the skies over Afghanistan every night, and their controllers called me to see what targets I had available. One night when I did not have anything else to hit I gave them the grids for a network of eleven radio repeater masts that the Taliban used to communicate, and they hit them all. The next day I realized that was not such a smart move because we could no longer listen to the Taliban. We may have disrupted their ability to communicate, but we lost a stream of intelligence.

I also needed to rotate troops who needed a break. That was something that the Afghan army had often failed to do, but I wanted well-motivated fighters, and that meant treating them well and ensuring they had rest when they needed it, as well as new equipment. Major General Chris Donahue called.

"Hi, CD," I said, using the name we called him.

"Hi, Sami. How's it going? Just hold the line while I sort something."

In the background I heard him call the special forces company commander, Major Paul Knudsen, at Camp Arena in Herat, the main international base in the west of the country.

"Hey, Paul. You know Sami Sadat?"

"Yes, sir. I do."

"From now on you are under Sami's command while he is over there in the west leading operations." That was as good a demonstration of someone who understood the role of the US as a supporting force that I had seen.

While I was shaping the space for a full operation in Farah I widened our ability to operate across the region. I employed a KKA unit to take a Taliban prison in a remote part of the badlands of Bala Murghab. The KKA, short for *Kita Khas Afghan*, were our most elite special forces, trained by the Green Berets and Delta Force to be a tier-one unit, on a par with the Delta Force itself. The KKA specialized in precision interdiction of vehicles and night raids, so they were the best unit for this highly sensitive operation where we did not want to kill our soldiers who were being held captive.

We planned the prison operation meticulously, rehearsing it in a mock facility. Colonel Khalid Amiri's KKA force would land in

Mi-17 helicopters with spare capacity, storm the prison and fly out with the prisoners. But the Taliban must have had a tip-off because shortly before the helicopters were due to land we saw the prisoners being loaded onto trucks and moved away. The trucks stopped about five kilometers away and took the prisoners inside a mosque.

Amiri said he needed to bring his men back to make a fresh plan.

"If we mount a night operation," he said, "it's usually seven hours of planning, and we need a surveillance aircraft."

I wanted to push on that night whatever the risks. "The prisoners will be shot if we don't get to them quickly," I said, "and the Americans already have a surveillance aircraft flying."

Reluctantly he agreed to send the troops straight back that night after refueling the helicopters. Shortly before the KKA force arrived, we saw the prisoners being moved to houses in the village round the mosque in groups of around ten, and once again their commander wanted to pull out to reassess. But I pushed him on, and when the force landed it could not have been easier. Some villagers voluntarily came out with their prisoners. Without clear command the small number of Taliban were quickly disarmed and taken prisoner themselves. But there were too many passengers for the helicopters available, so we brought out what we could and went back again for more. We needed to do four flights in all after one of the helicopters malfunctioned. It was daylight before the last flight. I did not tell Amiri that we had lost our air cover an hour earlier.

It was one of the most complex operations we had conducted to date, but if it was not for our young commanders, with US support, we would never have succeeded. I felt proud of serving alongside such a wonderful team of warriors.

I probably broke every military rule and every special operation rule by doing what I did. I had Americans calling me as the dawn was breaking and we were still taking out prisoners, saying, "Sir, I am advising you not to do this. I'll have to report that the Afghan forces conducted flight after flight into a dangerous, deep enemy zone without air support, and it was General Sadat who ordered them."

I responded, "Please let me focus on this." Major Paul Knudsen, who was coordinating American support, was worried he would be blamed too. As the last helicopter successfully lifted out prisoners he called again. "Sir, I got sick, I swear to God I got sick because of the pressure. My stomach was knotted because of the way you conducted the operation. But I will give you this, you're a hell of a leader. If it was for me and Colonel Amiri, we would never have authorized the rescue of these prisoners. So I am very proud of working with you. Next time you are in the US the coffee's on me." While I was in the US in 2023, he messaged me, and I reminded him he owed me a coffee.

We brought out eighty-seven of our soldiers, a morale booster to others to know that we would not leave them behind. And the Taliban's authority in the region was now seriously challenged because Afghan forces showed we could operate at will wherever we wanted to go—and in the toughest winter conditions. We could resupply our units, we reinforced Bala Murghab, we reopened the route to Ghor, and we rescued our prisoners.

Now I needed to focus on Herat in the south of the region, clearing the main highway to link to the ring road, the most commercially important route in the country. We had a convoy of 285 military vehicles carrying supplies waiting in Helmand to come west to Herat. The last military convoy that had tried to make the journey by this route suffered 40 percent casualties. The road was permanently damaged by improvised explosive devices and under constant watch from the Taliban. There was another route through the desert to the west, but it ran close to the Iranian border. It was forbidden to fly warplanes within ten nautical miles of the border, but Major

General Mike Martin came up with a great workaround on the edge of legality.

"Sami, why don't you move the convoy as you planned it down the border. I will have F-16s on standby. They can remain outside the ten-mile exclusion zone but are capable of hitting targets within it. We can't fly drones, but you still have cover." So we took the convoy, 400 vehicles in all including our 285 resupply vehicles, along the safe corridor, with only one casualty when a commando officer was run over by one of our own vehicles.

With the fresh supplies we could keep up momentum through the new year into 2020. I was inspired by the hundreds of Americans and Afghans working in bases all the way to Kabul to provide support. It was an amazing coalition to ensure we achieved our operational objective. This was the winning team.

On January 3, I had a late night watching a raid in Farah and was woken soon after getting to bed by my aide, Humayun, rapping loudly on the door.

"It's the minister, sir. He needs to talk to you immediately." I picked up the phone still nearly asleep.

"Sami, where are you?" Khalid asked urgently.

"In the corps headquarters."

"What's going on in Iraq?"

I thought I must have misheard him. "What? Nothing is going on in Herat."

"No, not Herat. Iraq, Iraq as a country." I said, "I don't know, sir, I'm not responsible for Iraq." He said, "Sami, wake up, check it out, and call me back. This is something very important."

I went on social media and found out soon enough why he was worried. Qasem Soleimani, the head of Iran's most powerful security force, the IRGC, had been killed by an American drone strike near Baghdad airport. I called the minister back.

"Sami, I think this will have strategic consequences for us," he said. "You're the closest Afghan force to the Iranian border. There is a likelihood that the Iranians will have a retribution attack on your 207 Corps. They might attack the headquarters and the NATO forces camp, Camp Arena. I want you to move out for a few days until we figure out what's going on."

"OK, sir. Let me assess the situation and find out, and then we can coordinate."

"Be prepared to leave the corps headquarters if you have to."

I called Colonel Antwan Dunmyer, the American deputy commander of the NATO detachment in the west, a great friend and ally in our campaigns.

"What is the plan if the Iranians attack in western Afghanistan and you're the most senior US officer?" I asked him. "You're the number one target. Do you want to go back to Bagram or Kabul for a few days?"

"I don't know, man. I need to talk to General Miller." And he paused. "I think the Italians also have a deal with the Iranians." We both laughed.

The Italian contingent, the main NATO force in the west, rarely went out on the ground, were rumored to pay the Taliban not to attack them, and all their dealings with Major General Junbish and his staff were by video link. They would not go to his base fearing retribution after an Italian soldier shot an Afghan sergeant in a misunderstanding.

"Maybe the Italians have a value for once," I said. "I don't think the Iranians will attack me because the Italians and Iranians do certainly have some kind of relationship."

Dunmyer said, "They should attack you because you are a general, and sending their puppet army, the Taliban, straight to hell."

"Thanks," I said. "Perhaps you should call them and tell them where I am."

He laughed. We both stayed in our bases for now and watched as recriminations flew over our heads between Washington and Tehran, but there was no escalation by Iran on the ground in Afghanistan.

That winter was the only time in my command years in Afghanistan that I really saw the fruits of military success. The counterinsurgency manuals talked about the need to "clear, hold, and build" so that victory could be permanent. We now held enough ground and had opened trading routes so we could see the effect of what we had done to change lives for the better. Business across the west was booming. I went to bazaars where people were happy to see Afghan forces. The Taliban were pushed to the margins, and even in the badlands of Bala Murghab, our troops were operating with less opposition than at any time for many years.

A few days after the scare over Iran, I had an incomprehensible call that fighter jets were bombing friendly forces in Shindand, a district of Herat province, close to the NATO airbase. I called Mike Martin at the CSAR, and he knew nothing about it. He called back soon after and said, "Sir, I found out that those planes are flown by US Navy SEALS in support of an Afghan unit on the ground."

"Well, get them to stop," I shouted. "They're slaughtering some good people."

"I'll see what I can do," he said.

It took a while, but finally the strikes stopped and we could find out what happened. It was a really tangled tale. Earlier in the day fourteen KKA fighters, including two women, flew into Shindand on the trail of an Afghan weapons dealer suspected of bringing Iranian surface-to-air missiles into the country. In the heightened tension since the death of Qasem Soleimani, there was urgency in tracking down the weapons. The KKA team, posing as civilians, tracked down the weapons dealer, and he ran for safety to a checkpoint that happened to be manned by forces of a pro-government militia group that had broken away from the Taliban. They did not know the KKA team were a government force, as they carried no identifying marks, and in the confusion there were exchanges of fire between the this pro-government militia and the KKA. The breakaway Taliban group, led by Tooryalai Zirkohy, still flew the Taliban flag, and when they called in reinforcements, truck after truck arrived flying the flag. That's when the air assault started.

The worst thing was that the breakaway Taliban leader, Zirkohy, was a friend of the minister of defense.

He called me. "Who told the Americans to start bombing?" he shouted.

"I have no idea."

"I know who told them," Khalid said. "You told them because you don't like anyone who is sympathetic to local tribal leaders outside your command. You had a problem with these guys."

"Sir, I have no idea who ordered this." Sometimes there was no reasoning with him.

"Sami, how is it possible that the American Air Force is bombing a location that's close to you? You're in charge of operations and they wouldn't tell you? Of course they would tell you. This is a strategic mistake and will have consequences for western Afghanistan."

He was right in that last assessment. Zirkohy's group were permanently weakened by the onslaught, and losing that anti-Taliban presence would later have consequences for the region. For now, I had to send vehicles and helicopters to bring back the dead and wounded. Locally at least people did not blame me for the attack.

While Afghan forces regained the initiative in the war and we pushed the Taliban back across the country in 2019 there were political moves happening at the same time that would have a direct impact on the war. A dispute over the result of the presidential election in September dragged on through the winter. The campaign had been fought between the same two candidates as the 2014 election, Ashraf Ghani and Abdullah Abdullah. But there was little enthusiasm for either of them. On the face of it Ghani had a slender lead, but the turnout was so low—less than 20 percent of eligible voters—that the result had little legitimacy, and Abdullah contested it for six months.

President Trump stepped into that power vacuum, ignoring the Afghan political drama to try to get a direct deal with the Taliban. He was a year away from his own re-election bid and wanted to be able to claim he had been the president who ended America's longest war. His negotiator, the Afghan-born diplomat Zalmay Khalilzad, had tried and failed to get a deal in 2018. When he tried again in 2019 the Taliban were more receptive. The release of Anas Haqqani was one of the sweeteners offered by Washington. But we had changed the calculus by winning on the battlefield as well. For the first time in many years we had turned the tide of conflict against them. They were taking a punishment and losing a lot of leaders and were now more willing to consider negotiation.

Unlike conflicts between states with uniformed armies, I knew that the calculus of insurgency warfare was always in favor of the insurgent. Tactical battlefield success for government forces rarely brought victory without a political settlement. Henry Kissinger put it best: "The conventional army loses if it does not win. The guerrilla wins if he does not lose." I wanted to kill as many of them as I could, but we were only shaping the space for negotiations. What we did not know was the severe time pressure that the talks would impose on our capacity to fight the war, just as we were making progress.

I was recalled to Kabul at the end of January 2020 after changing the way we fought in the winter and reopening the west. I knew that the Americans had nominated me to head a new beefed-up Joint Special Operations Coordination Center, JSOCC, which would have all special forces and the CSAR under it. I wanted to harvest the lessons I had learned to take the war to the Taliban across the country.

Chapter Nine

GIVE PEACE A CHANCE (2020)

"Sami, I miss your coffee. Can you make me a coffee?"

I did not expect a victory parade, but I guess I thought there would be more of a welcome than that. The minister of defense, Asadullah Khalid, was sitting with some other people in his office, and there was no greeting when I returned from months out of Kabul, other than a request to make coffee. When his guests left I said, "What was that all about?"

"I did it intentionally, Sami. So you don't get too cocky."

"You might say something like 'how are you?' or 'thank you.'"

"Sami, if you're doing these operations for appreciation, you have the wrong motivation." He demanded a lot. "Make sure you do this for your army and for your country. The right people will always know. We have to be selfless and we have to serve our country."

I guess I knew he was right, although it was like a bucket of cold water. It reminded me of my lessons in the British officer academy—to be selfless, respectable, professional, and serve the country. It resonated.

My phone buzzed, and I went out of the room to take a call from Colonel Alokozai, one of the better commanders in the western region. He had been chasing the Taliban around the Farah desert and came upon a convoy of vehicles full of armed men. He was requesting air support. I called CSAR to get at least a drone to cover them. They said they were already tracking the convoy and they saw twelve vehicles, including some top-of-the-range pickups. They could see men with guns, all in civilian clothes.

"How many missiles do you have in the drone?" I asked the CSAR controller.

"Four, but we have F-16s not far away."

"Reroute them and tell me when they are on target. Let me just get a confirmation on the ground, and then I'll give you a shoot-to-kill order and eliminate all of them."

Colonel Alokozai called back on his satellite phone. He said, "Sir, we have stopped the convoy. We jumped in front of them and we're now moving close to these people. We can see armed men but they are not shooting at this point."

"Can you handle it? It's a lot of people."

"Let me try," he said. "We have tanks as well, so we have better protection and more firepower than them."

"OK. If the firefight becomes too serious, then back off and I'll send in the air strikes."

The line went dead for ten minutes, enough time for the F-16s to be in range.

My phone rang again. "Sir, these guys are Arabs and Afghans." That could only mean al-Qaeda.

"OK, back off. We want a clear field of fire."

"No, sir," he said. "Hold on. It seems this an Arab hunting party. We can see hawks on the backs of the seats."

That was not what I was expecting.

"Take their weapons and report back to me."

It turned out that there were around thirty armed Afghans protecting a small group of Arabs led by Sheikh Ali bin Abdullah al-Thani, the cousin of the emir of Qatar and a former government minister. For ten years he had brought his family to Farah in the winter months. He owned tens of thousands of acres with a remote private desert airstrip and a villa with ornate gardens. And he was a close friend of President Ghani.

"Holy shit." There was no other response. They had come so close to being killed. If Alokozai had not said he could handle it I would have pushed the button and caused a major international incident. I told the American aircraft to back off as the suspects were friendly, and I told Alokozai to hold onto to the group for now until I knew just what was going on.

The next moment my phone exploded with calls from the president's chief of staff, MPs in western Afghanistan, and lots of other powerbrokers to say, "Oh, sir—your forces just arrested my friend."

It took some time to track down the minister of interior, Massoud Andarabi, who had sanctioned the trip but without telling the army. It turned out that Sheikh Ali had more than 150 Afghan police he used as his bodyguards whenever he visited. But he was also very close to the Taliban. On days he went hunting he told the Taliban and they cleared the roads of improvised explosive devices. Alokozai had saved his life and those of his companions. Such was the reality of Afghanistan. While we were fighting for the survival of our nation, men like Sheikh Ali were using it as an adventure playground.

His presence symbolized what Qatar would do to our country, by promoting the Taliban in the 2020 Doha deal and paying hundreds of millions of dollars to empower them after it was signed. The Qataris even paid people in America to lobby for the legitimacy of the deal, casting our nation into the deepest misery of our history.

Khalid could not stop laughing. He kept asking, "Who did you guys arrest?" I told him I was getting all these calls.

"So am I," he said, still laughing. His phone buzzed again, and it was the president's chief of staff. "Tell the president to call me himself if he wants to talk to me," he said. "Never call me again," and he cut off the call. It showed the lack of trust across the Ghani administration. His closest staff lived in an isolated bubble, remote even from the senior players in the government he led. Khalid did not care what they thought of him.

A minute later his phone buzzed again, and it was the president with a personal appeal for the release. The hunting party were his special guests, and we had not paid enough respect.

I called Colonel Alokozai and ordered their release. He had saved their lives. "You know, we are really happy with this," he said. "Now we know there are no improvised explosive devices in the region we can do some hunting of our own, and we are not chasing animals."

JOINT SPECIAL OPERATIONS *COMMAND*

The day after I nearly killed a senior member of the Qatari ruling family, the minister Asadullah Khalid appointed me head of the Joint Special Operations Coordination Center, JSOCC. It was not the job I wanted as then configured. The JSOCC was a clearing house to handle messages, with a staff of around eighty people who liked sitting in an office and had no ambition to join the fight.

Until then JSOCC's only job was to receive target packages from NDS and choose which unit should get the package. All the decisions on how to manage the targeting were made by the units, who would come back to JSOCC if they needed air support. JSOCC would ask the Americans, who had their own decision loop before they would accede to a request for support. The process was lengthy and ineffective, and JSOCC did not have the authority it needed to action some of the most important targets where forces were acting on their own. It meant they were left with routine easy targets and were not given the quick calls that would make the decisive change if we were going to win the war.

I wanted to be out on the ground commanding special forces, but instead I was inducted into a shabby office full of the same old has-beens, colonels serving out their time, that I had seen in other Afghan offices.

General Miller and Asadullah Khalid came to my induction into the shabby low-ceilinged plywood warren of rooms which housed the JSOCC. Khalid told me that he had ambitions for the role. "You know what? Change it the way you think will make it more aggressive. Isn't this what you want? And however it shakes down I want you to be in the forefront of managing the relationship with the US military, with oversight of every one of our special forces operations."

"In that case," I said, "I want to make it a command position because then I'll have legal authority to authorize operations rather than just moving around messages. Let's rename it so it is no longer the coordinating center but the Joint Special Operations *Command*." Khalid approved my change of title as well as a jump in rank. I would not be the director of the new JSOC but its commander, which came with legal responsibilities. I could own more risk and have more authority to order strikes. There had been hard fighting to put the Taliban on the back foot in 2019. The right use of our special forces capability now could make that permanent. I told the minister that I wanted to make the new JSOC the "center of excellence for Afghan warfighting," and he agreed.

A couple of weeks later I saw my chance to make the change I wanted. The president disbanded the Kabul garrison, a coordinating body under a three-star general, which had responsibility of controlling law and order in the capital city. It had been set up by the former national security adviser, Hanif Atmar, as part of his personal empire-building project, and the president saw no use for it, as it so obviously replicated other military capabilities. It was in a series of newly fitted-out buildings with modern communications facilities in its own large grounds inside the airport perimeter. With very good security and a short walk to the flight line, it was a prime piece of real estate, perfect for the headquarters of a reformed JSOC.

Khalid approved my land grab, and the next day I had expanded my staff by around six times, with the cooks, security, administration, and other support staff I took over. But I did not bring any of the colonels from the old JSOCC. I wanted to build a new operation from the top down with people who were capable, aggressive, and with wild ideas.

The new organizational plan was quickly approved. Khalid sidestepped the team around the president to get him to sign it off. But I still had to fight lengthy bureaucratic battles to get the people I wanted. Afghan defense bureaucracy seemed designed to prevent swift, effective decision-making. If you wanted to get approval for one person they would do a trade and ask you to appoint another person elsewhere—trying to balance tribes rather than reward merit. Khalid helped me navigate that, but it was not easy.

I had three deputies—from the NDS, ministry of interior, and the air force. The air deputy was an American-educated head of the MD-530 attack squadron, Lieutenant Colonel Shahpur Bakhshi, who was working on a plan for full night capability for the MD-530s. My NDS deputy was Colonel Khalid Mazloomyar. Trained as an officer in the UK, he was a smart guy. And Colonel Khalid Wardak became the key link between our operations and the ministry of interior. A brave warrior, he had lost a leg fighting in Wardak, and had been chief of police in Ghazni during our successful campaign there in 2019. I thought he would be effective at the staff level.

The CSAR would move under my command and to head it I appointed Major Javed Salim. It was a one-star post, two ranks above him, and I had to fight HR. I succeeded in promoting him one rank up to lieutenant colonel.

I added another coordination cell to take responsibility for targeting with a one-star post to head it, and again I had to fight to put a major in the post, Sohrab Azimi, two ranks below what was required, but an aggressive commando who had proved himself in several roles. This cell would assess intelligence and go after top-tier targets working against Afghanistan. Lieutenant Colonel Hayatullah Parwani from Defense Intelligence took over the joint intelligence fusion, and my closest adviser and loyal friend, Reza Sarwary, who had been with me on a number of operations, took the joint information operation fusion cell. A lot of these gifted individuals would stay with me when I moved on.

These were smart alpha players, and it was not easy to get them to work together. They were not the most polite or obedient military commanders, but they were the most effective. To turn them into a team, we spent long days and nights together, eating, going to the gym, running round the grounds of the new JSOC. I did not want to control every decision they made as we devised new ways to get after the Taliban. I wanted confident decision-making at the right level by this capable, knowledgeable, patriotic cadre of officers, the new generation who could have saved their country given the right support for long enough.

But just as we were ready to employ the new capabilities of JSOC in the 2020 fighting season to build on the advances of the year before, America changed the rules so the situation on the ground shifted decisively in favor of the Taliban.

THE POLITICAL LANE

"Sami, I need to you come to Brussels." Khalid was already on the way to address a meeting of NATO defense ministers when he called to ask me to join him to talk about my plans.

"I'm in Ghazni on an operation," I protested, "and I don't have a visa." I was only a few weeks into my new role. And I was already on the ground ensuring we kept up relentless momentum against the Taliban after our successes the year before. A talented commander who had been instrumental in that success, Colonel Mobin, had been killed by a rogue police officer in an insider attack, and I wanted to make sure his death was not in vain. I left the operation and managed to get a visa that same day. The following morning I was in a meeting in Brussels with Khalid, General Miller, and the US secretary of defense, Mark Esper, who said, "I've heard about you. How's it going?" And he asked some questions about interoperability and how we were using intelligence further down the chain for better effect.

In the main meeting in the afternoon in front of all the ministers of the alliance Khalid spoke about how much progress had been made and how the Taliban were now under extreme pressure from the Afghan military and the US military. He had a lot of applause from the room. Good news from Afghanistan was rare. Miller spoke briefly. I knew that he did not enjoy the political lane; he was a soldier's soldier. But he outlined the changes at JSOC and how he hoped this could be part of a shift that could potentially push the Taliban into full negotiations with the Afghan government.

After the briefing from the military side, the head of the UN mission to Kabul, Tadamichi Yamamoto, was supposed to report on the political side of international intervention. All eyes in the room turned to a large video screen connecting to his office to find him sound asleep, slumped back in his chair. All we could hear on the sound track was gentle snoring. There were stifled laughs around the room, while a voice off screen in a stage whisper said urgently, "Mister Yamamoto, Mister Yamamoto."

He pulled himself up in a startled way. He was quiet-spoken at the best of times and just managed to stammer an apology, "I'm so tired working out the politics here."

It was such a powerful symbol of what had gone wrong. We were doing our part to win the war, and the international politicians who were supposed to be taking advantage of it were literally asleep on the job, while our political leaders were in an endless struggle over the result of six-month-old election. When Yamamoto read his statement it was just another pious hope that a national unity government might emerge from the arguments over the election.

We had heard so many platitudes like it over twenty years. The international community still played the same power-broking games. It was all they had. Abdullah Abdullah won more votes in the 2014 election, but he was our man and not someone Washington wanted, so the election was rigged in favor of Ashraf Ghani. The Obama administration then pushed Abdullah into a national unity government under Ghani, but the one thing it had not brought was "national unity." For five years we had been living with the consequences—constant horse-trading and competing patronage for positions across government. And now the same thing was happening in arguments over the 2019 election, weakening the Afghan administration just when it needed to be strong and with a unity of purpose for our new young nation as we went onto the offensive.

The American team was going on from Brussels to the Munich Security Conference in Germany. "Hey, Sami," said General Miller. "You wanna jump in the plane with us so we can continue to talk?"

"You go, Sami," said Khalid. "I hate planes. I'm driving to Munich."

I was really tired after an overnight flight, but I could not leave him on his own. "I'm going with my minister." So I turned down the chance of a longer one-on-one chat with the US secretary of defense for an eight-hour car journey to Munich. On the way Khalid was listening to Ghani Khan poetry set to music.

"Wake up, Sami," he said, when I looked like nodding off. And it was worth hearing what he had to say. Ghani Khan was a Pashtun poet from the northwest frontier region of Pakistan, prominent in the 1960s and '70s. His father, Abdul Ghaffar Khan, had been a famous independence activist against British control of the region before independence in 1947. The poetry asked why there was continuous foreign intervention in our region. Ghani Khan's answer was to blame religious fanatics, extremist mullahs, who he said were the biggest impediment to freedom. To him religious extremists were the number one enemy of the very Islam they claimed to represent. He loved freedom and cooperation. Given the challenge we were facing with the Taliban it felt like a very contemporary message.

When we arrived in Munich we heard that President Ghani had made a last-minute decision to leave the arguments over the election and was now on his way to join us at the security conference. His unpredictable temper had swung against Khalid in recent weeks, and I saw it as a good opportunity for the minister to make it up with the president. But I knew that Ghani would not want me anywhere around. He still harbored crazy ideas about me and suspected my patriotism. He may have formally forgiven me when Khalid went to his house, but he did not trust me. I headed for another hotel and told Khalid I would pick him up after the conference was over.

When I came back after spending a lot of money on a long leather German coat, Khalid told me that he had had to head off one potential problem. The secretary of defense met President Ghani and was enthusiastically talking about this young Afghan general he had met. Ghani turned to General Miller, "So who is this?" Fortunately at that moment Zalmay Khalilzad appeared in the room, so no one had to mention my name.

Khalilzad was in Munich to tell Ghani the terms of the deal he was about to sign in Doha with the Taliban. He was not consulting him; he was informing him of a deal already done. It confirmed just how bad the Afghan government's relations with the US had become that Ghani had been cut out of the talks. It would have been unthinkable only a few years earlier for the American government to make a deal with the Taliban without involving Kabul.

To President Trump we were yesterday's war, a problem to be off the table if possible ahead of the election later in the year. Esper was his fourth secretary of defense since Jim Mattis had left the post a year earlier, and it was hard for us to get focused political attention. Despite his long years living in exile in America and enthusiastic lobbying of Washington, Ashraf Ghani had few friends there. America had created his presidency and now realized it was a mistake. His national security adviser, Hamdullah Mohib, was seen as a joke, and the Trump administration had not even talked to him for a year after he publicly accused Khalilzad of being a "viceroy," a loaded term going back to the days of the British empire, implying that Khalilzad wanted to govern Afghanistan for himself under the control of Washington. This was a fatal dislocation in our administration. At the time we were making progress on the battlefield we needed our politicians to be able to make our case at the top in Washington. Instead they were frozen out through their own incompetence and high-handed behavior.

BETRAYAL AT DOHA

I was back in JSOC at the end of February when America's deal with the Taliban was made public after a high-profile signing ceremony in Doha. Something like an electric shock went through my staff as we watched it streamed live on TV. We could not have imagined that so much would be conceded for so little return. A very brief document outlined how Khalilzad had agreed to a timetable for withdrawal of American troops and achieved nothing from the Taliban except a vague promise to sever links with al-Qaeda and other international terrorists. There was no mechanism to enforce compliance with this, or with a Taliban offer of a ceasefire and talks with the Afghan government. Even given Trump's tight schedule to try to get troops out before the US election, it was a terrible plan: a deal not for peace but withdrawal.

I felt an overwhelming sense of betrayal. I was bitter and could not believe that the United States, after fighting the Taliban for twenty years, had cut such a one-sided deal. I could not really grasp what had happened, but we experienced the consequences soon enough. In a remarkable act of deception that showed the deep contempt the American administration now had for President Ghani, they agreed secret annexes to the deal with the Taliban that were not shared with the Afghan government. Under these, America agreed that it would not attack the Taliban across vast swathes of the Afghan countryside, as long as the Taliban did not attack American bases or try to take provincial capitals.

Overnight we lost nearly all the US air support that had been instrumental in changing the course of the war in our favor the year before. The momentum of success had given our forces so much confidence as they improved day by day. But now, while there were the same number of American aircraft in country, and they would still fly, they could drop bombs only in very limited circumstances. The new rules of engagement meant that when the Taliban mobilized in large groups they would no longer be a target, nor would Taliban fighters seen moving with their weapons. American forces would watch pictures from drones tracking truckloads of explosives and convoys of pickups full of fighters moving across the country but could not target them.

The Taliban could only be targeted if they were attacking an Afghan outpost, and even that was limited. They had to be within three hundred meters of the outpost, and if they stopped fighting, the US aircraft was not allowed to engage. The Taliban quickly worked this out and it became a deadly game of cat and mouse. An Afghan position would be attacked and within twenty minutes or so US planes would arrive. The Taliban would stop fighting, then wait maybe half an hour before resuming the attack, the cycle would begin again, and there was nothing the American air controllers could do to help under the new rules of engagement.

We saw what this meant while the ink was still wet on the deal. We saw American drone pictures of the Taliban attacking one of our outposts in Zabul province, and burning the bodies of the dead, an attack which days before would have led to an air strike, and there was no response. It was hard to understand, let alone explain to our forces what had happened.

The figures told the whole story. During the crucial months of the main Afghan fighting season across the country in 2020, from April to September, American warplanes dropped just 227 missiles or bombs. That was compared to almost 4,000 in the same period the year before and was the lowest number for any year since the Taliban's reemergence as a fighting force in 2006.

America effectively abandoned Afghanistan to the Taliban in 2020; the chaos at the airport in the final pullout a year later was just the final death throes caused by a knife plunged into the heart of the Afghan republic at Doha. After the deal was signed it was as if our war effort was forced into slow motion, made more shocking as it was in contrast to the aggressive pace we had achieved with engaged American support the year before.

Whatever we did, it became much harder to keep momentum going in the campaign, and we were hit by a number of other events. COVID-19 swept unchecked across Afghanistan and across our headquarters. The innovative CSAR commander Chris Donahue was replaced by an officer who did things much more by the book, just as the rules for Afghan as well as American operations became far stricter. Not only did we lose almost all American air support overnight, but were told to cease our own offensive operations to "give peace a chance." The slogan became the new American bumper sticker, for use in any engagement with us. It threw away the advances we had made the year before.

Given the right supplies and the right leadership, our forces could have prevailed in 2020. But instead of building on success, we were ordered into a defensive posture, being hit without hitting back. As well as losing most American air support, our own air capacity was restricted as the supply of smart bombs was stopped. When I asked for more I was told, "You have had your quota." It was the first time anyone had mentioned any limit to their use. When it later came to Ukraine, all of a sudden supplies seemed limitless, but in Afghanistan we were reduced to dropping dumb bombs, which meant a higher risk to our aircraft as they needed to fly lower to release them, with a higher rate of civilian casualties as they lacked accurate targeting capability. Minister Khalid spent months trying to buy GBU smart bombs from the United Arab Emirates but could never seal the deal. We even ran out of artillery shells for our D-30 field guns, one of the most important weapons in achieving dominance over the Taliban.

At the same time as weakening our offensive capacity, America forced us to release seven thousand high-value Taliban and al-Qaeda prisoners as a "confidence-building measure." I knew these men too well. I had put some of them behind bars myself when I worked in intelligence. They were some of the darkest people on the face of the earth, including the mastermind of an attack on a children's hospital. On the list of people they wanted released, the Taliban also put in the names of hundreds of drug dealers. They may not have been Taliban before, but release bought returns. The Taliban put them on the list to get a slice of opium profits, a new cash stream. We secured the release of some of our own people in return, but the Taliban did not hold many prisoners. Many of those they released were just civilians from highway buses who had been seized in order for them to have a bargaining chip when it came to talks.

This did nothing to "build confidence" ahead of talks as intended. All it did was to strengthen the Taliban. We got little advantage from the "swap." Many of the prisoners the Taliban released in return were civilians held ready for this exchange. For months they had been stopping buses across the country and conducting mass arrests.

Afghan troops felt abandoned, confused, and lost their sense of direction, asking questions no one could answer. The loss of effective air support was very damaging for morale. Our troops would see an American airplane or drone overhead but not attacking Taliban in plain sight. It led to a sense of betrayal that sapped their will to fight. They would call CSAR and say things like, "Why is this airplane not shooting and this Taliban force has just killed two of my men, five of my men, and they're lying dead."

Our own small air-strike capability was now stretched as never before, trying to conserve its limited stocks while every unit across the country was calling on support, and we were getting instructions not to conduct offensive operations. The Taliban were mobilizing in larger groups than before, with attacks of hundreds hitting remote isolated checkpoints and bases. Alongside "give peace a chance," the Americans promoted a general theme that summer of "RIV," reduction in violence. But the only reduction was on our side. Afghan forces moved into a defensive position and the Taliban took their chance to increase violence.

As uncertainty spread, the Taliban sensed opportunity, and the mood in the Afghan countryside moved in their favor. War is a contest of wills, where moral capacity to fight is as important as the hardware available. As we communicated weakness, the Taliban capitalized on failure. People did not sign up to their ideology but saw the way the wind blew and switched sides for their survival and for personal gain. That was how war had always been fought in Afghanistan—not with decisive battles, but a power game where people tended to support the winner, whoever they may be. The many years of corruption which had enriched a small Kabul elite now had fatal consequences for the republic as people turned their back on them.

The Doha deal legitimized the Taliban as never before. They were sitting as equals with the most powerful country in the world. Many Afghan politicians and senior officials calculated that perhaps they would prosper if they switched sides. The seeds of the fall of the republic were sown at Doha.

KEEPING THE HIGHWAYS OPEN

By summer 2020, we were watching districts fall to the Taliban and we could do little to stop the collapse. Villages were handed over intact without fighting by elders who could see the way the wind was blowing and had no fight left in them. Rather than pushing the Taliban back across Afghanistan, my main task at JSOC became purely defensive, ensuring that no city or provincial capital fell and keeping the highways open to military supplies. I flew up to the north where the Taliban were mounting checkpoints on the main north-south highway, extorting cash from drivers and taking random people prisoner to keep up their stocks for any later exchanges. We were concerned with keeping the northern route open and having access to the northeast, the main recruiting ground for the Afghan army. If the road was blocked to Badakhshan province it would sap the morale of Badakhshani soldiers fighting in the south.

When I went up to support the road-clearing operation, just after I landed I was told that an Afghan A-29 attack plane had gone down in the mountains in Baghlan province. The commander of the air force, General Fahim Ramin, came on the line.

"This is urgent."

"OK, brother," I said. "So what happened?"

"The pilot of the A-29 that went down was an American instructor. He was working with the Afghan air wing in Mazar-e-Sharif in the north. We don't know his condition. I want you to help us recover him, dead or alive."

"Do you have a location?" So they tracked down the last location where his GPS locator was still on and gave me the grid. My Black Hawk pilots had just settled down to lunch when I called them.

"I need you back in the air now," I said, and explained our mission. "Go back to the aircraft and turn the engine on. I'll join you."

I took two bodyguards and went out to the helicopter. The crew were already going back through the drills to get the rotors moving. When the pilot saw the grid, he whistled. "This is high altitude, sir. We can only carry six people up there."

Where the plane came down was a Taliban-controlled area. Six people in each aircraft, twelve in all, was by no means enough to provide sufficient cover for any rescue operation. Nonetheless I said, "OK, we'll try. Let's go with twelve people."

Baghlan is part of the Hindu Kush belt of mountains that go across the north of Afghanistan. The highest peaks are at 21,000 feet, or 6,400 meters, higher than the flight ceiling of a Black Hawk. We would be pushing the air frames to their limit, plunging into valleys, then climbing to scrape ridges and peaks covered with snow as we flew over to plunge down to the next. Looked at from 4,000 meters up, the last known location of the plane could be in any one of a number of valleys. So we had to go from valley to valley, fly down, look around, and move on. After about half an hour of this, one of my bodyguards spotted a group of people around a man lying down. As we got closer we could see he was wearing a flying suit. It took our pilot three attempts against strong wind to land close to him.

The people on the ground were not hostile but curious shepherds. There were several children among them. They were thin mountain people, and the big American on the ground looked like a giant among them. I jumped out and walked over to the pilot. He looked up, relieved to have been found. But he lay motionless.

"Can you move?"

"My back hurts. I am afraid to move."

"Where's your communication equipment?" I knew he would be carrying sensitive kit that could not fall into the hands of the Taliban. He opened his vest and gave it to me. We carried him back to the Black Hawk, stumbling in the snow. We were only minutes ahead of the Taliban.

As we were flying back I read a message on my cell phone from the American commander at the CSAR, Brigadier General Marcus Evans.

"Sami, I need your help urgently. We need to conduct a search-and-rescue mission for one of our pilots who went down in Baghlan province."

I responded by sending a picture of the pilot lying in our helicopter, with the message, "Is this your guy?" We had recovered him before his own side even knew he was missing.

The pilot was called Major Marco Scott and because he was an instructor was allowed to fly alone. I asked him a few times why his flight had not been registered ahead of time, but he never had an answer. I guess he was bored with limited work to do during the worst days of COVID. He wanted to test himself against the Hindu Kush, and the mountains won.

We went back to the road-opening operation, and after briefing commandos for a raid on a Taliban checkpoint on the highway, we suddenly saw a group of Taliban firing machine guns and rocket-propelled-grenade-launchers. I could hear the helicopter taking hits, and on our return we found that seven heavy machine gun rounds had hit us in all, one coming very close to the main control system in the tail. The Taliban were getting more confident every day as we were forced to fight with one hand tied behind our back.

THE MISSING VIDEO

In the summer, General Yasin Zia took over as chief of the general staff. He was an experienced fighter who had worked in intelligence for the resistance against the Taliban in the 1990s. He rose quickly through the ranks in the new Afghanistan after 9/11 and was trained in Australia and the US. I liked him, and we had a good working relationship. But as he was an assertive commander who wanted control of the war, friction grew over my wide range of responsibilities. Often his corps commanders would call me first when they needed support, knowing I had flexibility to respond where the bureaucratic MOD machine did not.

I knew people would die if I did not get support to them quickly and cut corners to save lives. But it meant that Zia was not in the command loop for fast-moving operations. And because I had streamlined decision-making, my lower commanders had more authority that other Afghan officers at that level, so it sometimes seemed as if they were out of my control. Zia would call me to try to coordinate priorities better, but our approaches were so different that it was hard to do.

With the war going badly for us, because of the loss of American air support and constant pressure not to go on the offensive, there were bound to be tensions at the top of the armed forces. A lot of the problems were political. Zia would get calls from politicians who called for troops to attack the Taliban in their area. And I might already have tasked them for a larger and more complex operation where there was a more immediate threat. They would call me to ask which operation they should go on. My personal relations with Zia were good. We had a shared ambition to reform the army, rotating troops to give them a break, bringing in new people, and inspiring leaders. I knew that, like me, he would sometimes pay from his own pocket when troops did not have what they needed. But however we tried to prioritize operations, our different ways of working led to friction.

I clashed, too, with the deputy minister of defense, Munira Yusufzada, over staff appointments and her management of wounded soldiers. Of course I had made other enemies as well, usually people who did not want to be pushed as hard as I pushed them in order to win the war. Corps commanders would complain against me if I called them to ask why they were not more aggressive against the Taliban.

Tension increased over how we managed scarcer resources, just as the war began to go the wrong way because of America's deal with the Taliban. And Minister Khalid had a close relationship with Zia that went back to the days when Khalid was director of operations at the NDS and Zia stood in for him when he was wounded by a suicide bomber.

Things came to a head over a new operation in September to hit Taliban checkpoints to cut one of their revenue streams—extorting money from drivers. We developed a plan to use KKA troops in plain clothes to approach checkpoints in civilian vehicles, then jump out and attack the Taliban. The first raid of this sort, early in the morning on the highway in Baghlan, went smoothly. The KKA guys killed seven Taliban at the checkpoint, jumped back in their cars, and drove to a nearby location where they were safely picked up by helicopter. It was a highly risky operation. We could not have air cover for these raids because that would give the game away. But Khalid was unhappy when I reported back to him because we had not filmed the raid from a drone as planned. We wanted to amplify the effect of the raid by publicizing our success, but the drone we planned to use had malfunctioned on the day. I said that we did have video of traffic now safely moving through the area, and pictures of the guys training and setting off.

"This is not what I wanted. I wanted video proof."

"I understand, sir," I said. "But this was the first operation. Next time we will make sure we have the video."

"It's not just that. I wanted the guys to go inside the customs house, find all their papers, and get their phones."

That had been in the plan, but on the day it was decided that remaining for that long would be too dangerous.

"Sir, this is the heart of the enemy. They did what they could. Once the boys leave the headquarters, I can't micromanage the operation, because it will get them all killed. Once they're on the ground, they see real-time threats and opportunities and make decisions based on that."

He was in an unreasonable mood and wanted to blame me—whatever.

"Well, it seems you don't have control over your guys, and if you don't have control over them, why am I asking you to do this? I should probably ask someone else."

"I do have control, but I don't want to kill them myself by giving them orders that make it harder for them to make decisions." On top of the criticism and sniping I had faced from Zia and the deputy minister for months, and a president who did not trust me, the minister was now having his turn. I was not happy with the way the war was going either, but not recording this operation on video did not seem to merit the importance he attached to it that day.

"For me, as a commander, the most important thing is to keep my soldiers alive," I said. "It's not bringing videos to you or to anyone else."

"Well, maybe that shows how incompetent you are."

"If I'm incompetent, then why do you keep me as a commander? Maybe you should appoint someone else."

"Maybe I should," he said.

"Well, excellent, I think you just did, congratulations." And I walked out of his office. He kept calling me as I walked down to get my car. And when he called me at home I turned off the phone.

For the next three weeks I was at home and saw friends. It was my first break for a year. By good fortune my son was born at that time, so I had time for that.

I watched as districts kept falling to the Taliban and confusion arose among special forces. The next KKA checkpoint operation was abandoned at the last minute as the commander did not trust the plan. Zia tried to solve the logjams but did not have enough commanders who could think in the way that my team did. JSOC had achieved an almost legendary status with the police, NDS, and with the army. Soldiers wanted to work with JSOC, or be attached to JSOC, because JSOC delivered success; not because of me, but because of my team. I brought the best Afghan officers to JSOC, and however junior they were, I listened to their ideas. I brought aggressive people who thought out of the box, who were ruthless against the enemy, and who also had the guts to join in combat operations that went into the heart of the enemy to eliminate any kind of threat. JSOC was a new role model for every Afghan commander and soldier. I don't think many people at the headquarters level in Kabul liked that. I was the tall poppy, and they wanted to cut me down to size.

But I knew they would call me back.

Battle of Helmand 2021

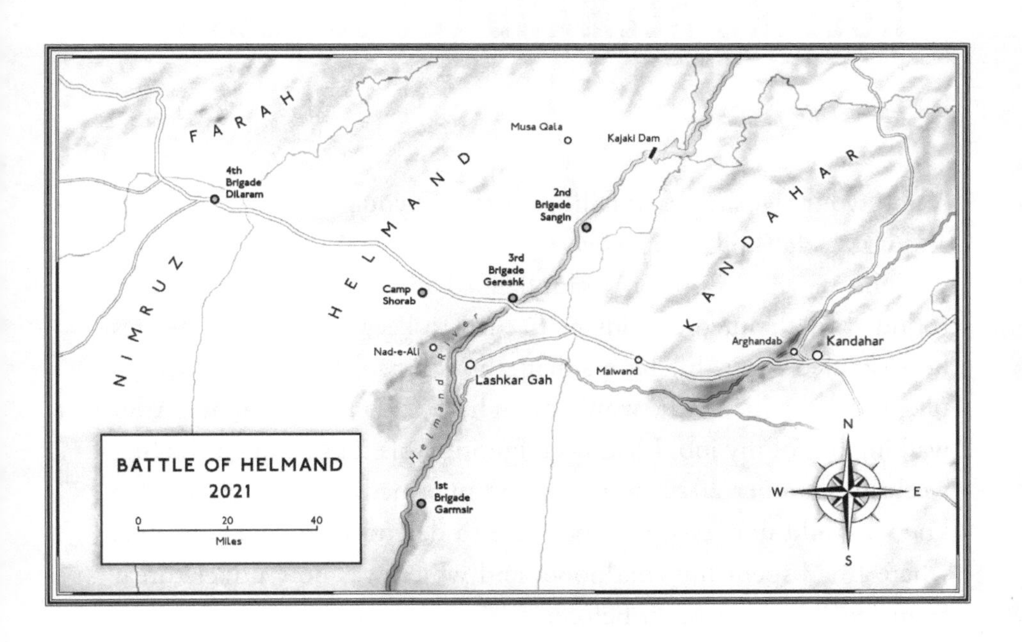

Chapter Ten

HOLDING HELMAND (2020–2021)

"Sami, your favorite city is falling apart. Are you going to sit at home and watch the Taliban take over?"

The defense minister, Asadullah Khalid, lay on his bed, surrounded by the medical aids he needed to keep going. The injuries he sustained when hit by a suicide bomber in 2012 continued to plague his health, and he would often have to collapse at home. After walking out of my job, I had been ignoring his calls through the first weeks of October 2020, so he sent an intermediary to fetch me. He knew I could not resist the challenge to defend Helmand province, where I had spent my childhood, and which was now under threat from the Taliban as never before.

In the brief time I had been away the Taliban had made their most determined advance since the Doha peace deal in February, killing hundreds of Afghan soldiers and advancing across most of Helmand until they were at the gates of the capital, Lashkar Gah. They had surrounded the city, cutting it off from the regional army headquarters in the desert to the north, and paralyzing the most important trade route in the country. Its loss would be a powerful symbol of failure.

"I thought we had trust issues," I said. "Why would you want me back disrupting things?"

"Let's leave that for now. There'll be plenty of time to discuss it." He was ashen-faced from pain, and raised himself onto his elbows. "I'm going to Lashkar Gah to try to save it, and I want you to come with me."

You could not fault Khalid for bravery. He was going to fight his way out of his sickbed and lead the war from the front. It was not difficult to decide to go with him.

That night we were in the military headquarters at Camp Shorab, the desert base in Helmand, where we had a bleak briefing from the corps commander. Next door was a small US special forces detachment in what had once been the largest foreign base in the country, called Leatherneck on the American side, Bastion on the British side—now a vast empty wasteland of abandoned buildings. The remaining Americans worked as advisers, but under the post-Doha rules of engagement they could not attack the thousands of Taliban fighters who streamed in from Pakistan, although they still had planes in the air. Afghan forces were overwhelmed across the south, in an offensive now concentrated on Helmand.

The Afghan corps commander, Lieutenant General Wali Muhammad Ahmadzai, had no fight left in him. "We may have to pull back our last forces out of Laskhar Gah," he said. "It's only a matter of time before it falls to the Taliban."

"It can't fall," said Khalid. "I have to go in there."

The corps commander was taken aback. "That's impossible," he said. "The Taliban have spies everywhere, and as soon as they know you're there, they'll do anything to kill you."

I turned to Khalid. "Sir, you're right. We need to rebuild confidence in our forces, and the best way to do that is to go and show that all is not lost."

"I disagree," said Ahmadzai. "I'm in command here, and I can't allow the risk of a car bomb or any other attempt to kill the minister."

We left the meeting. The minister was still sick and unsure what to do.

"You have to go," I said. "Show resolve. People know you have come to the south. If you leave now, Lashkar Gah will certainly fall. The hit on morale would not just be here but have a domino effect across the country. We can't show weakness."

Khalid agreed, and after a short helicopter ride we were in the governor's compound in the besieged provincial capital. The minister had a briefing from military, police, and political leaders, each at the end of what they could tolerate. Fear had eaten its way across the Helmand command. The minister was not on the ground long. He called some brigade commanders, and as we prepared to leave, the governor, who had formerly been in the NDS, said, "Sir, could you leave Sami behind when you go?"

The minister turned him down, but back in headquarters, I argued I should stay. Apart from anything, I could see this was a target-rich environment. Thousands of Taliban fighters were now in Helmand, and with the right coordination we could inflict a lot of damage on them. Khalid was concerned that I would be blamed if the city fell. The conventional army commanders would say that I disrupted their efforts; without me interfering they could have won.

"Well, that's the kind of risk I am prepared to take," I said. "And if the city does fall," I paused and smiled, "well, then, there is no Sami to blame, because I'll be dead."

The next day, October 14, 2020, the minister returned to Kabul and left me in command in Helmand. Once again I was his trouble-shooting adviser, back in the role I had played before I went to JSOC. I returned to Lashkar Gah and set up a joint command center, flying down key members of my team from JSOC. Until then the army, police, and NDS all had different commands, and the army had further divisions for artillery and other assets. I replicated what I had done elsewhere—centralized coordination of intelligence, planning, and overall command, so my intent was well understood, but with substantial authority delegated down to every unit to take action on their own initiative. I had learned that this was the best way to have maximum combat effect—centralized planning, but with local authority to act. It was a principle called mission command I picked up from our allies that went back to the Second World War, but it was alien to the tight top-down command structures normal in Afghanistan.

To make it clear that holding Helmand was now the main effort for the Afghan armed forces, the minister sent down the army chief of staff, General Yasin Zia, with several other generals to take overall command. This had potential challenges. I had left the military the previous month after clashes with Zia over prioritization of resources and the application of force.

Inevitably we soon ran into a problem when I ordered helicopters in one direction to find they had been sent elsewhere by Zia. I called the commander of 777 Brigade, the special mission air wing, Brigadier General Ziarmal.

"What happened, why did you change this plan?"

"The chief of staff gave me an order."

"You answer to me, not him, on operational matters. You are breaking your command."

"I am sitting with him," he said. "You had better ask him what you want."

I walked over to their office. I needed to sort this out.

"Sir, you call me twenty times a day for resupply, support, offensive strikes, and deployment of commanders," I said to General Zia. "I deliver what you need and always on time. But if you call commanders directly it could hinder the sequence of larger operation. Those helicopters you have taken away were due to pick up casualties—and had two other tasks tonight."

I turned to Ziarmal, the 777 commander.

"What makes you think you can countermand my orders? Even if General Zia tells you to do something, you can walk over to the command center and request it through the normal system."

I was mad at him for letting this happen. "Anyway, what are you doing in Helmand? You should be at 777 HQ in Kabul."

"I came as a pilot for the chief of army staff."

"You're a commander, not a personal pilot for some general."

"Hey, Hey," Zia intervened. "I'm sitting right here, guys."

He did not want a confrontation. He wanted to make this relationship work. "I told Ziarmal to come with me, Agha Jan," he said, using a personal name I was known by. "I know he has command responsibilities, and he has been able to fulfill them."

"Sir, here is my proposal," I replied. "You are, of course, in overall command, but I have operational command. Whatever you need, you tell me, I will make sure it happens. Talking to the units, making specific decisions, which helicopter should go where, what special forces should go where, please leave that to me. You can be involved at the political level and decide priorities, we'll make sure that we deliver effectively so everyone is happy."

He smiled and said, "It's a deal, you're the operational commander, I have oversight."

The war was not going our way. Our casualties were unsustainable. We were losing soldiers at a rate of up to thirty a day, killed and wounded. In a symbol of how bad leadership had been in Helmand, I discovered that some remote bases had to hold onto bodies because they could not be recovered. Because of the restrictions on the way we could operate, in 2020 the Afghan army was bleeding to death.

The loss of American air support, slowdown in their ammunition supply, orders to us to halt offensive operations under the stupid rules of "Give Peace a Chance," and the weakness and indecision of Ghani's national security team, all contributed to a loss of morale and a change in atmosphere.

We were willing to fight, but during 2020 watched as many of the hard-won gains of the year before were lost—squandered by the political environment. And although the Afghan government had not been allowed to see the secret annexes of the US deal with the Taliban, it was clear enough by now what was in them, and they were being flagrantly broken every day. The Taliban had committed not to attack major highways or provincial capitals. And yet here they were with roadblocks on Highway One, the main ring road across the south of Afghanistan, and troops threatening Lashkar Gah.

When I pointed out this breach to our American partners, I had more success than in recent months in calling on air support. We now had US air strikes every night. With that and some renewed drive with special forces support on the ground, we changed the momentum of the campaign. A couple of weeks after my arrival, the Taliban were pushed back and had lost many combat troops and commanders, giving us some breathing space.

On October 23, at around midnight, two Chinook helicopters landed in Lashkar Gah stadium, next to the governor's compound, carrying more than seventy US soldiers. They were finally showing up to support their partner on the ground. It was heartwarming, giving us confidence that things could change and we could go on the offensive against the Taliban again. The unit was led by Brigadier General Marcus Evans. While he sat with General Zia and his team in the governor's compound, I walked with two majors to my command center in a separate compound some four hundred feet away.

They had come to do a detailed assessment of how they could help, within the limited resources they still had in the country.

As we walked through the calm dark of the city night from the governor's compound I said casually, "Before we go to the command center, I was planning to clear a compound of Taliban that is not far away. Perhaps your guys could join us in the assault."

One of the Americans turned to me with a worried expression. "Sir, we have been told we can't engage. And if there are Taliban around, don't you think we should go in vehicles and not walk?"

"It's OK," I said. "I'm only joking. I know the rules."

"That's an acquired sense of humor," he said, with no hint of a smile. The two majors did write a recommendation that we needed a rule change so that US special forces could go on joint operations alongside their Afghan comrades. General Miller sent it to Washington, but it was turned down. President Trump was only days away from seeking reelection and did not want the distraction of American casualties in Afghanistan.

As I was trying to reassert control of the war in Helmand, in the parallel universe of politics, Washington had turned its back on us. And when Joe Biden won the election, President Ghani made the fatal miscalculation that he would reassess the situation and keep American forces in Afghanistan. Anybody could see that the Taliban had not been serious about peace talks with the Afghan government that spluttered on through 2020 after the Americans signed the Doha withdrawal deal. But in the period between the November vote for the American president and January inauguration, Ghani ordered an actual pause in the talks, believing that Biden would reset the terms in January and keep American troops in the country. It was naïve wishful thinking which would cost Afghan lives. Biden had only contempt for Afghanistan and would do nothing to prevent it falling into the hands of the Taliban.

AMBUSH AT CHANJIR

My initial assessment in Helmand was that we needed to push out of Lashkar Gah to dominate more of the landscape and reopen ground lines of communication to our more isolated bases. I began with Camp Chanjir, on an important crossroads to the north. The operation was planned to start with an Afghan Border Force move to the police headquarters in District Ten, three kilometers from Chanjir. Late in the evening they reported that they had successfully achieved that objective. I told them to ensure swift evacuation of police casualties and arrange resupply, and they assured me that was done.

The next morning I set out to join them with Captain Mirzada of JSOC operations, Captain Asem, my aide de camp, and a small force of my bodyguards. Traveling in one armored vehicle and one pickup truck, we drove through streets which did not tell a good story. There were no Afghan troops in sight, men watched us warily, and children ran away on our approach. That suggested they knew there were roadside bombs planted, or we were heading for an ambush.

As we neared the police headquarters we came under ferocious sustained attack by a large Taliban force. We raced through the ambush only to find the police opening fire on us with large-caliber machine guns as they did not know what was going on. Both vehicles were hit. We yelled over the shooting. "Open the gates. Open the gates. We are Afghan forces."

We got into their yard with Taliban bullets ricocheting around us. My head of security had a bad shoulder wound, and the vehicles were peppered with bullet holes. The police were wearing civilian clothes, so you would not have known whether they were police or the Taliban. They were dusty and looked beaten after days of punishing attacks with no support. Some parts of their compound could be raked by Taliban gunfire. Once we were in a safe corner sheltered from the incoming rounds, the police commander, Colonel Shawali Popal, asked us how we had come.

"Up the main road," I said.

He and his officers looked at each other. He thought I was joking. "No, seriously," he said. "How did you get here? The main road is with the Taliban."

"Well, that's the way we came." I paused. "What happened to the force I sent yesterday?"

"They couldn't make it. They couldn't break through Taliban lines. By late night, around twenty-two hundred, they pulled back." And he looked around at my men. "How much force did you bring to break the ambush?"

"What you see is what we have. Ten, twelve people."

"You're crazy," he said. "Who are you, what do you do?"

"I am Sami Sadat. I am in overall command in Helmand under the direct authority of the minister."

He found the information hard to compute. He had never met a senior officer who traveled so lightly or went so far forward.

I called the ground force I was supposed to link up with to reach Chanjir.

"Where are you? You confirmed to me last night that you were in police HQ in District Ten."

"We were close, but we couldn't link up with them, the Taliban resistance was too strong, so we had to push back and in fact, we're preparing to assault those positions now."

It was now around noon.

"Son of a bitch. So you lied to me. Do you know where I am?"

"No, sir."

"I'm in the police headquarters in District Ten, but I nearly got killed on the way, along with everyone driving with me. Why would you lie to me?"

I cut off his apology.

"I don't want to hear explanations now. I want your sorry ass up here, along with all the force you can bring."

I turned to the police colonel. "Shawali, do you know the exact location of Taliban outposts?"

"Yes, every one. We've been fighting them these past two weeks."

"How about local civilians?"

"Sir, they all left two weeks ago when the fighting began."

I had a little drone in my backpack and Mirzada flew it around, while we watched images on a tablet, and the policemen sitting around me pinpointed the Taliban positions one by one.

I called the base at Shorab where a good friend, Major Lotfullah, was leading air operations.

"Sir, I am really glad to talk to you. We had wild reports that Sami Sadat went on this operation and was injured in a firefight. The Americans are calling and they're pushing aircraft our way."

"That's good to hear. We have some targets for them."

Mirzada gave him the grid references of Taliban positions around us and coordinated radio frequencies for ground to air communications, and for the next few hours, we were on the radio, talking to pilots, while the police gave us what information they could from the ground. Most of the air strikes were by our own MD-530 helicopters and A-29 planes. They flew sortie after sortie, returning to base to rearm and refuel before coming back to hit the Taliban in compounds and large trenches they had dug across the town.

Late in the afternoon, the ground force finally joined us, and I stayed until we had killed every Taliban fighter on the road to Chanjir. Before sunset there was no more incoming fire. The police headed out and gathered weapons and ammunition from dead Taliban across the town.

At the end of November, I went to Kandahar, which was facing the most determined push by the Taliban from the north and northwest for many years. As Afghan forces withdrew, the Taliban retook Arghandab district. Arghandab is one of the most populated districts of Kandahar province with a venerable past as "Arachosia" under Alexander the Great, when he set up his capital in Kandahar. It had changed hands several times during the war. Its dense undergrowth of pomegranate plantations and fruit trees, in a fertile landscape crisscrossed by a lattice of mud walls, made it difficult ground to fight in.

While on the Kandahar campaign I handed back operational leadership in Helmand to Lieutenant General Ahmadzai, leaving Khalid Amiri, the commanding officer of the KKA, in charge of special ground operations and Lieutenant Colonel Parwani leading the mobile targeting team, so we did not lose momentum.

General Zia, the chief of the general staff, was already in Kandahar when I arrived with my small team. We followed the same pattern we had set in Helmand, where I led operations while he provided overall oversight and liaised with politicians. My team established our command center in the part of Arghandab still under Afghan control and began our operations. We had great local intelligence assets, and the head of the air force, Fahim Ramin, had informed me that his first batch of "night stalkers," MD-530 attack helicopters capable of flying at night, had just graduated, and he sent them to support our operation.

My deployment to Arghandab did not last long. By December the president seemed to have changed his mind about me because now he wanted me to take formal command of 215 Corps in Helmand, no longer as a mobile adviser for the minister. I argued that Helmand should be amalgamated with 205 Corps in Kandahar in order to have a coherent security policy for the whole south. General Zia agreed, but he lost the argument with the president, who was by now beginning to lose contact with reality, shouting orders and believing a smaller and smaller group of advisers, none with the experience needed for this moment of critical danger for the republic.

My appointment was part of a general reorganization. President Ghani and his national security adviser, Hamdullah Mohib, were the worst kind of micromanagers. Apart from my appointment, most of the new commanders were in the same tribe as the president, who was building his personal power base.

I could see there was no way back to JSOC. Its operational effectiveness was severely reduced after I left, and it was folded into the Afghan special forces command, where the brightest and most original minds I had encouraged were crushed under old-guard communist-era officers. Many in the ministry of defense had resented the way it operated on its own and wanted to cut it down to size. My best people were being killed when they were sent on what were really conventional operations. In a long operation to push the Taliban out of the dense farmland of Arghandab around one hundred commandos were injured and killed. Those leading the operation depended solely on the troops they brought down from Kabul—employing special operators where they should have used conventional forces. The way I had used commandos under JSOC was as a small agile force, employing intelligence from people who knew the ground, effectively applying air and artillery as well as special forces. But that approach had been replaced by brute force instead of smart strategy, wasting the lives of our best troops.

215 ARMY COMMAND

The Helmand campaign tested me to the marrow of my bones. I came out of it a different man than when I went in. I took command on December 13, and it was hard to be hopeful. That first night there was an attack on our gates, killing a guard. When I slept it was cold, and I had only one blanket and no power. In the morning I was told there had been no electricity across the whole corps for two months, and there was fuel for generators for only two hours a day. I called in our logistics team, whose brief audit of essentials told its own story. In 215 Corps, we had 18 percent of our fuel requirements, 40 percent of vehicles, and 60 percent food. And we were well below our effective fighting strength. There were only around half of the soldiers available who were nominally on the payroll. This was the big picture of what was known. When I traveled round what the soldiers told me scared me. They revealed it was even worse on the ground than the bare figures I had been given. Some had gone months without meat or fruit, eating the most basic of diets which would not sustain a fighting force.

I took trips to remote bases, surrounded by the enemy, with no secure ground lines of communication, where they had never seen a corps commander before. I made some immediate decisions to wrest back control of the campaign. I tasked Command Sergeant Major Mohibullah to recommend frankly what we needed to give our soldiers their best fighting chance. The role of a sergeant major at the corps level was new in the Afghan army, but I had seen its effectiveness in American and other NATO forces. This was the voice of the ordinary soldier at the top table. Mohibullah was honest, he knew the psychology of soldiers, and he also had ideas about how to fix certain problems.

"I want to start with the soldiers," I told Mohibullah. "I want to know how they think, what they need. The officers often lie, but soldiers will not be shy about telling you the truth. I want to know what they want to turn the tide in their favor."

"Yes sir," he said, smiling at my dig at officers.

"And there's another thing."

"Sir?"

"Tell me immediately if one of my soldiers dies. We need them to know their lives matter."

I wanted to signal to the Taliban that there was a new commander in town; things would be different from now on. In the moral contest of wills at the heart of warfare I wanted the Taliban to begin to doubt themselves. To go on the offensive, I set up a mobile targeting team to coordinate intelligence, planning, and command functions, calling in some of the best people from JSOC. And I brought down 4th Company, KKA, as a strike force. They had been my praetorian guard since I took over JSOC and had most recently retrained for the high-risk operations in civilian clothing we had run against Taliban checkpoints. Half of them had been based in Helmand with Navy SEALS, so they knew the area.

I had to argue hard to move 4th Company to Helmand. But I had done the MOD a favor by taking on 215 Corps, the toughest fight in the country, and they caved in when I pushed. For our first operations, we moved conventional forces east from Shorab and west from Gereshk along Highway One, aiming to meet in the middle, using 4th Company as a flexible strike force to enable the move. At the same time my executive officer, Brigadier General Latif commanded a similar operation to open Highway 601 from the capital, Lashkar Gah, northeast to Maiwand.

To keep control of Highway One once we had opened it, I took the hard decision to destroy hundreds of properties built close to the road, against protests by local people. I knew it was unpopular, but the Taliban had been using the buildings as cover, and we needed to be able to move on our own terms.

These early operations were about shaping the battle space. Following the principle that while "amateurs talk strategy, professionals talk logistics," I set my most competent and loyal adviser, Reza Sarwary, onto dealing with the supply challenges, which involved liaising with our American partners to curb corruption. The war would not be won without a major change in the delivery of equipment and food.

There were other supply issues, which were down to incompetence and the rigidity of army structures. The way the ministry of defense was set up, there were supply depots located inside my corps that were not under my command. If I wanted something from the depot next door I had to request it through Kabul. Even a reply, let alone delivery, would sometimes take more than a week, a clearly unacceptable delay given the intensity of the war. I went to the depot and insisted they open the gates so I could see what they had.

Inside I found a warfighting Aladdin's cave. There were hundreds of unused sniper rifles, laptops with sensors that could identify the location of improvised explosive devices, and small robotic tanks that could defuse them. I immediately emptied the warehouse, sending the equipment to my hard-pressed troops.

And I needed to do more to stem our casualty flow. First thing every morning I would go to the hospital and watch as lines of coffins were taken out and loaded onto a C-130 transport plane to be flown out of Helmand. A lot of our casualties were killed by Taliban "Red Unit" snipers at night, equipped with thermal sights on their rifles, which gave them night vision capability. They could pick off our soldiers at will, and we would not even know they were there. Things had gotten so bad that in some technical areas the Taliban now had superiority to us, using equipment seized from the Afghan army in defeats and bought through corrupt routes.

I wanted to even this up and called the minister.

"I need funding to buy thermal scopes for my snipers. The casualty rate in Helmand is unsustainable."

"I don't have that kind of money," he said. "But I could ask the president for a special grant."

I could see that getting bogged down in bureaucracy.

"If I buy these myself, can you repay me?" I had more than one million dollars in an account in Dubai, made from my risk management company.

"Sure," he said. "It it's that urgent then go ahead, and we can repay you later." There never was a "later," and the Afghan army still owes me more than a million dollars for the sixty-two thermal sights I bought, along with other equipment. It shows how much our troops were let down by the system that I was now spending my own money in order for them to be equipped as well as the Taliban.

The thermal sights immediately cut our casualty figures. Our American partners had fitted what they called RAID towers at several bases, where cameras would give 360-degree surveillance for several kilometers around. As soon as the Taliban approached at night, they would now be identified from the RAID tower cameras, and our snipers, with their new thermal sights, could pick them off. And we began to fly our ScanEagle drones at night, giving real-time information of potential targets. This was sent to MD-530s, now fully confident on night operations, and to mortars and artillery guns, whose commanders now had authority to open fire without referring upwards. The result was a huge drop in our casualty rate—down from around thirty a day to just one on average.

At the same time I ensured that food supplies improved and upgraded the defenses of every base. I used my long-term connections in Helmand to get honest local contractors to do the work. It was personal for me. I love Lashkar Gah; my heart pounded when I defended it until the very last days of the Republic. I would look at drone pictures of the Taliban in places where I had been for a picnic or with my friends after school. I knew the owners of houses we could see occupied by Taliban commanders. Some of the police who were killed I knew from my schooldays. I would constantly get calls from people I knew who expected me to do more, and I was already working 110 percent. I had pride in my heart that I could do something to stop the Taliban destroying the homes of people I had known all my life.

On the other side of our headquarters, across the vast expanse of the empty base, where thousands of American and British troops had once lived, lay an airstrip that had once been international standard. It was 3.5 kilometers long, but the equipment for the control tower and landing lights had gone, so we could make only limited use of it. Again spending my own money, I tasked a colonel to improve it and he bought in equipment from Germany. The night came when he called me over and I saw thousands of lights illuminating the airstrip, giving us the ability to fly whatever aircraft we wanted round the clock. It meant we doubled our supply capability and could rotate troops far more flexibly than before. Even President Ghani heard about it and called me to ask how it had been done. Finally he was getting the idea that I may be competent. When I asked for my JSOC deputy, Colonel Khalid Wardak, to be appointed Helmand police chief, he was sent down the next day.

Since my days in the NDS I had known the value of good intelligence. And we desperately needed to get ahead of the Taliban to cut casualties. I came to realize that they had informants across the command, giving them details of weak points they could exploit. One night I was told there would be an attack on one of our checkpoints where there were only seven soldiers, rather than the fifteen who should have been there. That was an uncomfortable level of detail. We tracked down the informant, and he quickly confessed that he had been recruited when serving in Nimruz province, on the border with Iran. He confirmed that the Taliban were sharing detailed information with the Iranian Revolutionary Guard Council and receiving funds and weapons from them. He gave us the names of four other Taliban informants, and we arrested them that night. They knew a lot about us, and in particular about me: where I slept, ate, how often I moved out. I discovered that a nurse who attended me had been working for the Taliban for two years.

I recruited my own sources in the Taliban by working through their relatives who were in the city. I would approach them and appeal to their patriotism, saying something like, "We know your cousin is in the Taliban, but I am sure you don't support these Pakistani-backed attacks." Or we worked with tribal elders and mullahs to question whether the Taliban were loyal Afghans. Money was a big persuader. I was paying a lot out of my own pocket to listen to anything that gave us an insight into the Taliban command structure and ability of individual commanders—their strengths and weaknesses, and where opportunities lay to turn them or kill them.

I had friends in Afghan intelligence who would pass me their own sources, and I had friends among tribal leaders who would call me and say things like, "Commander, you know, there is my cousin who is a local Taliban commander or Taliban operator, he wants to help." Even low-level contacts helped. They might say, "My cousin is a driver, he's driving Taliban from Pakistan to Afghanistan. Do you need him for anything?"

Where I could I would meet sources myself. I surprised low-level Taliban commanders by praying with them. They would say "Oh, Commander, we're so happy that you're praying."

I replied, "Of course I'm praying. I'm a Muslim, I pray five times a day, and I obey all the rules, and it's you guys who are not obeying the true path of the faith." And then I would open a religious discussion, which would lead onto a wider conversation about how we were all Afghans: why did we fight each other when we could benefit from being united and at peace and prosperity? I would always say that the Taliban and al-Qaeda brought shame and misery to Muslims, and I played on Helmandi customs and traditions of friendship. If we bonded like that, they would be loyal to me, not to the Taliban.

Once the intelligence flow began it became a constant stream, from people disillusioned with the fighting, opposed to Pakistan, or short of money. If information about a significant Taliban commander led to his kill or capture, I would pay up to $15,000, a huge incentive in a poor place. The intelligence enabled us to get ahead of Taliban planning, so we knew when there were large forces coming in from Pakistan which we could target.

We developed a constant flow of information that was followed up either by my KKA shock troops or local regular army commanders in a series of targeted attacks behind Taliban lines. We killed many key al-Qaeda and Taliban leaders in this way, including shadow governors, constantly disrupting their command capacity.

TAKING THE FIGHT TO THE TALIBAN

With our defensive capacity improved and the morale of troops raised by better supplies and reduced casualties, we went on the offensive. Unlike in northern Afghanistan where the snow slowed the momentum of war in the winter, in Helmand it was possible to keep up pressure during the winter months. And because the Taliban had become used to operating without much opposition, they had massed into larger fighting groups, so it was the target-rich environment I had anticipated. In the first two months of my Helmand command around 1500 Taliban fighters were killed, mostly by air strikes. We kept up a ruthless strike rate against their known meeting places, destroying more than eighty of them. We wanted them to think there was nowhere safe to run.

We did not yet have the strength to take and hold ground, so rather than large-scale offensive operations, we devised a campaign of surprise, with frequent daring raids by the KKA commandos of 4th Company behind Taliban lines. They hit several prisons in the Taliban-held densely populated zone on either side of the Helmand River, releasing thirty of our soldiers taken captive in one operation, sixty in another. Again this was a morale-booster as our troops began to realize that we cared about them.

Gaining in confidence, we planned to hit the Taliban in their effective capital, Musa Qala, way up in the desert in the north of Helmand, close to the central mountain range. The remoteness of the town gave the Taliban security. British and American forces had both failed to hold it, even during the years when there were hundreds of thousands of foreign troops in the country, and it had become a safe haven for drug dealers and weapons smugglers as well as the Taliban's al-Qaeda allies. The Taliban shadow minister for defense, Sadr Ibrahim, was known to spend a lot of time there.

Now that we had airport lighting we could reliably conduct night operations, and late one night around seventy men, including nearly all of our effective commando strength, set off for Musa Qala in four Mi-17s and two Black Hawks. Along with 4th Company, KKA, the force was made up of what was left of 10th Battalion, a specialist commando battalion attached to 215 Corps. It had started out in 2016 with 1200 men and was now reduced to around 100, showing the hammering the war had taken out of our best troops. The ground force assault team was KKA, while Commandos from 10th Battalion made the landing zone secure. With cover from a ScanEagle drone, and close air support from MD-530 attack helicopters and AC-208s, this was one of the most complex operations we conducted.

There were many moving parts, with four layers of airspace assigned for different aircraft operating in the same area. For me the most important part of the operation was to get all the boys back alive. Previous raids by both British and American special forces teams had sustained casualties. One advantage we had on our side was surprise. Since the Doha deal the Taliban would never have thought that we would attack them in Musa Qala. I watched images from the command center all night. The raid went like clockwork. We took the prison and repulsed wave after wave of Taliban attacks all night, as the prisoners were taken to safety in transport helicopters rotating in and out.

We were still holding Musa Qala bazaar at dawn, sending a powerful message to Taliban headquarters and their paymasters in Pakistan that we could operate at will and strike deep at their heart. I did not have the forces to hold Musa Qala, and it was a long way to the north of my area at the end of a vulnerable supply route, so we pulled out during the morning, but we had made the point.

The Taliban put sustained pressure on Maiwand, reversing our early successes at opening the road and surrounding the town. The desert town has a totemic importance in Afghan history as the scene of the defeat of a British invasion force in 1880—the biggest defeat of British forces on the battlefield during the whole period of their empire in Asia. It left us with a legendary heroine, Malalai Noorzai, "Malalai of Maiwand," who urged on the Afghan troops, picking up the flag when its bearer was killed and waving it as a battle standard before she was killed in her turn. This history gives Maiwand a mythical symbolic value out of proportion to its strategic location: all Afghans know that control of Maiwand is crucial to control of the south. The Taliban had been founded near here in 1994 as it was the home territory of their secretive leader, Mullah Omar. As part of the contest of wills, we needed to hold Maiwand.

Maiwand district was just beyond the border of my command area but came under Kandahar, and its weakness showed why it would have better for the whole south to be under one command. I called Major Gorzang, now deputy police chief for Kandahar in the neighboring 205 Corps, headquartered in Kandahar. He had been a close aide to my friend General Raziq, who was killed in 2019. When Gorzang landed in the center of Maiwand his helicopter came under attack and could not leave again. I arrived the next day, and my own helicopter took heavy fire from Taliban as we tried to land. We saw the black turbans of the Taliban firing up at us from positions in the open. The pilot hovered a little but agreed to land, and as soon as we were on the ground, our side gunners opened fire with heavy machine guns, giving us the ability to take control of our immediate surroundings.

We walked through empty streets, not knowing the location of the police headquarters. My troops jumped on one man in civilian clothes and were putting handcuffs on him when he said, "I am a police officer. I wanted to make myself known to you."

"That's great, so take us to police headquarters," I asked.

A few minutes later we were in the headquarters and made a plan to push conventional troops east from Helmand and west from Kandahar along Highway One to relieve Maiwand, and northeast from Lashkar Gah along Highway 601. After getting an assessment, I flew back to base, taking Major Gorzang with me. The next day we secured Maiwand bazaar, and troops connected with each other along Highway One in both directions. But we still faced threats from a region in the desert south of the main road, where a drug baron, Mullah Tawab, was paying the Taliban to fight against us. We had far more confidence to conduct our own night raids now, which in the past we could do only with American support. Commandos dropped at his home and killed everyone inside, including Tawab and two of his brothers, and that effectively ended opposition in the Maiwand region.

Whatever we did, though, our successes were not matched elsewhere in the country, and the Taliban were given a new lease of life when President Biden abandoned Afghanistan with his announcement in April of the final withdrawal date of August. He had been arguing for withdrawal since he was vice president in the Obama administration a decade before. As president he could finally deliver it.

Legitimized by the Trump deal at Doha, and now handed Afghanistan on a plate by Biden, the Taliban moved in strength across the country, backed by thousands of Pakistanis fighting alongside them. They had millions of dollars from Gulf backers to buy off whole Afghan tribes, taking much of the country with major deception operations and little resistance from Afghan forces who were exhausted, under-supplied, and felt abandoned.

Our winter success had foiled their battle plan to take the south first, so they concentrated on the north. And despite constant breaches of the commitments the Taliban had made at Doha, American troops continued to plan only for their own withdrawal. There was such powerful political pressure coming from Washington to get troops out that our partners reluctantly turned a blind eye to what they could see happening around them.

My US special forces detachment left at the beginning of May, two weeks after the president's announcement. Before they left they destroyed a huge amount of equipment. I could understand that they would not hand over computers, which might have contained sensitive information—these were destroyed with a sledgehammer. But it was harder to listen every day to them blowing up unused ammunition. Their orders were clear: "No ammunition to be handed over to partner forces." At a time when we were rationing every round, the sight of mortar shells being fired uselessly into the desert, one after another, was demoralizing.

The Americans themselves were desperately sorry to leave and had an emotional evening with some of my men, sharing stories of fights they had been in. Many had served multiple tours of Afghanistan, sacrificing time with their families to support us. There was a strong wind blowing as they took down the last American flag to fly over Helmand and folded it away, helping us mount a new flagpole to fly the Afghan flag over their part of the base. I felt more pressure than ever before that it was now down to me to hold southwestern Afghanistan together. I did not have time to reflect. The Taliban knew the date of the American departure as well as anybody.

ALL-OUT WAR

On May 2, the day after the last American left Helmand, and just after we had stabilized Maiwand and reopened the roads, the Taliban began their most sustained assault since I had taken command. They came in wave after wave, down from the mountains in the north, up from the south across the Baluch desert, but most directly from Pakistan to the east, well-armed and supported by the Pakistani army with what felt like a bottomless armory of rockets, artillery shells, and rounds for small arms. Later we heard that Iran, too, sent them weapons, including rocket-propelled grenades and mortar shells. Helmand was the epicenter of a hurricane that did not blow itself out. It felt like being in the grip of a mythical beast who never slept.

In the first twenty-four hours of the new Taliban offensive there were 194 separate attacks on Lashkar Gah and the other key strategic town, Gereshk. The campaign went on day and night without pause.

We destroyed unit after unit of incoming Taliban, with large numbers of Punjabi fighters loyal to AQIS among them.

It did not seem to quell the tide that they could see we were not the Afghan army they were defeating elsewhere in the country, where poorly led, poorly equipped troops were crumbling. My troops now had night vision goggles, sniper rifles, and were well fed and supplied with properly maintained vehicles, vital force multipliers because we had far less artillery and fewer aircraft than some other parts of the Afghan army. Helmand had always been at the end of the line when it came to the supply of heavy weapons and aircraft. I had only two Black Hawks and two MD-530 helicopters of my own. They cut through Taliban ranks where they could. But there were always more Taliban to come. And American air support had now all but gone.

Leaving Brigadier General Latif in charge of the Shorab headquarters I led from the front, in the operational mobile strike team. We would land in a Black Hawk and I would take my turn firing the heavy machine guns mounted on each side to give cover to pick up injured troops, killing Taliban commanders behind their lines, destroying their vehicles, and burning ammunition dumps. This gave confidence to my men, who became hardened warriors that year. They trusted me because I never lied to them. And I trusted them because I knew they would not collapse as some other parts of the Afghan army did that spring. If you take care of your men when they need you, they'll take care of you when you need them. It is human nature, and I saw how doing it right turned men into teams and teams into fighting machines.

The new Taliban assault was initially led by Mullah Talib, a religious fanatic who was one of those we were forced to release from jail against our will under the US deal with the Taliban at Doha. He had been arrested by 215 Corps in Sangin district of Helmand and was sent back to the battlefield. Ten days into the new campaign, we had halted the Taliban advance on Lashkar Gah and killed most of the Taliban tactical commanders. Through May and June we killed over 1500 Taliban fighters and injured hundreds more. But still they kept coming.

Every night I held a video conference with my five brigade commanders, wanting to hear what each was planning for the next twenty-four hours, so we kept up a relentless pressure across the whole area of operations, even as we came under attack as never before. They were all taking hits. Four of the brigades stood at 30 percent capacity, while the one in southern Helmand was at over 60 percent.

We carried out dozens of operations every night: ambushes, extra checkpoints, raids on houses, and artillery strikes, along with aggressive patrolling. Command Sergeant Major Mohibullah gave me daily reports of what the troops needed, and I made sure they got it. I drew down several hundred thousand dollars more from my business account to buy another batch of thermal scopes and sent them out to the police and other units. I bought civilian vehicles as basic troop carriers, paid to fix broken electricity lines, made payments to wounded soldiers, and bought food in the market for troops when our supplies failed. In those months it was all-out war of an intensity none of us had experienced before.

At the time I thought that once we had secured the south of Afghanistan, we would unite with Kabul and push the Taliban back elsewhere. I thought we would be in one hell of a fight for perhaps a year, but then we would get through it and clean up the country. For the southwest, I had no worries that we would prevail. I knew this was a hard fight, and thousands of people would die. But I saw victory at the end of it. And I felt like this needed to happen. Once the Afghan Army had won the war, then we could clean up Afghanistan. We had been failed by our political elites, but now we could remake the country. Each of the commanders who fought with me would be a role model for other commands across Afghanistan.

This is why men fought so hard. If I had thought we were going to lose, I would not have fought as I did. I was in this to win the war, and I gave it everything. No matter what they threw at me—and almost every day we had credible reports of suicide bombers on their way to target me—I would fight to the end. Once a car bomb did get through and exploded close to me. It would be more than a year until my hearing recovered. But despite the risks I felt the destiny of the nation in our hands. The dedication of army, police officers, and local young men in Lashkar Gah motivated me to stay with them and fight on.

The Taliban made it personal. Hashim Alokozay was the chairman of the armed services committee of the Afghan Senate, and a distant cousin of the Taliban defense minister, Sadr Ibrahim. He made many appearances on TV calling me a child killer, with wild claims that I dealt in drugs, was profiting from my command, had killed thousands of civilians, and destroyed property. Off air, behind the scenes, he used his influence to blacken my name to the president, calling on him to remove me because I was said to be needlessly sacrificing the lives of Afghan soldiers. The NDS director general told me he was paid by the Taliban to tell these lies. Some of the dirt stuck, and he damaged my reputation. But he did not succeed in having me removed from command.

The only pause in the fighting that year came in the three days of the Eid holiday in the middle of May, nearly two weeks after the Taliban onslaught began. In the past after such ceasefires, it had taken a few days for the momentum of the campaign to take off again. But this time it was going to be different. I maneuvered troops relentlessly during the ceasefire, carving up my region into three combat zones, and sent artillery shells and mortar rounds where they were needed. As the clock turned to zero hundred hours on the third day I launched an overnight offensive in all three zones, with A-29 attack planes coming from Kandahar in the east to pound Taliban positions. Among those we killed that night was a notorious Taliban Red Unit commander called Mullah Juma. We had watched him taking up new positions to launch an assault at the end of the ceasefire, but we pre-empted him and annihilated his force.

We kept on the offensive throughout May. I had learned that it was easier to attack first, instead of waiting to be hit. It meant we kept the initiative. But still the Taliban kept coming, and there were so many of them that inevitably they made ground. I was constantly on the move, carrying a backpack full of my own money to pay off informers, and supplying loyalists with weapons to hold off the Taliban.

We were now really feeling the lack of maintenance for our Black Hawk fleet. At the end of April, just as we were moving onto the offensive, we experienced the next stage in America's betrayal. I came out one morning to be told by my Black Hawk pilot that he could not fly because the contractors who kept his aircraft in the air had left overnight. They did not taper out or do a gradual handover. They all went. Our American partners said it was part of the Doha deal to pull out all contractors at the same time.

If we had some notice, we might have replaced them with contractors from eastern Europe or some other country that flew Black Hawks. We could do about 30 percent of the work needed on Black Hawks with our own engineers. But they had not been trained for some of the tasks. For weekly checks our Black Hawks now had to fly to Kabul, where there were just four hard-working Afghans trained to the level required. It meant four hours in the air, get the check, and then fly back next day. So we lost two days every week, and by the time the Black Hawks arrived back they had already burnt through eight hours of flight time.

There were nearly twice as many foreign contractors as foreign troops by 2021, and their loss was a serious blow to our ability to win. And we did not lose only aircraft engineers. We had been trained and configured to fight in the American way. That meant we needed software to keep in touch with our troops and their vehicles and to target missile systems, both for offense and defense. The special mission wing helicopters of 777 Brigade lost infrared radar and flare system to protect them from surface-to-air missiles. When the contractors went, we effectively lost the air superiority we had enjoyed. We lost surveillance from balloons and towers that protected bases, as well as more mundane, but nonetheless essential systems.

The ministry of defense lost several highly sophisticated software packages. One was an intelligence management system that managed the huge dataflow of information coming in round the clock, compartmentalizing it and classifying its secrecy level. Another software loss meant that we could no longer follow the GPS trackers fitted to every vehicle and aircraft as well as some individual soldiers. It needed constant maintenance and protection from cyberattacks. Our ScanEagle drone surveillance software was user-friendly and worked for a while, but that, too, began to fail as it needed constant maintenance and new sites where we were actually fighting to keep the system operational.

The cumulative effect was of an individual turned blind and deaf at the same time, and then asked to fight against an agile opponent. Since the fall of the republic, some people have said that it was a mistake to give us sophisticated systems. But they are wrong. We needed twenty-first-century kit to prevail, fighting a complex multifaceted war in a difficult country. America was right to equip us well as they could, but they should have anticipated the disastrous impact of the sudden pullout. Contractors were not in active combat zones but lived inside secure bases—Kabul, Kandahar, Mazar—that were under no threat until the very end of the republic. President Biden never mentioned that he would pull them all out in his April announcement ending American involvement.

It was around June 10 that the Taliban's next Helmand offensive began, to take the city of Gereshk, the crossroads of the province, where the main north/south road across Helmand met Highway One.

BATTLE OF GERESHK

By the time I arrived in Gereshk, most of the city had fallen to the Taliban, leaving our forces in isolated pockets in the governor's compound, and police and NDS headquarters. Before landing in the city, I first went north to Sangin, conducting hit-and-run raids behind Taliban lines, following intelligence. Each time we landed we killed groups of Taliban fighters who were preparing to advance on Gereshk. From the air, we followed one car driving fast towards Sangin, which stopped at a house on our approach. We flew low and saw three men jump out of the vehicle carrying AK-47 rifles. Two rushed inside for safety. The third, a big man with a black turban, also carrying a rifle, ran round the back in an attempt to hide. Hovering just two feet from the ground, we fired through the dust cloud kicked up by the helicopter and killed him. After landing in front of the house my KKA troops went inside and killed other people. We seized weapons, Pakistani cash, and equipment, including thermal scopes. After taking off again we moved to a final house where we landed and destroyed nine vehicles. Our second Black Hawk pilot who was circling then radioed that he had been hit.

"Can you land?" I shouted back. His voice was steady, although he did not know if he was badly wounded.

"Yes, I can. But we have very little fuel."

As he landed, more Taliban appeared, firing rocket-propelled grenades in our direction. Fortunately none exploded near the helicopter. The pilot found he had a scratch with a little bleeding on his neck. We returned to Camp Shorab to refuel and check the helicopters. Both had taken hits but there was no serious damage.

Although the pilot had been millimeters away from death, he brushed off my suggestion that he take time off, and with no delay we flew to the center of Gereshk. When we landed the governor and police chief were laughing.

"We are listening to Taliban radios, and they are all leaving."

It turned out that in one of the raids we had killed three of their district governors, who had gathered for the assault on Gereshk from towns across the north of Helmand. Our raid behind their lines had decapitated the command, and leaderless troops abandoned their positions across the city. Nothing scared the Taliban more than gunfire behind their backs.

"And there's another thing, sir," said the governor.

"What's that?" I said.

"They know it was Sami Sadat carrying out those raids."

"So what are you waiting for?" I asked. "Do you need me to tell you to do everything? Press home the advantage and retake lost ground. Begin by clearing lines of communication between our key bases so we can move at will."

Not all the Taliban had gone. As we drove out we came under attack, and my vehicle was hit with mortar rounds. But we fought them off and retook the city. Gereshk mattered to me not only for its strategic location, but because it was a civilized and developed part of the south. The people were very pro-government and wanted their daughters educated as well as their sons. Helmand was not the backward place of Taliban imagination, and this was one of the signs of that. I spent a week there, ensuring that we had reasserted our authority. I wanted to keep it in our hands. When I returned to Lashkar Gah, the governor held a meeting with tribal elders, putting a turban on my head as a mark of esteem.

There were lots of very young men in the crowd at the ceremony, teenagers carrying polished assault rifles, almost as status symbols, that did not look as if they had seen combat use. We were going to need them in the battles to come. We were recruiting new soldiers all the time, and I had cut the basic training period down from three months to twelve days. But we needed the whole population on our side. I appointed a key powerbroker, Abdur Rahman Jan, as head of a brigade. He was sixty-five years old and knew the tribal dynamics of Helmand better than anyone. He was a divisive figure, marginalized by our American and British partners who did not trust him. But I knew that in the tribal power play that underpinned the battles between the government and the Taliban, he was on the government side. And it turned out to be a good appointment as his men held their positions until the end.

And my other conventionally appointed commanders were taking sick leave. My deputy, Colonel Musazai, who had been in Gereshk when it came under attack, requested time off to see a doctor and did not come back. My executive officer, a key role in any command, Brigadier General Latif, also took time to see a doctor in Kabul. The war was hard on all of us, and we were all exhausted and tired, but when they left they never returned. These absences meant I was stretched even more, relying more on my civilian adviser, Reza Sarwary, to do the important administration in headquarters, while I was out every day, fighting an increasingly tough campaign.

My own command appointments were not confirmed by Kabul, but I carried on. I had the legal right to appoint someone for 90 days without confirmation. Apart from Abdur Rahman Jan, I mostly promoted younger officers who had proved themselves in the field, showing courage, dedication, and bravery. The two youngest were colonel Javed Salim, my most loyal commander, who took 4th Brigade in Dilaram in the west, and Haitullah Ahmadzai, who now commanded 3rd Brigade in Gereshk. Massoom Sadat took 1st Brigade in Garmsir in the south, and colonel Jawid Naderi commanded 2nd Brigade in Sangin in the north. By June 2021, Helmand was the only place in Afghanistan where the Taliban were still facing a hard fight, as so much of the rest of the country had collapsed. Soldiers and officers wanted to join me in the fight, which I still thought we could win, and then reclaim the rest of Afghanistan.

BATTLE OF LASHKAR GAH

At the end of June we needed to shore up the defenses of Lashkar Gah again. The Taliban had penetrated the west of the city, and once again we pushed them back. They had developed a new weapon, hanging explosives under a small gas-filled balloon and then hurling them towards us with a catapult. If the explosives detonated they would ignite the gas and then burn everything around them. Some days about one hundred of these improvised weapons would come across our lines, the sound of the boom as they ignited crashing across the city.

We were now facing renewed onslaughts across the province. All four brigades were already fully committed round the clock when the Taliban began a new campaign way down in the southwestern desert in Nimruz province, three hundred kilometers from Lashkar Gah. We had no spare capacity, so I flew down there myself and prepared a ground assault, using conventional forces, with my KKA team as usual carrying out daring commando raids to rock the Taliban on their axis. I wanted to show them that there was nowhere in my region that they could operate without facing an attack from us. Just after I arrived I had an unexpected call from Camp Shorab. An anti-corruption team had appeared at Garmsir in the south of my region, on the trail of some vehicles and other equipment that American forces had left behind in Camp Dwyer. Not content with calling me a murderer daily on live TV, my enemies had spread a rumor that I had taken the vehicles for my own use.

My staff were furious, swearing down the phone and saying they would shoot them or lock them up.

"Don't do that," I said. "Send them to Camp Dwyer to see for themselves." I sent a reliable officer to accompany them, and they found everything as it had been when the Americans left, including fuel, apart from twelve vehicles I had given to commanders in Lashkar Gah to replace those damaged in the fighting.

After dealing with this distraction, I flew 150 miles to Nimruz, a province in the far west of the region, on the Iranian border, the location of the Taliban's next advance. It was now 120 degrees for most of the day in this all-desert province, and we could hardly breathe. Having the energy to walk while wearing body armor was a tough trial, let alone fighting. We covered our heads with makeshift turbans and poured water over ourselves when we could. But it was tough for the Taliban as well, and after some days we recovered the lost district, inflicting severe casualties on the Taliban.

When we were back within cellphone coverage the president called me. It was a surreal moment in the searing heat of the Nimruz desert.

"General, I am sitting here with the National Security Council around me."

"Yes, sir. Please go ahead. How can I help?"

"I have heard that an investigation team has been to investigate you and your staff."

"Yes, Mister President, they have done their job and returned to Kabul two days ago. I hope you have read their report."

"You should have arrested these guys and detained them in the worst dungeon you have. Nobody should mess with my war commanders, and you are a respected man. We're very proud of you. I'm grateful for everything you're doing. This is wrong, and nobody should mess with the Afghan army." I did not catch the rest of what he said as he started yelling.

"Mister President," I replied, when the yelling had stopped. "There was clearly some confusion or misunderstanding in Kabul. I'm very happy that this is now fixed. However, I have a request."

"Go ahead," he said. "I will provide anything you need."

"I want you to see and interrogate the person who made these accusations. That is who should be brought to justice."

"Absolutely," said the president. "I will do it right away."

I knew that the order had come directly from him. Nobody would send such a team into an active military headquarters without signoff from the top. And that was confirmed when Amrullah Saleh, now vice president, called me an hour later. When he had heard of the investigation, he complained to the president, and Saleh said the president had used his exact words when he called me.

"I told him this is not the way we should treat our war generals. Sami Sadat could be dead today or tomorrow. The president just repeated what I said."

"Well, thank you," I said. "I figured someone must have got to the president to make him change his mind like that." And from then on, until the end of the republic, Saleh was a supportive voice in the presidential palace, pushing for what we needed, and helping me fight against the bureaucracy.

But by now there was too much against us to win. We had done what we could to hold onto Nimruz, but two weeks later, the whole province fell to the Taliban, the first permanent loss in my region. And then the president's deeply inexperienced and incompetent national security adviser, Hamdullah Mohib, began to make disastrous appointments that weakened our ability to resist. The first of these was the removal of General Yasin Zia, one of the best commanders of the new generation, as chief of the general staff. He was replaced by General Wali Ahmadzai, a corrupt and drug-addicted relic of the past. I had succeeded Ahmadzai in Helmand, although I never called him out as I could have done for the corruption I discovered when I took over.

The reason for the change in a number of top jobs was growing paranoia from the president that he may be under personal threat. For much of his time in office he had promoted his own cronies to senior positions, rather than people promoted on merit. Now it was not enough to be cronies: they needed to be fully loyal. Ghani did not fear a military collapse, he feared a military coup, and rather than worrying about whether we could defeat the Taliban and protect the republic he thought only of his own skin. Never forget that his full name is Ashraf Ghani *Ahmadzai*, and he was putting tribal Ahmadzai allies into key positions, pulling the wagons into an ever-smaller circle—revealing the hypocrisy of his claim to legitimacy as a democratically elected leader. He lacked the human warmth and empathy that was needed for good tribal politics. He always felt more like a guest lecturer than the leader of the country.

I never played tribal politics myself. As a Sadat, a direct descendant of the Prophet Muhammad, I had no tribe. My mother was a Tajik from Badakhshan in the northeast, but my upbringing was in Pashtun Helmand, so I was not identified with any tribe or interest. I had myself appointed an Ahmadzai, Colonel Haitullah, to command in Gereshk, the second most important brigade in my region, not because of any tribal connections to the president, but his military ability.

The Ahmadzai who now became chief of the general staff was a retread, a reminder of Afghanistan's failure in past campaigns. Whatever morale remained among younger officers, it drained away when such incompetent figures were put into the top jobs.

General Ahmadzai resented my appointments in Helmand, which had sidelined his people, and as soon as he was put at the top of the army he did what he could to undermine my authority. He ordered the recall of 4th Company KKA, the unit I had brought to Helmand as my bodyguard. As well as that task, they were the most effective commando force in the country, as I had proved in numerous operations with them. I appealed to my friend General Haibatullah Alizai, commander of Afghan special forces, but there was nothing he could do. I immediately felt vulnerable and was far more exposed whenever I moved out of the base. Then I discovered I could no longer call in air support, particularly at night. We were now the most active war zone in the country, but after Ahmadzai arrived we received the least air support. One of the reasons Nimruz fell was because of the lack of air cover, and we felt it keenly. Sometimes night-capable MD-530 helicopters would be heading our way from their base in Kandahar before being recalled when Ahmadzai heard where they were going.

He issued contradictory orders to me, sending me to three different locations on the same day. I ignored them and did what I needed to do. But it was a distracting contest over authority that had a material effect on our ability to fight.

One night we were evacuating a base in Nad Ali, where 160 troops were surrounded by the Taliban. I had called in KKA troops from Kandahar to carry out the operation, who came in helicopters from 777 Brigade, the special mission wing. They needed to establish a helicopter landing zone, then secure a corridor for the troops to leave. They came under fierce attack, taking casualties as soon as they landed. They made it to the district center and brought the small force out to a helicopter landing zone. But the first helicopter that attempted an approach was forced down in an emergency landing, badly damaged by Taliban gunfire. The second helicopter landed briefly, only long enough to take out the pilots, leaving the damaged helicopter behind.

I got a call from the 777 commander.

"Sami, we are requesting that your troops protect the helicopter until the morning, when we can retrieve it."

"Do you know where this helicopter is?" I said. "It was shot down and any attempt to remain with it or recover it will cost lives. If they remained to guard it, every soldier would be dead by morning. I am not going to sacrifice my men for your helicopter."

It did not stop there. The next call came from the chief of the general staff, the useless General Ahmadzai.

"My orders are that your troops protect that Mi-17 at all costs, because I need it fixed by tomorrow."

"If I obey, that will put my soldiers at risk of death. In fact they may anyway be dead by the morning because they are in grave danger, and then you can hang me later. Right now I'm going to burn this Mi-17." And I cut the call.

The KKA pushed ammunition inside the helicopter, but the fighting got so intense they could not get close enough again to set it alight, so they rerouted to the emergency landing zone, three kilometers away. The remaining helicopter could still not land because of incoming fire, so they walked another four kilometers to a second emergency landing zone, navigating through the night while carrying two casualties, one dead and one wounded. They made it successfully and by dawn were all returned to Camp Shorab after three rescue flights shuttled in and out to collect them.

I ordered MD-530s to go back and destroy the downed helicopter. They shot several rockets, and it was destroyed. The next day an investigation team came to ask the cause of the crash and who had ordered the mission. After they made their report, I found that I was now liable for a bill of $30 million for destroying a helicopter against the orders of my superiors. I was past caring.

All the arguments about losing a helicopter obscured the main issue. Nad Ali was not a long drive from the center of Lashkar Gah. If we were withdrawing from there, then the Taliban really were at the gates of the provincial capital they wanted most. And by July they could sense victory. Any time I went out we had credible reports of suicide bombers in vehicles searching for me. I began to receive daily calls from worried Americans telling me to leave. I could not take one call from an American friend who was an adviser to the new American commander in the country, Rear Admiral Peter Vasely, because I was in a firefight to the north of Lashkar Gah. He sent a message, which read,

"Sami, there are four reasons why you might not leave. One, you want to die fighting for Lashkar Gah; two, you are not leaving because you don't have orders; three, you can not leave because you think you will die leaving; and four, you are not answering my call to just tell me to fuck off. Which one of these four is correct?"

I replied with a one-line message: "It's one. I will die fighting here."

That led to Vasely going directly to the president to request that I should be taken out of Lashkar Gah immediately as I had a death wish. The president had seen the rest of the country collapsing, and knew we were still just holding out. He called in the key security ministers, interior, defense, and the NDS, for their advice. They all agreed that the surrender of Lashkar Gah was only a matter of time, and it would be better to pull troops out now to prevent further loss of life.

"What does Sami Sadat say?" asked the president.

"We haven't spoken to him yet on this," said the minister of defense, Bismillah Khan Muhammadi.

The president said, "I will leave it to him. The fate of Helmand rests on the decision of Sami Sadat. Whatever he decides, that's my decision. Go talk to him."

I was called the next day for a video conference with the three security ministers. On my side were the chief of police, governor, and director of NDS for Helmand.

I had been staying in Lashkar Gah all the time by then. We would have lost the city if I had left. They told me that their advice was that it was time to leave, but the president left the final decision to me.

"So now it's up to you, Sami, whether you leave or stay." I had known Bismillah Khan a long time and I could hear the emotion in his voice. A tough fighter from the 1980s generation, he became minister of defense for the second time in the spring of 2021 when Asadullah Khalid's health prevented him from carrying on.

The pressure of the decision was overwhelming.

"I am not going to take a decision to leave and go down in history as the man who abandoned Lashkar Gah to the Taliban. I'm going to fight to my death before they take the city."

They asked the chief of police what he would do, and we were all getting emotional as he said, "Sami is our leader. If he's not leaving, I'm not leaving either."

The governor was next. "I would like to die with Sami here in the city. We cannot leave the city."

"I've never seen such courage. God bless you," said Bismillah Khan. We will do what we can to support your decision." And we continued to fight into July, as thousands upon thousands of Taliban fighters were thrown at our positions, which became increasingly isolated. We lost most of the city, but still held key locations—the airfield, police headquarters, NDS, and the governor's compound. And we could not move out on the ground.

We still held important strategic sites across the province—Gereshk and Sangin all the way up to Kajaki, as well as Dilaram in the west and Garmsir in the south. And as word of my stand spread, hundreds of the best troops in the country went to their headquarters and requested a transfer to Helmand. It was the most moving demonstration of bravery and pride in the nation you could ever witness. The army was collapsing everywhere except for our last stand. When some air force pilots were refused permission to transfer, they went on strike and said that if they could not fly under my command they would not fly at all. So in the next five days I got some of the best Afghan pilots for the A-29 attack planes, Mi-17 helicopters, and night-capable MD-530s. They included the best Afghan special forces pilots, like Colonel Khalid Amiri and some of my other close friends.

General Alizai moved his special forces control room into my operation in Lashkar Gah. He is a good friend and one of the bravest men I know. He is the same age as me, and had a similar career, graduating from the UK command course a few years after me and spending time at the NDS. He is one of life's optimists, seeing opportunity not threat in every challenge. His men loved him. He is a Pashtun from northern Helmand, but ethnically neutral, the best advert for the new Afghanistan. He literally saved my life coming to Helmand, bringing the strength of the commandos to buttress our fightback.

Through the end of July into August we carried out a sustained campaign that rocked the Taliban backwards, killing hundreds and restoring our ability to move to the airport and the other strategic locations we still held. We linked up with Abdur Rahman Jan's border forces to the west. Morale was good; we were all convinced once again that we could prevail, and the confidence was infectious. We had intelligence that Amir Khan Muttaqi, who would later become the Taliban's acting minister of foreign affairs, had turned up in northern Helmand to appeal to tribal leaders to send their sons to fight because the Taliban were running out of reinforcements. I tried to fix on him for an air strike, but he escaped.

We had proved that we could fight successfully without American support, and despite all the obstacles thrown in my way, I had successfully retaken a provincial capital. This could be the springboard for a national fightback. But by the second week of August, events rapidly moved out of our control.

Chapter Eleven

TWELVE DAYS IN AUGUST (9–20 AUGUST 2021)

Hamdullah Mohib's tone was light. "So, Sami, how are things going in 215 Corps? I have good news for you." It was Monday, August 9, the beginning of what would turn out to be the last week of the Afghan republic. I still thought we could hold the country for a fightback and wanted him to share that confidence. Mohib was a weak man, appointed only for his unquestioning loyalty to President Ashraf Ghani, ineffectual and worse, interfering, as a national security adviser.

"We're winning here," I said. "Just hold on elsewhere and we can fight off the Taliban advance."

"I'm very happy to hear that." He paused, expecting me to ask what the good news was. His tone was of someone passing the time of day, not instructing a general in a war zone.

"I'm glad to talk to you," he said. "The guy you hate most will be fired by end of today."

"Who's that?" I asked.

"General Ahmadzai. He's out as chief of the general staff."

"So who's coming in?"

The constant reshuffling of people at the top had unnerved the army. Neither the president nor his national security adviser had any military knowledge or experience. They compensated for their lack of strategic understanding by attempting to micromanage army affairs, destabilizing the ministry of defense to its core. I guess I should have expected that this change at the top would not be any better than the last. But even I was surprised by the answer.

"General Zabi Mohmand."

"You mean the Zabi Mohmand who lost all the territory in Herat to the Taliban, who you appointed to command 209 Corps in the north literally three days ago? The same guy?"

There was silence on the line, then he replied, "Yes, that's him."

I was past trying to show respect. "Mohib, fuck that. If you're always going to find another old communist to put in charge of our army, then why have us fight at all? If that's your best appointment then you are looking for another commander to come and take over 215 Corps, because I will not be fighting under Zabi Mohmand."

I could see no sense in it. First Ahmadzai who was from the same tribe as the president, and now Mohmand, who was from the same hometown as Mohib: it seemed they did not care about the impact of such major appointments but were interested only in keeping hold of the army. Mohmand had proved his incompetence. They were swapping one tribal ally for another, with no improvement in what we so urgently needed—capable direction at the top.

"Well, Sami, we understand your frustration. But the president is confused."

What he said next showed just how far he and the president were from any grip on reality. It turned out that General Haibatullah Alizai and I were both in the frame to be appointed chief of general staff. He was currently head of Afghan special forces, which had absorbed JSOC, the Joint Special Operations Command I had established to coordinate the war. Alizai had moved his command center to Helmand to support my operations, and he was sitting alongside me on the call. According to Mohib, the president thought I would be upset if he appointed Alizai, and Alizai in his turn would be unhappy if I got the top job; he was treating the role of head of the Afghan army like a high school talent contest.

"Look, please go and tell the president to appoint General Alizai," I told Mohib. He was making a problem where there was none.

"I'm happy to serve under General Alizai. He's from our generation. He thinks like us, and the army, from its top commanders to the newest recruits, will follow him. Nobody trusts General Mohmand. He is from three generations ago, and our young soldiers have no idea who he is."

Alizai spoke up. "Doctor Mohib, I had a discussion in Kabul last week with the commander of the Afghan air force, the director of operations, and the director of military intelligence. There was no disagreement. We all accepted Sami to be the next chief of the general staff because we respect him and see him as a natural leader."

I knew the president would not want to hear this. To the end he did not trust me. And half an hour later Mohib called Alizai to appoint him as chief of the general staff while I was to take over special forces. I knew that once the news was out he would come under even more severe threat, as suicide bombers would want to kill the head of the army. Alizai flew late night to Camp Shorab, and the following morning, Tuesday, August 10, he flew to Kabul.

I planned to follow him to take over his role as head of special forces but was faced with a stream of resignations by WhatsApp. They came from commanders across the 215 Corps region—from Abdur Rahman Jan, the tribal powerbroker I had put in charge of the border brigade, to conventional commanders I had appointed in the field when they proved capable. Their message was simple. "If you're leaving, no one else will fight."

I spent the morning calling each of them to convince them that I could do more for them as head of special forces with the capacity to call in air support. Now that General Ahmadzai had gone, there would be no obstacle to us moving from Helmand to retake the south.

I told each of them, "I am appointing Javed Salim to command the corps. I want you to work under his leadership." He was the best of my brigade commanders, who had proved himself in combat time and again.

But the change of leadership knocked away a vital pillar of morale. They knew I had a plan to capitalize on our success in Lashkar Gah by garrisoning the city. I had five hundred soldiers in reserve, ready to take on police roles. But like air slowly coming out of a tire, our soldiers lost their belief in their ability to win. I had inspired them to great things, but if I was leaving, they took other choices. My command sergeant major, the lightning rod of the view of the soldiers, said that there was a general view that the government was removing me from this command in order to hand over the province. The troops heard the news of Taliban advances across the country and were no longer willing to fight, as they thought of their families and their future. Despite the advances we had made in previous weeks, on the morning of Wednesday, August 11, I took the tough decision to abandon Lashkar Gah and pull back to Camp Shorab.

The news had a domino effect across the province. Without any orders, officers in 3rd Brigade in Gereshk began to load up their own vehicles to head for safety in Camp Shorab. Realizing he had effectively lost control, the commander ordered a general evacuation of the base. They made it to Shorab without much fighting on the way.

We made plans to leave Lashkar Gah, commandeering civilian vehicles. We had taken so many hits that we had only one functioning armored Humvee and four military strike vehicles left. The police headquarters had been hit the week before with a huge bomb at the gates, causing many casualties, and the survivors were in our base in the governor's compound.

A young officer, Nasrullah Alizai, standing in for the police commander injured in the blast, came up with a proposal.

"Sir, are you planning to fight your way out?"

"Yes," I said. "There's no other way."

"Don't you think that if the Taliban hear that Sami Sadat is leaving Lashkar Gah they will garland your way with flowers?"

I did not like the sound of any kind of deal. I did not trust the Taliban. But I gave him permission to sound them out. He approached an elder, Haji Ahmed, who I had known all my life. He was a friend of the family from my childhood, so I trusted him. Ahmed spoke directly to Mullah Yaqoob, one of the most senior Taliban commanders, the son of the founder, Mullah Omar. His initial response was a mirror of mine. "Can we trust Sami Sadat?"

Negotiations went on through the day, and by evening it looked as if Nasrullah had made a deal. Mullah Yaqoob ordered that no units would attack us as we moved to Camp Shorab, and I demanded that they remove all the improvised explosive devices on the road. We intercepted his orders and he followed them to the letter, telling his men that if even a land mine left over from the Russian war exploded, then Sami Sadat would call in air strikes on every Taliban position.

The plan was that the conventional forces would travel by road, a journey of some four hours, while Alizai's special forces would go to the airfield on the edge of town and helicopters would ferry them to Camp Shorab. We started after nightfall, and there were no incidents, except that the roads were full of Taliban getting in the way and shouting at our troops. This slowed the move, and around 11:00 p.m., I threatened to call in air strikes to get the Taliban away. The Taliban called Nasrullah and promised to back off. They suggested that we stop overnight and travel by day, but I did not want them to have videos of our departure for propaganda and insisted we keep going.

Once all the forces had left the governor's compound, our last redoubt in Lashkar Gah, I walked with the governor to a helicopter, holding hands in the dark as I had the only pair of night vision goggles. I remained awake most of the night to see all the vehicles into Camp Shorab.

On the morning of Thursday, August 12, Javed Salim arrived with his brigade from Dilaram in the west. We had negotiated a three-day ceasefire with the Taliban for the moves, and I told Nasrullah to pass on to the Taliban that we were going to hold onto our remaining bases beyond that. We may have left from the provincial capital, but in addition to Shorab, we still held Kajaki and Sangin in the north of the province, and Garmsir in the south. If they attacked any of those positions I would bomb their new headquarters in Lashkar Gah. They accepted quickly. We had caused huge casualties on their side in the battle of Lashkar Gah, during the weeks when the best troops in the country had come alongside me to show what the Afghan army could do. The Taliban were tired and had no fight left in them in Helmand.

Around midnight I flew to Kabul in a PC-12, a small cargo plane that was one of the workhorses of the war. In the early hours of Friday, August 13, I landed close to the JSOC headquarters I had set up the previous year and walked five minutes across the airstrip to the office to go straight to work.

The team were busy all night, ensuring that there were no compromises of electronic security as bases collapsed and disconnecting the surveillance systems so the Taliban could not use them. I had asked the staff to prepare a briefing, and it could not have been much worse. One after another, all the corps commands outside Kabul, except for my base in Camp Shorab, had fallen. As they collapsed, special forces commandos were scattered, and JSOC had lost touch with around 80 percent of them. Some units were still said to be fighting in isolated pockets, but we lacked the means to support them and lost vital streams of intelligence. In the north, hundreds of commandos had crossed the river into safety in Uzbekistan.

"So what's the plan for Kabul?" I asked, sitting in the large pine-walled office I knew so well, with a map on the table marked with black chinagraph which told the whole grim story. The Taliban were at the gates, and the Afghan army was scattered and in disarray.

"General Alizai has brought what troops could move back from the corps headquarters as they fell," the briefer said. "The plan is for each corps to be reconfigured under whatever commanders remain. They will be responsible for a single sector of the defense of Kabul." And he pointed on the map to where 217 Corps would go to the north of the city, 205 Corps to the south, and so on.

Beyond Kabul, a lot of ground was still in our hands, including the eastern gateway from Sarobi. This was the route the Taliban had taken into Kabul when they last entered the city in 1996. But the troops who were holding that perimeter lacked supplies and had been fighting for months without relief. Alizai planned layered defense, supported by special operations commando raids, to give the capital city its best fighting chance of survival.

I slept little that night, aware of the responsibilities that lay ahead. It was not all over. Bismillah Khan Muhammadi, an experienced warrior with more than three decades experience, was still minister of defense, and General Alizai was the best we could have as chief of general staff. At first light on Friday, August 13, I met them in the ministry, where they outlined the plans: the layers of defense around the capital and concentration of forces at all the entry points. There was a large concentration of government defense assets in Kabul in the NDS and armed police, and most of the air force had now flown in from regional air bases.

My role was about to become a whole lot more complicated.

When I arrived back at JSOC, my political adviser, Reza Sarwary, shared some news that had just been announced on Twitter. I had been put in overall command of the defense of Kabul. I was furious, with Mohib for just putting it on Twitter without telling me; for the two men I had just met who must have known and did not say anything; and most of all, I was mad at the president for handing me such a pile of steaming manure. The entire Afghan defense establishment had failed, and they were using my popularity to cover up their mistakes while they planned their own routes out of the country. I was being made the fall guy. If it all went wrong, that would be OK, because it would be Sami Sadat's fault.

I called Alizai. "Why didn't you tell me five minutes ago in your office?"

"It was the Americans' idea," he said. "They told the president they needed one guy in charge of overall security."

I knew I could not turn it down because it was already public. That was the reason for the Twitter announcement. I also knew that if I asked any of my friends they would say I had to do it. There was no one else who could give confidence to the army and air force to believe that all was not lost. Kabul might fall even if I took the job. If I did not, it would certainly fall.

Building on Alizai's plans, I set about organizing quick reaction forces across the city who could respond if one of the defense lines was breached or if the Taliban succeeded in sabotage or inciting a riot. These new forces were supplemented by students and instructors from the special operations school, which I now ordered to be closed.

I had another troubled night. Some shrapnel had cut into my upper body when a mortar shell exploded nearby during the last days in Helmand. I had not told anyone about it because I thought that would damage morale, and I was changing the bandage alone every night. But the pain and infection were getting worse. I could sleep only on one side. On the morning of Saturday, August 14, I went to see my friend Matin Bek. He was loyal to President Ghani at the time and worked as his chief of staff, although he later regretted it. I had been out of Kabul for some time and wanted to get a sense of the politics. There was a lot of activity at the airport as planes returned from around the country. But I ordered that all routine activity for commandos must stop as we prepared the layers of defense for the city. I even issued rifles to the cooks, drivers, and cleaners to be ready to operate as a quick reaction force.

I had come from Helmand where we were fighting all the time. I had no space in my head for any talk of reconciliation, power-sharing, or surrender. We had good men on the ground, including three commando battalions, who were the best troops not just in Afghanistan, but across the region. One was in Kapisa province, protecting the northeast of the city, one was the KKA quick reaction force in Kabul, and the third was still down in Camp Shorab. And there were two thousand NDS special strike forces holding defensive lines in the south of the city.

In the evening I was called to suppress a riot in Pul-e-Charkhi, the large prison to the east of Kabul. This was not the job of special forces soldiers, but reluctantly I sent a unit of KKA troops to put down the riot. I was working until 2:00 a.m., talking to survivors of the fall of Mazar and Herat who were now in Kabul and talking to units around the country where we still had contact.

On Sunday, August 15, I planned to start the day with a coordination meeting for all the security chiefs who would be responsible for the defense of the city. The first sign that this might not be a normal day was when there was no one there either from the NDS or Kabul police. The meeting was short. I had a clear plan I wanted to share. I appointed Lieutenant General Habib Hisari, the chief of staff at the MOD, as head of the joint command center coordinating the campaign at JSOC, and I told all the heads of different security services to relocate to JSOC. I said it was important to avoid misunderstandings and confusion in the city, and we needed unity of command.

After the meeting I went to talk to the media who were waiting outside the office. I explained the new command structure and, looking down the barrel of a TOLO TV news camera, I said, "I'm asking the citizens of Kabul not to be scared. We'll fight and we'll protect you and the city. I can assure you that every soldier will do their utmost to make sure that Kabul city is protected and you live safely. I'm asking you not to create confusion and not make unnecessary journeys so we can keep the roads clear for security forces."

It was a brief statement and I took no questions. The head of American forces in the country, Rear Admiral Peter Vasely, had called a meeting at short notice just after mine. I asked Alizai to brief me on what was said. But since my meeting was so short, I set out down the airport road, less than a mile to the American headquarters, to join the end of Vasely's meeting. We could hardly get out of the airport, let alone to the American base; the roads were already clogged with cars, loaded up with household goods as people headed out of the city. So I walked back into the base, abandoning the plan to join the American meeting. That afternoon I planned to travel to Camp Morehead, the special forces headquarters in the south of the city, and went over to 777 Brigade, the special mission wing, to secure a helicopter. The commander, General Ziarmal, was sitting down to lunch and asked me to join him. General Yasin Zia, the former chief of general staff, was with him. He was in civilian clothes and I was surprised to see him.

"What are you doing here?" I asked.

"Just coming to check on you guys," Zia said.

"I heard you were in London."

"I returned a couple of days ago."

It was a strangely casual conversation given the events unfolding around us. We had a quick lunch and then I walked out to a helicopter. A lot of pilots were there wanting selfies.

"Hey, sir. Welcome back. Glad to see you're alive," they shouted. Some were emotional. It had been the toughest time any of us could remember.

Before I boarded the helicopter I called General Hisari, now in operational command at JSOC, to hear the latest. He said that some tribal leaders had approached our defenses in the east of the city and asked the men to surrender. I told Hisari to go and assess what was going on, then join me on my visit to the south of the city. As I was walking towards the helicopter, my cellphone rang.

It was 1:45 p.m. on Saturday, August 15.

"Sami, where are you?" It was Asadullah Khalid.

"I'm in Kabul. In my headquarters."

"Sami, I have just heard that the president has fled the country."

I felt as if the ground had fallen away beneath me and I was flying unaided into a clear blue sky on a journey without maps.

"I need to check it. But I trust the guy who told me."

Khalid was a serious man, and he would not bullshit me. "Listen, Sami. Listen hard. What if he has really gone? What are you going to do?"

I had no hesitation in answering that.

"I will secure the presidential palace and announce martial law."

He must have thought I would do something like that. That is why he called me.

"Are you out of your mind?" he said. "That's crazy. Nobody's fighting anymore. Across the country they've all given up. You can't hold the palace on your own. You need to make a plan for yourself. The country's finished."

"Well, call me if you hear anything else." I cut the call and walked back to JSOC.

The helicopters that went to take out the president and his closest staff must have left from the airport while I was having lunch. But in all of the other movement, nobody noticed.

Rumors spread quickly. The president was in the US embassy, he had come to JSOC HQ, he was already across the border in Tashkent. That third rumor turned out to be true. Order fell apart. Across Kabul there were reports of police throwing down their weapons, putting on civilian clothes, and leaving their posts. I sent a trusted KKA unit to go out and see what was happening—and collect any discarded weapons on their way.

I instructed all bases to close their gates and block all access. I effectively declared martial law, ordering that anyone engaged in sabotage, such as pulling down our flag or raising a Taliban flag, should be immediately shot. And that included senior members of the Afghan army. But it was unclear if anyone heard it. My team tried to bring order out of chaos, working the phones as things collapsed around us. They began to lose contact with army units, one after another. I tried to get hold of the vice president, Amrullah Saleh, and install him as president ahead of making a public announcement to try to control the chaos inside the city, but he was nowhere to be found. At around 4:00 p.m. General Fahim Ramin, the head of the air force, came in with the chief of general staff, General Alizai, along with two other senior commanders.

"What are you doing here?" I asked.

"Well, you know, everything is screwed up since the president fled," said Alizai.

"Are you kidding? So how will we get out of this if you are not at your posts? You should be in the MOD, and you, Fahim, in air force headquarters."

Alizai said "Sami, there's no one in the MOD. There's no one trying to control anything. It's over."

"We're not going to let this happen," I said.

"Brother, what are you going to do alone? Let's go together."

I drove with Alizai to the palace. I had a standoff with a couple of presidential security guards standing at the gate, at one point drawing my pistol. They called on the radio and were given permission to let us in. "It's OK," said the guard. "I know you're Sami Sadat." It turned out that they had orders to shoot anyone trying to enter apart from the Taliban. The orders came from Masoom Stanekzai, the former head of the NDS and recently a top government negotiator with the Taliban. He was the man whose life I had saved the night that former president Burhanuddin Rabbani was killed. He had told them not allow anyone into the palace except the Taliban.

We found no one inside, and it was the same story in the MOD next across the street. We raced down the half mile of the still-secure street linking the Afghan seats of power to the American base. Inside, Rear Admiral Peter Vasely was waiting with a couple of his officers. In the situation awareness room, there were pictures on the big screen coming from multiple sources across the city that told the whole story. It was chaos everywhere.

In his meeting that morning Vasely had announced that three thousand American troops were on their way.

"I want American patrols out on the streets," I said. "That's the only way to restore confidence among my troops that their partners are here."

"I can't do that, Sami. You don't have a government anymore. Who are you fighting for?"

That hit me hard. I was fighting for principles, for a republic. If the president had abandoned it, we would not give it up.

Vasely did not share my view. "My orders are to evacuate this base and go to the airport. The extra troops are here only to enable our orderly departure. It's over. And there's a seat on the helicopter for you. I've been told to take you with me."

"Fuck that," I said, grateful once again for the drill sergeant in Germany all those years ago who taught me to swear like a US marine.

"The whole city will be slaughtered if you leave. That's thousands of Afghans, members of parliament, women leaders, civil society activists, journalists. We can't leave a capital city with no one in charge."

This was getting heated, but I was mad at him and America for this final act of betrayal. "I have my own helicopter, thank you," I said. "We are on our own."

"Sami, don't be stupid. The Pentagon told me to take you to HKIA, [Hamid Karzai International Airport]. There's no security on the road now."

"Let's head out, brother," I said to Alizai. "The Americans aren't going to help us."

His reply was what I expected of this great warrior. "I want to go fight."

As we walked out, Vasely was still yelling. "Let me put you on a helicopter to the airport. Those are my orders."

Driving back to the airport, I called Fahim and ordered him to load up every aircraft with night-flying capability with all the ammunition we had. "I am authorizing air strikes into urban areas of Kabul tonight. Any Taliban fighter who raises his head will wish he was not born."

His voice was weak and distant in reply. "Commander, we don't have any aircraft."

"What do you mean, we don't have any aircraft?" I said. "We have hundreds of aircraft."

"They've gone. The pilots flew them out of the country, mostly to Uzbekistan, some to Tajikistan." They had saved the aircraft and their own lives. But their departure made collapse inevitable. We had no offensive capacity left. That's why Zia was having lunch with Ziarmal. They were planning their own exit. After I left, they had boarded the PC-12 aircraft that had brought me in from Helmand less than sixty hours before and flown with all the other 777 Brigade pilots and their aircraft to Uzbekistan. The departure of the special mission wing precipitated a general rush for aircrews to take out every plane that could fly, carrying whoever could jump on board with them.

Alizai and I were both in shock; rational thinking was hard in the face of the enormity of the challenge. He wanted to drive to the special forces base at Camp Morehead to command the defense of the south of the city. It took me a lot to persuade him not to go. I begged him, even threatening to restrain him.

"What you say is noble," I said. "But what I foresee is you being killed—or captured and tortured. As a friend, and a brother officer, I can't support your stand. We have lost the war. You will only get yourself killed, and others with you. Our job has to be to get as many good men out of the country to fight another day."

I ordered an inventory of what we had left: two damaged Black Hawks, one operative C-130 transport plane, and one barely functioning. The minister of defense, Bismillah Khan, had tried to leave on the good C-130, but my praetorian guard, 4th Company, KKA, had surrounded the aircraft and not allowed it to take off without my permission.

That was it. The end.

The president had abandoned the nation. Even if our best special forces held perimeter defenses, the police behind them had disappeared, conventional army units everywhere were faltering. Our partner force, the Americans, had abandoned us, and we had no air support. We have a saying in my language, I guess it is the same in English, that I wished the earth would open up and swallow me. That is how it felt.

I called all of the key assets, JSOC and MOD intelligence, and told them to come to JSOC headquarters. I found the minister of defense, Bismillah Khan, in the VIP area of the public terminal. As well as his present position, his former role as a commander in the mujahidin forces who had fought against the Taliban in the 1990s meant they would kill him on sight. He told me that he had waited at the MOD that morning and had been expecting the president to cross the road from the palace and come to the MOD to tell his senior staff what to do. When he heard the president had fled, he jumped in a vehicle and came to the airport.

He was leaving and tried to persuade me to join him.

"I'm not going anywhere," I said. "I have a lot of people still trapped in the city as well as my headquarters in Camp Shorab. I will find a way to fight for them. I'm not leaving them at the mercy of the Taliban."

He boarded a plane sent by the United Arab Emirates. They were sending flights to pick up their embassy staff, and Asadullah Khalid persuaded them to put on an extra one for senior Afghan military personnel. He wanted me to leave with him, but I refused. A few senior officers, good men, Fahim, Salari, Alizai, and Naseri, all said that if I was not leaving, they would stay too.

That night two pilots worked on the damaged C-130, fixing two engines. They calculated that it could take around twenty-five passengers safely, less than a quarter of its normal payload. Alizai and Fahim took the operational C-130 and flew to Kandahar to pick up soldiers from the so-called "Zero Units," named because they were numbered Zero-One, Zero-Two, and so on.

These forces operated in the shadows, carrying out night raids with little public attention. Set up by the CIA, even after they were handed over to full Afghan control they were never accepted fully into the Afghan system. Any Zero Unit soldier caught by the Taliban was immediately executed. The CIA had arranged a local ceasefire with the Taliban to allow them to leave. But even for these, their closest comrades, America would not send its own planes. The Afghan C-130 flew to Kandahar, bringing back 170 Zero Unit commandos, well beyond its published payload, led by Colonel Eqbal, who I knew well from the battle of Arghandab. It was good to see him alive. The Zero Units would go on to provide the last security for Kabul airport as chaos hit.

The CIA then prepared to pick us all up to go the US, but I said I needed the planes to get my men out of Camp Shorab. I called Javed Salim.

"There's no way you could get a plane in and out of here, sir. There are thousands of soldiers in the base and it would be mobbed on the tarmac."

I called the American control room again to request their support to evacuate Camp Shorab, and I received the same curt answer as from Vasely. They could not support us because we did not have a government. I was mad at them. Their rationing of support had reversed all the advances we had made the year before. Now they were cutting us off. They stopped taking my calls after that.

Javed Salim carried on fighting until Tuesday, August 17, two days after the rest of the country had fallen. Of course the Taliban did not stick to the promise they had made not to attack the base after I left. My 215 Corps troops held off assaults on Camp Shorab, and on all the bases we still held from Kajaki in the north to Garmsir in the south. They staged the last stand against the Taliban. I was so proud of them.

On August 17, Salim could see that it was pointless to go on. He negotiated an end to hostilities and safe passage for himself and senior commanders. They put on civilian clothes and drove to Kabul. They were stopped at every checkpoint by Taliban fighters looking for Sami Sadat.

By August 18, when Salim led his convoy into Kabul airport, it was already besieged by thousands of desperate people, and the international evacuation operation, that became familiar on TV screens across the world, had begun. I had given a list of the key soldiers and commandos who should come in, but the Americans at the gate did not accept all of them.

I had saved those I most cared about. I could do no more. On Wednesday, August 19, I accepted an offer from Britain to get medical treatment for my shrapnel wound and a flight out. General Giles Hill, who had been the British deputy commander of international forces the year before and was a good friend, had arranged for me to travel to the UK. I succeeded in getting flights to the US for 4th Company, KKA, led by Captain Fazal, the soldiers who had been most loyal to me, and some others who were most vulnerable to retribution from the Taliban. Once they were safely away I took the British offer of a new home. I felt betrayed by President Biden who abandoned us in our darkest hour.

While I was waiting to leave, I had a strange call.

"Sami's a brave man. He's just been fighting for the wrong side. We can tell him how to reach us and get protection for himself and his family."

The speaker was Mullah Muttasim, a former senior figure in the Taliban, acting as an intermediary. "I have been asked to give you that message from the young Malawi." It was the way Afghans referred to people often called Mullahs.

"Who's the young Malawi?" I asked Muttasim.

"Mullah Yaqoob," he said. I knew who Yaqoob was well enough: the son of the founder of the Taliban, Mullah Omar. We had been negotiating with him the previous week for safe passage out for some of our troops. He would soon be appointed as minister of defense in the new Taliban administration.

"He asked me to call you to ask you to stay behind. There are safe places in Kabul already under Taliban control."

The Taliban were offering an amnesty.

"The answer is no," I said, without hesitation. "I don't need Taliban help, and I don't need Taliban protection."

He called back an hour later.

"The Malawi wants to make it easy for you. He says he will send his deputy to wherever you are to give you protection."

I wanted to stop this quickly. "Tell him we're not friends. We lost the war not because he won but because we were betrayed. Tell him I'll meet him again on the battlefield." I ended the call abruptly.

I left the country I love on a clear blue morning, Thursday, August 20. I was driven across to a waiting C-17 by two British special forces commandos with Massoud Andar, the director of counterintelligence in the NDS. I took a last look at the mountains rising above the Shomali plain to the north...and vowed to return.

Chapter Twelve

"CHAOS-ISTAN"

Twenty years after 9/11, the Taliban were back in power, after a war costing more than two trillion dollars, taking the lives of sixty-three hundred brave young service members and contractors from the US and its coalition partners, and more than two hundred thousand troops and fifty thousand civilians from our side.

The war was lost not because the Taliban were strong but because for twenty years it was not treated as a war but as a short-term intervention. The better American officials knew the problem. They had a saying: "It's not year twenty. It's year one for the twentieth time."

President Biden has spoken contemptuously about the capacity of our armed forces, saying that Afghanistan could not expect Americans to die in its cause if Afghans were not willing to fight. But our army's capacity to fight was removed by him in an act of betrayal that made defeat inevitable.

The Taliban have broken the main condition they agreed in order to secure US and allied withdrawal: that they would not support al-Qaeda, who have been able to regroup and recruit in Afghanistan to make this their most successful international cell. General Stan McChrystal was right all those years ago when he said what would happen if US troops were withdrawn. Biden's policies have indeed delivered "Chaos-istan."

Al-Qaeda gained credibility among jihadi fighters by supporting the ouster of US forces from Afghanistan—a blow against what their doctrine describes as the "far enemy." Now from safe and secure bases in Afghanistan they are able to plan attacks on the governments in the Middle East they call the "near enemy." They have the ability and will to kill or kidnap American soldiers, business leaders, and diplomats in the Middle East and Africa and disrupt international trade.

We have a patriotic duty to kick out the Taliban, recover Afghanistan for its people, and prevent further terrorist attacks on the world. But mobilizing forces has taken time. Those who could have led a quick fightback were in shock, too preoccupied with resettling their families and starting again abroad. They may have hoped it would be temporary exile, but even with competent leadership it would have been hard to coordinate an insurgency against the Taliban in those early months. The country was tired of war, and the Taliban benefited from a peace dividend, as people could move around in more security—not least because the Taliban were no longer attacking them.

But that consent is time-limited as the full horror of Taliban rule is being realized. The Taliban have proved themselves incapable of running any kind of economy, and savage restrictions imposed on all freedoms, particularly affecting women, have led to widespread discontent. They rule only by fear; their support is shallow. At the same time Afghanistan has once again become a crucible of international terrorism, under Taliban protection. As time has passed the Taliban have provoked opposition to their rule by their failure to build an inclusive government, with only a handful of non-Pashtuns in senior positions, and no women in any role. All they have is a misguided, misquoted, and misapplied sense of the Quran, deployed against the very people who take pride and honor both in the depth of their religious tradition and their tribal roots. In the Taliban regime, there is no space for women, no respect for a head of a tribe or for a wise man or scholar, no respect for ordinary citizens, and no space for the values and hopes of the modern generation educated since 9/11. The only respect and privileged status is given to Taliban fighters, whose loyalty is to their warped ideas, not the society or normal religion of the Afghan nation.

This leaves a gap for an opposition movement to mobilize the new generation of Afghan citizens who saw a vision of a new country in the twenty years of the republic. People tasted equality, freedom, democracy, and development, and want to return to a country that is not isolated from the world, and where everybody is educated. We had many factions in the past, but now people are more willing to coexist with one another to end the cycles of violence of the past fifty years. And if we get this right, we can connect the new generation to the traditional pillars of authority—religious and tribal leaders who have been sidelined by the Taliban—and forge a new society.

Afghanistan's best generation was atomized by the fall of the Ghani administration. Its military and civilian leaders live scattered as refugees across the planet or hide in Afghanistan with no prospect of earning money to keep their families alive. But those of us who left carry with us our education—and a burning desire to return. The new generation, my generation, have the motivation to take back Afghanistan and change it once and for all in the direction of peace and prosperity. We share a sense of loss of the constitution of the republic that brought progress with the support of our international partners.

For now I am a general without an army. And I am constantly meeting politicians without a parliament, women's leaders who are campaigning for a return to the equality we enjoyed, and businesspeople who mourn the ruin of the Afghan economy. We know what it is like to lose our country, not to have a vote, to stay in places where we do not belong and are often not welcome. And this feeling is translating into a wider commitment among hundreds of thousands of Afghans to take our country back and kick the terrorists out.

For all the faults of our leaders in the twenty years of the Afghan republic, people saw the value of having a government that sought to deliver education, jobs and a functioning economy, and an army that fought for honor and the flag. All that has gone.

So I believe this is a strategic opportunity that can ultimately unite the nation to find an alternative to the Taliban and a lasting settlement to bring peace. And this time we need to do it our way—learning from the mistakes of the past and without American boots on the ground. It is time to raise the banner for a new Afghanistan, based on the foundations of the 2004 constitution that was endorsed by old and new pillars of Afghan power, including Islamic scholars. It was even signed by our revered former king, Zahir Shah, who returned from Rome, where he had been exiled since the 1973 coup, to die in his homeland soon afterwards.

Everyone has a view of what they think could be changed in the constitution: it is centralized and perhaps the president is too strong; there should be more power for local government. It is open to change. But we need to start somewhere and base our fightback on a return to constitutional order, open to a process to amend the constitution with a consensus of the people once order is restored.

The existing constitution is founded on Islamic principles, but with a liberal view of today's world, accommodating human rights, the rights of women, freedom of speech, freedom of religion, freedom of politics. That should be the basis of a return to order. We have proud traditions of meeting in *jirgas*, both at the local and national level, to resolve issues. Afghans have ways of finding consensus, and we will do it again. Afghanistan needs reform and capable reformers to come together to build government and the state and liberate the country to encourage international investment for development to serve the greater good.

That is the offer, that is what we are preparing to fight for, and it may be necessary to fight to take back our country. The Taliban are not strong, and internal divisions have weakened them further, but I do not underestimate the scale of the task. In stark contrast to the outward-looking, more progressive values of the republic that molded the minds of the post-9/11 generation, the next generation are having a very different experience. There is a risk that the whole country could become a terrorist hub, as schools turn into propaganda machines for the death cult that is the Taliban today. They are nihilists who value martyrdom in their cause above all else. The best thing that young people can do in their eyes is to die. I see this on social media, where there is far more talk of death than before. In Taliban Afghanistan, people are being groomed to die.

It is frightening for a country with so many young people to have the minds of the next generation polluted. Tens of thousands are trapped in this death cult. So we need to act. And we need to act with good preparation so we know we can win. Nobody wants war, but to reach a stable peace, there is a need for a final war to end all other smalls wars in our country.

I spent most of 2023 in the United States, where I discovered a network of supporters for a return to rebuild the Afghan republic, outraged by the way their government abandoned Afghanistan in 2021. I held a series of strategic discussions with a wide range of people to decide how to go about restoring Afghanistan to its rightful place in the world and end fifty years of conflict. I discovered a reservoir of support, particularly among military veterans and their families. There is a deep moral injury in the heart of many veterans and active military service members who sacrificed so much for our country and saw it thrown away by their government. It was a relief to realize that America is not the Biden administration, and in meetings across the country I had a warm reception.

I often traveled with three great warriors. First, the counterinsurgency and strategy expert Doctor David Kilcullen, who helps show the possibilities in the realm of strategy as we craft the way forward. Second, a former Green Beret, Thomas Kasza, who left the forces after the collapse of Afghanistan in 2021 and now heads the 1208 Foundation, supporting Afghans who saved many American lives clearing mines. And third, and one of the best commanders of the Afghan special forces, Brigadier General Khoshal (Kosh) Sadat. He is the master tactician and practical leader for our cause, allowing me to focus on the broader horizon of our task and prioritize what to do next. Kosh brings a wealth of experience as the best-connected Afghan general in America, whose friendships with many senior players in the US military, politics, and business will serve our people well.

We traveled forty thousand miles across sixteen different states, conducting hundreds of meetings, in thinktanks, in Ivy League schools and other campuses, in private sessions, and with financial institutions. Everywhere we were enthusiastically welcomed by American and Afghan veterans who planned conferences and events. All that work began to pay off. We wanted to persuade Congress to stop engaging and legitimizing the Taliban, and some senior politicians began to take notice. The chairman of the Foreign Affairs Committee, Mike McCaul, invited me to give testimony. The State Department had been moving towards engagement with the Taliban and possible full recognition of the Taliban as the government of Afghanistan. But we reduced the political space for that to happen as we robustly lobbied and reminded people that Afghans refuse to accept the Taliban, who are a global threat. We have had more traction with Republican politicians, since the approved line among Democrats is to forget about Afghanistan after the debacle of the withdrawal. But it was wonderful when we received the support and prayers of Democrats who reached out to us.

To deliver the change we need, we have formed the Afghanistan United Front with friends and comrades dedicated to progress in a new and reformed Afghanistan. This is above all a political organization, dedicated to restoring the Afghan republic, one nation, united and with equality for all its citizens, governed under a constitution and by a government appointed with the consent of its people. We draw support from across Afghanistan. At the launch of the AUF in Virginia, we raised an Afghan flag that was lowered in the governor's office in Helmand province, the last city to fall when we left it in August 2021. Our promise is to take back the same flag to free Helmand and hang it up there once again.

Our political office is headed by former provincial governor Massoud Bakhtawar, whose family have deep roots in southwest Afghanistan. We also have with us another former governor, Qayum Rahimi, a seasoned Afghan politician and intellectual, who fought to the last bullet in western Afghanistan. Governor Rahimi serves as my national security adviser, bringing unmatched knowledge of religious extremism. And from the northwest, we have the support of Ziauddin Akazai, a former member of parliament. As well as being a place to engage with American political leaders and other circles of influence, our Virginia office provides a space for Afghan groups to meet and plan the future, sharing ideas for business or culture. And it is a clearing house for Americans who want to help Afghanistan.

But as a last resort, we are ready to fight if necessary. So we are working to establish a military office in a country neighboring Afghanistan. A young leadership of patriotic officers will reestablish the Afghan National Army, with a Joint Special Operations

Command, while training ground forces to liberate our country. It is only when we get into Afghanistan, taking and holding ground, that people will realize that the Taliban are not there forever, and this will shift opinions across Afghanistan, moving tectonic plates that change mindsets among our people, as well as policymakers in the region, and blow a wind of change to Washington. President Biden may have turned his back on us, but military success against the Taliban will change the calculus for others. We do not need Americans to support us, but we want them to stop legitimizing the Taliban, at least making it a level playing field so that Afghans can choose their own future.

We have the support of several brave warriors from the army of the republic, including Major General Mustafa Wardak, former commander of 209 Corps in the north; General Mahmud Noorzai, former commander of NDS special forces; General Muhammad Ali Yazdani, former commander of 217 Corps; Major General Jalal Yaftali, founder of the elite KKA Force; General Sharif Yaftali, former chief of the general staff of the army; and Major General Noorullah Qaderi, former commander of 207 Corps in western Afghanistan. My most loyal inner team of comrades are also with me on this journey: Colonel Hayat Parwani, Colonel Salahudin Dawood, son of the famous late General Dawood from the northeast, Captain Asem Shukoori, Major Naqib Mirzada, and Reza Sarwary, my most trusted political adviser and all-time friend. And there are many tribal leaders on the ground in Afghanistan, and women's leaders who support us but who I cannot name for security reasons.

Many of my closest lieutenants are intelligence professionals, and we have maintained and expanded our networks across Afghanistan. We also have intelligence capacity into Iran and Pakistan, with reach to Turkey and Iraq. That means we have been tracking terrorists coming and going from Afghanistan as well as keeping across Taliban links with foreign governments.

The Taliban are not without some support, and until we have made gains on the ground we will not rally the numbers of people we will need to retake the whole country. But we need to make the case for freedom in Afghan minds before we take to the battlefield. We have already begun a campaign to shape the information space, with three messages: that the Taliban are widely rejected by the people of Afghanistan; that they do not represent the culture and traditions of any tribe; and that everything they do is against the people and interests of our country. We have a proud history of standing against invaders, and the Taliban are foreign invaders from Pakistan. They do not have any sense that they are responsible for a functioning economy to keep our people fed. And they do not understand or practice Afghan customs or values. They rule only by violence.

We face the challenge that the opposition to the Taliban is fragmented, and some of those planning a fightback, particularly in the mainly Tajik National Resistance Front, are not in favor of a return to the united republic, but are instead fighting under an old flag from the mujahidin days in the 1980s. I have offered a joint leadership council with the NRF, but the idea was turned down. We can only change this attitude by delivering success for a united republic on the ground.

We have tried to shape public opinion among potential Western allies too, although for now America and Britain, as well as the European Union, have publicly said they will not support armed opposition to the Taliban. This is a mistake, but I realize that there will be no change while Joe Biden is president. In order to justify his lack of attention to the problem, he is deluding himself that the Taliban are backing America in stopping international terrorism and that al-Qaeda have no presence in Afghanistan. This is moral bankruptcy. A major UN investigation showed that links between the two organizations are 'strong and symbiotic,' and al-Qaeda is 'rebuilding operational capability' from its base in Afghanistan.

The UN report could not be clearer: 'Promises made by the Taliban in August 2021 to be more inclusive, break with terrorist groups…and not pose a security threat to other countries seem increasingly hollow, if not plain false, in 2023.' Given this disconnect between reality and the wishful thinking in the White House, a coherent American approach is not likely in the short term.

The US administration is ignoring the waves that were sent crashing across the world by the success of the Taliban. America's retreat from Afghanistan signaled weakness, so Vladimir Putin was emboldened to attack Ukraine because he thought there would be no response from Washington. And the Taliban victory provoked the rise of anti-Islamic parties who won elections across Europe, in the Netherlands, Hungary, and Slovakia. The extremism of Hamas in Gaza has made this situation worse. If we do not recover Afghanistan for moderate Islamic forces, my fear is this will translate into a wider mainstream conflict, dividing the world between Islam and Judeo-Christian traditions: a contest with no winners.

In our campaign to end terrorism in Afghanistan and recover the country, we see policy change in some regional countries, who have now realized their mistake after being initially sympathetic to a Taliban takeover. This includes Afghanistan's neighbors. Iran has been involved in several armed clashes with the Taliban on the border, and even the Taliban's long-term supporter, Pakistan, is having to face up to a terrorist state on its border and is reassessing its options. Pakistani intelligence, the ISI, made a serious miscalculation in backing a Taliban takeover. They mistakenly believed they had a deal with the Taliban, but it turned out to be worthless. Their calculation was that a Taliban takeover of Afghanistan would diminish the Pakistani Taliban, the TTP. The opposite has happened, as the change of government in Afghanistan has left the TTP significantly strengthened, with the infusion of hundreds of high-value prisoners released from Afghan jails. It has renewed itself under its leader, Noor Wali Mehsud, with a more coherent media strategy and a clearer focus on taking power in Pakistan, specifically talking about global terrorism launched from its safe haven in Afghanistan. The Taliban emir's vision is to take over Pakistan with his TTP brothers. He sees the existence of Pakistan as a co-existential threat to his Taliban rule; now Pakistan realizes this and sees the Taliban in the same manner. These intentions only help us predict a dire and violent next years between Pakistan and Taliban. It's going to be very bloody.

This is an opportunity for us, because if both Iran and Pakistan were actively supporting the Taliban, as they were when we were fighting for our lives in 2021, it would make our task far harder. We are looking for at least consent if not active support from all of Afghanistan's neighbors, who are worried about the clear threat of terrorism coming from Taliban-controlled Afghanistan. The likeliest jumping-off points are from the Central Asian states to the north of Afghanistan, Uzbekistan and Tajikistan, and I believe that as soon as they see a viable alternative to the Taliban they will support it. I am continuing to have discussions with Tajikistan in particular. This is complicated by their military alliance with Russia, although I do not believe Russia will oppose our plans. Russia is a great power, with interests across Central Asia, with Afghanistan near its zone of influence, and Moscow has been practical about the international threat of the Taliban, making clear objectives for engaging the Taliban.

Despite the Ukraine war, Russia and America could work together against the Taliban. I think the US administration understands very well that if they want to see a terrorist-free state in Afghanistan, Russia must be on board. My ideal scenario would be America putting pressure on Pakistan to let us have access to Afghanistan, and Russia helping to give us space in Central Asia. I think that will save a lot of bloodshed and time in defeating the Taliban.

But while we will take support where it is offered, we want this fightback to be an all-Afghan affair. We need international understanding, but we are fighting for our national interest, and are nobody's puppet.

We believe that we now have the right leadership to be able to mount a fight against the Taliban, coordinated with actions by armed groups who are already bravely fighting. We are beginning to mobilize and train troops, and we have the most important component in any military campaign—the will to win. This is an all-or-nothing fight to recover our country.

I am under no illusions. The first phase of fighting will be bloody and hard. We see posts on the media from various international organizations, including the UN, but it never changed anything in Afghanistan. It is the man on the battlefield with a gun who has made the difference. We will be at pains to avoid civilian casualties to keep the population on our side. But I know they will support us, and if we show we are determined to win, others will raise the flag of freedom across the country. People without work or freedom will join us because they know the only way to change this government is to fight. And once we have shown strength in the early phase, others will join. Power often changes hands in Afghanistan without much fighting as people see which way the wind is blowing.

We want to enter Afghanistan with clear military and political objectives, with a decisive strategy and disciplined force that could clear the area of the Taliban and operate a strong local and provincial administration. Once we hold some ground the next phase is to stabilize areas taken, with a plan to avoid a general breakdown of law and order. Afghanistan's past has too many uncomfortable and brutal examples of the country sliding into chaos and divided by warlords and criminal gangs. I watched it happen to my father's generation and do not want to see it again. It is important that we fight for a united Afghanistan, governed by the consent of its people, not for personal advantage. And that is why our work in building consent for a return to the constitutional order, one country united under one flag, is important. At Afghanistan United Front we have zero tolerance for warlords and foreign puppets who cause harm to our national security.

The Taliban's failure to govern the country is causing widespread poverty and starvation, and their narrow social restrictions against both men and women are increasing the will of Afghan people for change. That is putting fuel onto the fire of opposition inside the country, smoldering for now, but ready to burst into righteous flame against the evil that has overtaken our beloved country.

We know the support for change is there. Before the Taliban took power again, we took pride in the symbols of our national identity: the flag, the army, a cricket team that competed with the world's best. I saw that unity on display at a football game in Kabul back in 2014, the first to be played under floodlights. The location was powerfully symbolic: nobody could forget that the Taliban had staged public executions in this stadium during their years in power first time round in the 1990s. Back then women, pathetically covered from head to foot in the powder-blue sacking of burqas, knelt in the mud and were shot for crimes against Taliban morality. In 2014, in a powerful demonstration of how Afghanistan had changed, soldiers carried a huge black, green, and red tricolor Afghan flag onto the field before kickoff, while a top woman singer, Aryana Sayeed, sang a patriotic song.

That was the national unity and pride in our nation that Biden never saw in his blind contempt. If he had looked beyond the mismanagement, he would have seen that something of great value changed in Afghanistan in the twenty years after 9/11, putting the country on a new path. Our people had changed. I was one of a new generation of leaders capable of holding the country for ourselves in an enduring strategic partnership with the United States—until he pulled out the rug from under our feet. In July 2021, the month before the fall, there were huge demonstrations in defense of the values of the republic, with people flying the black, red, and green tricolor, chanting for the army and country they loved as they knew it faced its greatest threat. The rallies began spontaneously and spread through social media, not just in Kabul and the big cities but into the countryside, including the Taliban heartland in the south. People realized what they were losing and rallied around the flag. It was the stirring of a nation-state not determined by ethnic or religious divisions. The republic was never so loved as just before it fell. That is the spirit we need to harness to ignite an uprising and build a reformed country around the Afghan republic, flag, and constitution, and take revenge for the humiliation of defeat.

We are the youngest country in the region, and I want to tap the energy and creativity of that generation to turn Afghanistan into a country that contributes stability to its region and the world, whose citizens are welcomed abroad because we are seen as a strong nation—a bedrock of security, not a watchword for failure and terrorism. We want to be free from poverty, free from fear of not having good hospitals or schools, and above all free from fanaticism. And as we seek security my ideal scenario is that once we take back Afghanistan and establish a government, America will see the value of a strategic alliance. We can negotiate in a more transactional way. We will not rely on American security guarantees after what has happened to my generation, but I would like to see the US as our first choice for an alliance. I would like us to call Washington our friend.

Afghanistan is a land of opportunity, with the second largest untapped copper deposit in the world, mountainsides full of precious stones, including the world's only lapis lazuli, and untapped resources of lithium and the rare-earth metals essential to the new global economy. We could be a vibrant economic and trade bridge between Central and South Asia. But for now our people are literally starving to death in the incompetent and fanatical grip of people who have distorted the good name of our faith. We cannot allow this to go on and let the country once again become a failed state and hub for global terrorism. We want Afghanistan to take its rightful place among the peaceful nations of the world, exploiting its best resource: its people. And we do not need much to return and make the Taliban years a brief interruption in progress towards peace and prosperity. Our people are very brave, talented, committed, and loyal. This is the key asset we have for the changes envisioned. We will work with every Afghan and friends of Afghanistan to ensure our country is prosperous after being freed from the tyranny of terrorism.

I know it will not be easy, but I will gladly give the rest of my life for this cause. If I survive, and we free our country, I will be proud to see my countrymen grow in prosperity and peace. But if I do not make it, I would like to think I have already contributed to showing the way to the younger generation of Afghan people, how to free our country, and why it is important to fight for freedom.

ABOUT THE AUTHOR

Lieutenant General Sami Sadat is a highly decorated former senior commander in the Afghan Army. He worked in intelligence and special operations before taking command of a Corps. He was awarded a bronze star for saving the life of a US pilot who had come down in a Taliban-held area. He is currently leading opposition efforts against the Taliban from outside Afghanistan.

Sadat's writing has appeared in the *New York Times* and the *Huffington Post*, and he has been interviewed by and his story featured in the *New York Times*, NPR, AFP, CNN, and the BBC. He is the subject of the Emmy Award–winning National Geographic documentary *Retrograde*, by award-winning director Matthew Heineman.

The Last Commander was written with the assistance of David Loyn.

Loyn was an award-winning foreign correspondent for thirty years for the BBC, and is now a visiting senior fellow in the Department of War Studies at King's College London. Winner of Britain's leading awards in both TV and radio news—Sony Radio Reporter of the Year and Royal Television Society Journalist of the Year—he is an authority on Afghanistan, which he first visited in 1994. He writes regularly for the *Spectator*, among other publications. In 2017, he worked for a year as communication adviser to the Afghan president, Ashraf Ghani.

Loyn is the author of three books: *The Long War: The Inside Story of America and Afghanistan Since 9/11*, published in 2021; *In Afghanistan: Two Hundred Years of British, Russian and American Occupation*, published in 2009; and *Frontline: The True Story of the British Mavericks Who Changed the Face of War Reporting*, published in 2006. *Frontline* was shortlisted for the Orwell Prize.

Made in United States
Troutdale, OR
08/07/2024

21827068R40189